The Collegiate Function
of Community Colleges

Arthur M. Cohen
Florence B. Brawer

The Collegiate Function of Community Colleges

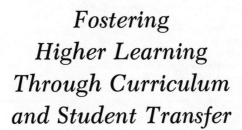

Fostering
Higher Learning
Through Curriculum
and Student Transfer

 Jossey-Bass Publishers

San Francisco • London • 1987

THE COLLEGIATE FUNCTION OF COMMUNITY COLLEGES
Fostering Higher Learning Through Curriculum and Student Transfer
by Arthur M. Cohen and Florence B. Brawer

Copyright © 1987 by: Jossey-Bass Inc., Publishers
433 California Street
San Francisco, California 94104
&
Jossey-Bass Limited
28 Banner Street
London EC1Y 8QE

Library of Congress Cataloging-in-Publication Data

Cohen, Arthur M.
    The collegiate function of community colleges.

    (The Jossey-Bass higher education series)
    Bibliography: p.
    Includes index.
    1. Community colleges—United States.
2. Universities and colleges—United States.
3. Students, Transfer of. 4. Community colleges—
United States—Curricula. I. Brawer, Florence B.,
1922-   . II. Title. III. Series.
LB2328.C557 1987   378'.052   87-45430
ISBN 1-55542-047-8

Published in cooperation with the ERIC Clearinghouse for Junior Colleges.

This publication was prepared with funding from the Office of Educational
Research and Improvement (OERI), U.S. Department of Education under contract
no. 400-83-0030. The opinions expressed in this publication do not necessarily
reflect the positions or policies of OERI or the Department of Education.

Alkaline paper ∞   Manufactured in the U.S.A.

JACKET DESIGN BY WILLI BAUM

FIRST EDITION

Code 8726

The Jossey-Bass
Higher Education Series

Contents

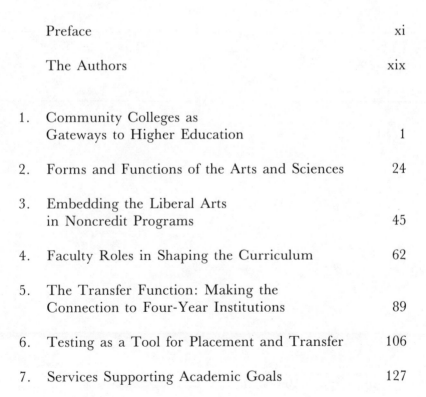

Preface

The American community college was founded to serve as a link between the lower schools and establishments of higher learning. Despite the many additional roles adopted by the colleges, that original function remains an essential component of their mission. It may be ignored by college leaders who would rather speak of their institution's role in assisting regional economic development or in providing lifelong learning opportunities for adults, but to the students seeking entry to institutions of higher education, it remains a cornerstone of the community college.

The collegiate connection, the linking function, rests on two sets of college operations: the liberal arts curriculum and the activities that support student flow into and through the community college and on into the universities. The liberal arts curriculum is provided for students seeking the first two years of a baccalaureate program, for the general education of those desiring vocational certification, and for the avocational interest of many others. The colleges' part in promoting student transfer includes academic support services, joint course planning and agreements with senior institutions for transferring course credits, student recruitment and placement in classes, and the numerous other formal and informal practices that affect student progress.

How effectively do the colleges perform their connecting role? How has it been modified to accommodate the needs of different student populations? How has it been maintained in the face of demands for a greater emphasis on occupational and adult education? Who are its supporters? Why should it survive? These questions are explored in this book.

We consider it essential to examine the transfer function and the teaching of liberal arts because those aspects of community colleges are too often either taken for granted or attacked as being archaic and irrelevant to the students who attend and the communities that support the colleges. By contrast, our position is that the collegiate connection reveals the community college at its finest. These institutions were originally organized around their programs of collegiate studies, and much of their growth and support have depended on their success in carrying out these programs. The collegiate connection influences the curriculum and its ancillary services, and the activities of the faculty and students, the expected institutional outcomes, and this function differentiates these colleges from proprietary trade schools, technical colleges, adult education centers, corporate learning efforts, and the numerous other forms of noncompulsory adult education available throughout the country. It is the rudder that keeps the colleges within the mainstream of graded education, stretching from kindergarten to graduate and professional school.

One of the book's main purposes is to disaggregate the institutions' provision of instruction in the liberal arts from the students' intentions and behavior regarding transfer. Much of the literature on community colleges confuses curricular content with student intent by calling the liberal arts ''transfer studies'' and by treating the students' transfer rate as a mark of curricular success. But one is a principle by which the curriculum is organized, the other a behavior manifested by the clients. The liberal arts curriculum has its own history, support groups, and rationale. It is based on a set of concepts that are central to our culture and that predate the colleges' establishment by many centuries. It is provided for all students, many who transfer to universities, most who do not. Students come to the community college seeking many things: credits enabling them to transfer, to be sure, but also job-entry skills and certification, studies enabling them to advance in occupations they have already entered, basic literacy skills, and recreational or avocational studies. Most of them study the liberal arts, many do not. We treat the liberal arts curriculum and student transfer rates separately as an aid to better understanding both.

We are advocates both of the liberal arts as a curriculum organizer and of the progression of students from the high schools into and through the community colleges. We have heard community college leaders insist that their institutions could do it all: provide liberal arts, occupational, recreational, and basic literacy studies and also serve students of any age, motivation or aptitude level, or aspiration. But we do not believe that everything can be accomplished with equal facility. We have observed the relative diminution of the collegiate connection as this linking role was subordinated to the task of providing access to everyone. The colleges attracted large numbers of people who were not sufficiently intellectually curious to study the liberal arts of their own volition, not sufficiently concerned with the making of a philosophy of life to study the liberal arts for their own value, and not so oriented toward traditional baccalaureate studies that they would accept the reading lists as worthy guides to follow. And the colleges mounted massive efforts to teach these individuals. Their opposing roles as open access institutions and as gatekeepers for the establishments of higher learning, the employers, and the professions generated a tension that the colleges have been able to ameliorate only by continually devising new programs.

College leaders have acted opportunistically to adjust their curriculum to fit the realities of the demands placed on it. They have modified the liberal arts in the degree-credit classes, built them into the occupational programs, and offered them in different ways in their continuing education programs. So changed, the liberal arts are designed to prepare people for further studies, recreation, the workplace, or to widen cultural exposure. As such, they may be more faithful to the heritage of the liberal arts than is the graduate, professional school or the academic discipline–dominated undergraduate curriculum in the university.

However, adaptability can be taken only so far as an organizational principle. Eventually, college leaders must choose among alternatives. Access mitigates gatekeeping; education for immediate employment runs counter to students' need to be flexible enough to climb career ladders; basic literacy training is different from an introduction to the pursuit of higher learning. We are encouraged by the way the collegiate connection has been maintained, but we think it should be strengthened. The liberal arts and practices that promote transfer can be at the heart of a college even while it remains open to all. In this book, we seek to show how this can be accomplished.

Data Sources

Since 1974 we have been studying the collegiate function of community colleges by analyzing the literature and by conducting projects of our own. The literature contains many reports of studies of the liberal arts and general education and of attempts to stimulate student learning through new course patterning and instructional techniques. It also includes studies of the transfer function: of the various activities designed to recruit and retain students in the colleges and of the policies and practices intended to ease the flow of students from secondary schools to community colleges and from community colleges to universities.

The studies we conducted at the Center for the Study of Community Colleges between 1979 and 1986 provide a second major source of information. These projects have yielded several comprehensive data sets on students, staff, and curriculum and have provided additional information from case studies, workshops, and staff interviews. We reported the findings of our earlier studies in *The Two-Year College Instructor Today* (1977) and *The American Community College* (1982). In this work we consolidate the findings from the following projects, listed along with the name of the sponsoring agency.

July 1, 1982 to   "Trends in the Humanities in Two-Year
June 30, 1984   Colleges." Tallied curriculum and surveyed
                     1,467 instructors in 172 colleges; spon-
                     sored by the National Endowment for the
                     Humanities

Oct. 1, 1979 to   "Revitalizing the Humanities in the Com-
Sept. 31, 1982   munity College." Surveyed 1,160 instruc-
                     tors and 6,162 students in 27 colleges; spon-
                     sored by the National Endowment for the
                     Humanities

July 1, 1981 to   "Helping Strengthen the Liberal Arts in
June 30, 1987   Community Colleges." Surveyed 403 in-
                     structors in 38 colleges and tested 8,026 stu-
                     dents in 23 colleges; sponsored by the Andrew
                     W. Mellon Foundation

Oct. 1, 1981 to   "Facilitating Transfer Through Commun-
Sept. 30, 1984   ity Colleges." Conducted case studies and
                     workshops in 38 colleges; sponsored by the
                     Ford Foundation

Jan. 1, 1983 to   "Transfer Education in American Com-
March 31, 1984   munity Colleges." Surveyed 347 instructors
                     and 1,613 students in 24 colleges; sponsored
                     by the Ford Foundation

Nov. 1, 1979 to   "Science Education for Women, Minority,
Dec. 31, 1982   and Handicapped Students in Community
                     Colleges." Surveyed 268 instructors and
                     6,426 students and analyzed 8,873 student
                     transcripts in 9 colleges; sponsored by the
                     National Science Foundation

April 1, 1985 to   "An Assessment of the Urban Community
Sept. 30, 1987   College Transfer Opportunities Program."
                     Analyzed student flow data in 5 colleges;
                     sponsored by the Ford Foundation

Overview of the Contents

Each chapter treats a specific facet of the collegiate connection. Chapter One explores the scope of collegiate studies and defines the collegiate function in community colleges as an amalgam of the liberal arts curriculum and efforts to promote student transfer. It presents reasons for the community college's emphasis on general education and discusses patterns of associate degree requirements. Chapter Two details the liberal arts curriculum, pointing up the enrollments and patterns of courses offered in the disciplines of science, social science, mathematics, humanities, composition, and fine and performing arts. Enrollment trends between 1975 and 1986 are presented for each of the disciplines.

Chapter Three considers liberal arts–related activities in the noncredit area, reporting on the scope of the arts and humanities presented through community services and outlining the difficulties in integrating those offerings into the credit curriculum. Examples of liberal arts–related continuing education programs are presented. Chapter Four discusses the faculty's relationship to the liberal arts. Data from seven nationwide studies of community college instructors reveal trends in faculty age, experience, ethnicity, and relationship to their professional activities. Detailed information on the faculty in separate disciplines is also presented.

Chapter Five introduces the transfer function as reflected in the intentions and behavior of students and explores answers to the questions concerning the number of students transferring, the number seeking to transfer, what happens after they transfer, and the reasons why many students fail to transfer. Chapter Six presents data on the use of tests to screen students entering the community colleges and summarizes some of the arguments for and against statewide uniformity in test administration. Details of the General Academic Assessment for evaluating students' knowledge in the liberal arts are presented.

Information on services that support the liberal arts curriculum and student transfer is presented in Chapter Seven. A review of trends in orientation, advising, remedial studies, tutorials and other supplemental instruction, and honors programs is provided along with specific recommendations for enhancing student use of supplemental services. Chapter Eight presents examples of ways in which community colleges have worked together with secondary schools and universities to coordinate the progress of students between institutions. Program coordination, joint agreements, and shared facilities are discussed, as are national, state, and local regulations governing interinstitutional cooperation.

Chapter Nine offers recommendations for strengthening the collegiate connection by reconceptualizing the curriculum, by measuring student intentions and relating them to student progress, and by rewarding community colleges for their students' progress. An appendix discusses in detail the liberal arts curriculum, including the percentage of colleges offering courses within each of five disciplines and the enrollments and patterns of instruction in each of these disciplines.

The Collegiate Function of Community Colleges analyzes all aspects of the collegiate connection: sources and content of the curriculum, the students served and the staff who serve them, patterns of support for collegiate studies, the enhancers and deterrents to student flow from high school to the baccalaureate, and ways of strengthening this connection.

Directed toward the leaders of community colleges and of the institutions sending students to them and receiving students from them, *The Collegiate Function of Community Colleges* will provide information and useful ideas for directors of instruction, admissions officers, curriculum planners, faculty members, counselors, and division chairs. State-level planners and members of governing boards may also profit from this analysis of the community colleges' basic role.

Acknowledgments

This book represents the efforts of several people—from agencies to colleges to ERIC staff members. We are especially grateful to Alison Bernstein, program officer at the Ford Foundation, and to Fred Crossland, formerly with the Ford Foundation, who supported our studies of community college transfer and minority populations. The Andrew W. Mellon Foundation, under President John E. Sawyer, funded our research on the liberal arts. Claire List, the foundation's program officer, provided sage counsel and assistance. We are also grateful to Stanley Turesky, formerly of the National Endowment for the Humanities Office of Planning and Analysis, and to Raymond Hannapel of the National Science Foundation, who assisted with earlier phases of the research. The concerns of these people are reflected in the analyses reported here.

Many people at City Colleges of Chicago, Dallas County Community College District, Los Angeles Community College District, Maricopa County Community College District, Miami-Dade Community College, and Saint Louis Community College helpfully assisted in compiling case studies and surveys and provided useful information. Primary among these were Donald Barshis, Hymen Chausow, Salvatore Rotella, and Oscar Shabot in Chicago; Jan LeCroy and Ruth Shaw in Dallas; Leslie Koltai and Norman Schneider in Los Angeles; Paul Elsner and Alfredo de los Santos in Maricopa; Jeffrey Lukenbill, J. Terence Kelly, and Robert McCabe in Miami-Dade; and Richard Greenfield and Gwendolyn Stephenson in St. Louis.

Glenda Childress of our center helped organize the copy, did much of the typing, and exhibited her patience and care in finding obscure items and missing information. James Palmer prepared the index.

Dorothy Berger of San Diego Mesa College and James Catanzaro, then at Lakeland College, now at Triton College, each critiqued the manuscript and shared their ideas with us. Their assistance is most appreciated.

This book is dedicated to all students who enjoy the liberal arts and profit from them in their own development.

Los Angeles, California   Arthur M. Cohen
July 1987   Florence B. Brawer

The Authors

Arthur M. Cohen has been a professor of higher education at the University of California, Los Angeles, since 1964. His teaching emphasizes curriculum and instruction in higher education and the community college as an institution. Cohen's bachelor's and master's degrees were in history at the University of Miami. His doctorate was taken in higher education at Florida State University.

As director of the ERIC Clearinghouse for Junior Colleges since 1966, Cohen has been involved with the literature about community colleges, stimulating writing in the field and disseminating information analysis papers to all practitioners. As president of the Center for the Study of Community Colleges since 1974, he has conducted several national research studies of faculty, curriculum, and instruction.

Cohen has been involved with numerous journals and professional associations and has written extensively. His books include *Dateline '79: Heretical Concepts for the Community College* and *Objectives for College Courses*.

Florence B. Brawer is research director of the Center for the Study of Community Colleges and was previously a research educationist at the ERIC Clearinghouse for Junior Colleges. A former psychometrist and counselor, she received her bachelor's in psychology from the University of Michigan. Her master's and doctorate were in educational psychology from the University of California, Los Angeles. She is the author of *New Perspectives on Personality Development in College Students* and the coeditor of *Developments in the Rorschach Technique, Volume Three.*

Cohen and Brawer together wrote *Confronting Identity: The Community College Instructor, The Two-Year College Instructor Today,* and *The American Community College.* They have also edited several series of monographs published by the Center for the Study of Community Colleges and the ERIC Clearinghouse for Junior Colleges. Since 1973 they have been editor-in-chief and associate editor, respectively, of the Jossey-Bass sourcebook series New Directions for Community Colleges. Together with other ERIC staff members they wrote *A Constant Variable: New Perspectives on the Community College and College Responses to Community Demands.*

The Collegiate Function
of Community Colleges

1

Community Colleges
as Gateways to
Higher Education

The strength of the community college as a connecting institution rests on two elements: its collegiate curriculum, organized around the liberal arts and culminating in the associate degree, and its students' tendencies to begin their collegiate studies at the college and then to transfer to senior institutions. The colleges' control over the curriculum and over the intentions and behavior of the students is not complete; both are influenced by external forces. University transfer requirements and the entering abilities of the students affect the curriculum. The percentage of local high school graduates choosing to begin higher education, and to do so in the community college, affects the transfer component. In this chapter, we sketch the community college as a linking agent by defining its collegiate function, outlining the sources of its liberal arts curriculum, discussing influences on that curriculum, and tracing patterns in the associate degree.

The Function of the Community College

Schooling and Sorting. The idea of mass schooling has been pursued more vigorously in the United States than in any other

1

country. This stems from a desire of businesspeople for employees trained at public expense, a constant striving for professional status on the part of numerous occupational groups, and the democratic ideal of a learned populace taking an active role in civic affairs. These forces merged with and supported the American notion of an open society, one in which every person should be given the chance to move between class strata, regardless of condition of birth.

When the last legal racial, religious, and sexist barriers to schooling had been broken in the mid 1960s, the ratio of college attendance reached 45 percent for the traditional eighteen- to twenty-four-year-old age group and remained constant for the ensuing twenty years. Among that 45 percent were a sizable number of young people whom the higher education institutions were unused to accommodating. As residential institutions, the older colleges were slow to adjust to commuters, part-time students, students employed elsewhere to earn college expenses, and students with family obligations keeping them in their home communities. The colleges were founded on traditions of literacy, and few could adjust to a generation for whom the major source of information was nonprint media. As hierarchical institutions, the colleges were structured around ideas of respect for authority that many students, used more to instant gratification and the destructive notion that everyone's beliefs are equally valid, were unready to adopt.

Enter the community college. Aptly labeled "democracy's college," it sought to provide access to higher education for people who might not otherwise attend. It accepted the diverse students and shaped itself to their form. Occupational programs were organized for students seeking job entry. Massive remedial programs were installed for students who could not read. Courses were offered at the students' convenience, day and night, on campus and off. Past academic sins were forgiven as the college accepted students who had done poorly in high school or in prior college studies. Course registration was simplified, and students took advantage of policies allowing them to drop out and in again at their whim. Adults seeking personal-interest activities, avocational pursuits, or occupational upgrading were welcomed. It became the college for everyone.

The community colleges serve all sorts of individuals as well as society as a whole. They are among the frontline institutions in the continuing war against illiteracy and irrationality. They defend an American culture, articulate it, filter people into it. They stand alongside the public libraries, museums, youth groups, and other community agencies in transmitting values and shared understandings. The colleges' societal role extends also to their serving as gatekeepers. They protect the universities by sorting the prospective students and sending on only those who have passed the various college-level initiatory rites: the courses, tests, and prescribed modes of conduct. They assist the community's employers by screening their prospective employees. Small businesses, which employ most American workers, rely on collegiate credentials that attest to the applicants' literacy and skills. And the colleges screen the support staff for the professions. The most highly developed and prestigious professions have a pyramidal shape, with each practitioner's activities underpinned by numerous technicians, paraprofessional aides, and record keepers, many of whom are certified in the community colleges.

Though gatekeeping is frequently unappreciated, some agency must do it. There is much similarity in this respect between the colleges and the police departments. The Los Angeles Police Department's motto, "To Protect and to Serve," could as well fit the Los Angeles (or any other) Community College District. Staff members in both agencies have similar perceptions of their roles. Many members of both groups feel that the public either does not understand or does not sufficiently value what they do in protecting the community. And both know that you do not hire choirboys to do the messy jobs, neither gentlemen as police officers nor scholars of the esoterica as community college instructors.

Organizing for Access. Prior to the 1960s, most observers would probably have agreed that schooling was designed to lead the students to the realization of a finite goal. The students could rightly expect an outcome for their investment: a higher-paying job, higher status among family or peers, or at least a ticket to the next level of schooling. The institution either provided those outcomes or lost its credibility. Most of the students at all grade levels either transferred to the next class in line or left to obtain jobs. Even those who dropped out before completing a program realized that they had reached their limits, gone as far as they could in the graded educational system.

Sometime after mid century, however, the concept of schooling primarily as an experience leading to a finite outcome suddenly shifted, and the idea of continuing education or lifelong learning gained prominence. People were never to fully complete their education, and the educational system was to stand ready to welcome them back. They could attend school sporadically throughout their lifetimes, returning whenever they felt the need to learn new skills or develop new insights. A student might move from course to course, program to program, without completing anything. The concept of lifelong learning allowed a total absence of formal academic goals.

The community colleges took the lead in offering these perpetual educational opportunities, and access to them became their hallmark. Students seeking job entry skills, cultural enrichment, university transfer credits, occupational upgrading, recreational activities, personal or career counseling, or basic literacy all were accommodated. The colleges offered a second chance for students whose high school academic records minimized their opportunity to enter the selective colleges. They welcomed those who could not pay high tuition, who had to work and attend part time, who had family responsibilities that precluded a total commitment to academic studies, who wanted to gain job entry skills in a collegiate environment. By the mid 1980s, the result was a student body of 4.5 million, most attending part time, all enrolled for reasons of their own.

A school that serves a broad sector of the public with noncompulsory education of necessity offers a varied curriculum. Singular curricular forms would serve the clients as poorly as would singular teaching patterns or entrance requirements. Each restriction limits access by denying some group the chance to participate. The more open the curriculum, the wider the audience.

Although the universities had organized continuing education or extension divisions to accommodate the casual learners, most community colleges disdained such distinctions and opened their degree-credit classes to everyone. Adults taking classes for their personal interest sat beside young people en route to the baccalaureate. Nor were occupationally oriented students entirely segregated; the program directors and their trades advisory committees might not agree with the graduation requirements, but, if they wished their degrees awarded by the college, they played by college rules, and their students took classes in science, social science, and the humanities.

From this fitting of the concepts of occupational and continuing education to courses and a curricular structure that had been designed originally in the liberal arts colleges, and the offering of freshman and sophomore classes to degree aspirants unready for the higher learning, there resulted a merger of ad hoc, student-centered activities and curricular concepts stemming from collegiate ideals of literacy and rationality. It is not recognizably the liberal arts as codified by the contemplative scholars. But it is the collegiate function of community colleges.

The Collegiate Function. The community colleges' collegiate function is an amalgam of liberal arts curriculum and efforts to promote student transfer. It is most pronounced in the colleges' activities designed first to provide a general education, then to pass students through to senior institutions. But students seeking only job training are also affected by the collegiate function; all occupational degree programs include a component of college-level studies. And most noncredit programs for special student groups are subject to faculty review and are accredited according to collegiate standards. The collegiate curriculum in community colleges centers on the academic disciplines, modified to fit students, staff, and programs. Since the students on average read less well than their university counterparts, their instructors demand less reading of them. Because the staff conducts little academic research, they may be unaware of the periodic changes in emphasis and direction in their disciplines. Since the purpose of these programs is to introduce freshmen and sophomores to basic principles and terminology or to point out practical applications to occupational students, the subjects are not taught with the same attention to theory and detail found in the university.

Just over 50 percent of the community college credit-course enrollment is in the humanities, sciences, social sciences, mathematics, and fine arts. This curriculum reflects the liberal arts as specified in the university freshman and sophomore studies that were adopted by the colleges in their early years and subsequently modified to accommodate their broader functions. The curriculum forms the core of transfer studies, the basis of preparation for students who would go on to the baccalaureate. It is required for graduation with the associate in arts or associate in science degree whether or not the student intends transferring; most institutions, either by state regulation or by their own internal rules, require between eighteen and thirty units in general education, usually interpreted as distribution in the liberal arts. Adult students attending for their own personal interest take liberal arts classes. And most community colleges maintain a liberal arts requirement for students in the occupational programs leading to the associate in applied science degree. The liberal arts enrollment of 50 percent is lower than the 75 percent share it enjoyed in the 1920s, but it has proved notably constant even with the growth in occupational studies that has marked the colleges in recent decades.

The Place of the Liberal Arts

Sources. Why have the liberal arts remained prominent in community colleges? The answer is rooted both in the place of the liberal arts in American colleges and in the place of the community colleges in American higher education. It relates also to the high schools' failure to complete their students' general education satisfactorily.

The liberal arts originally constituted that education suitable for a "free man"—that is, a man free from the necessity of labor, one with leisure to contemplate. In the early American colleges, the definition was further modified to include the higher culture, that which sets some people apart from their fellows and suits them to be leaders in the learned professions. As the universities developed in the late nineteenth century, their faculty banded together in academic departments, and the liberal arts were codified as discrete subjects of study. History, the fine arts, the social, physical, and behavioral sciences, literature, and modern foreign languages were added to the medieval definition of the liberal arts as the study of grammar, rhetoric, logic, arithmetic, astronomy, geometry, and music. Most recently, the liberal arts have been considered to include any academically or intellectually defensible area of course work other than one leading to immediate employment. In the community colleges, the liberal arts are sometimes considered to include any academic subject designated by the university or a state agency as acceptable for baccalaureate credit.

But such varied definition of the liberal arts betrays the concepts on which they are formed. The colleges—junior and senior alike—have maintained the liberal arts not only because of tradition but also because such studies are deemed basic to societal cohesion. The dominant American culture rests on literacy, shared values, common understandings, an appreciation for diverse points of view, respect for traditions. Each new generation must be acculturated, a process that occurs in the home, in sundry voluntary associations, among one's peers, and in the schools, traditionally the dominant archive and transmitter of the culture. The liberal arts curriculum teaches principles of rationality, language, judgment, criticism, inquiry, disciplined creativity, sensitivity to cultures and the environment, and awareness of history. It has the advantage of being generally understood. Staff and students can anticipate what a course in history or biology comprises. The class schedule with courses in physics or psychology is familiar to the public. These disciplinary areas are considered useful for purposes as diverse as training for professions, strengthening the mind, broadening outlooks, and developing better citizens.

The liberal arts form the core of the curricular canon, a body of rule as strict and authoritative as any dogma set down by a church or government. Some studies are acceptable; others are not. Much derives from the doctrine of contemplation. Weaving, painting, ceramics, and printmaking can be studied as art; college credit will rarely be awarded if they are done as recreation. Considering the essence of law, the history of peoples, or the influence of rulers is proper; stimulating the disenfranchised to gain control of their environment is not.

This separation of the *study about* from the *doing of* stems from the colleges' roots in the monastic orders. The medieval scholars isolated themselves from society and its temptations so that they could think, understand, know, approach the divine. Over the centuries, the rationale changed but the activity remained constant. Western society exalts order, logic, rationality, a government of laws, even as it rewards the entrepreneur in the market. It is founded on an amalgam of classical thought, church doctrine, and secular humanism, with technologically derived modifications. To understand it is to gain power within it. And it is best understood through the apprehension of its texts, the manipulation of its codes, the learning of the rules of its disciplines.

On a more limited basis, the culture of the workplace includes certain expectations for employers and employees. Employees are expected to show up regularly and on time, follow directions, discuss grievances, read instructions, interact with co-workers, and be aware of their environment. In the modern workplace, where information processing is central, employers value those who understand the subtleties of language: allusion, metaphor, idiom, irony. Language dominates, and the liberal arts are central to language.

The public recognizes the value of the liberal arts' contribution to social cohesion; community polls such as that done by Gallup (1981) repeatedly show liberal arts instruction high among the functions assigned to colleges. Studying the liberal arts enhances the shared expectations, understandings, and values that mark a people. The recent high enrollments of immigrant students whose cultural background differs from the American norm makes study of the liberal arts even more imperative.

Modifications in the Liberal Arts. The liberal arts curriculum in community colleges has always been influenced by the types of students attending the classes and the faculty teaching them. In the early years, when most of the faculty were recruited from secondary schools, liberal arts courses were frequently taught as modified versions of the same courses presented in the high schools. They were centered on the textbook, with little expectation that students would do independent study. In the middle years, the 1950s and 1960s, as more of the faculty entered directly from university graduate programs, they were inclined to teach college-type courses, with students expected to write papers and read beyond the assigned textbook; and the slogan ''Our courses are just like those offered in the universities'' was often heard.

When the full extent of the decline in student abilities was felt in the community college of the 1970s, expectations in the courses changed notably. These modifications were traced by Richardson, Fisk, and Okun (1983), who showed how the requirements for reading and writing had been reduced in one representative community college. Their findings were corroborated in several studies conducted by the Center for the Study of Community Colleges in the late 1970s showing that, nationwide, students were required to write papers only in one in four humanities classes and one in ten science classes (Cohen and Brawer, 1982, p. 156). While this phenomenon of attenuated course requirements afflicted all of higher education, it was accentuated in community colleges, which have always drawn their students from among the less well-prepared segments of those who did go to college. The declining abilities of high school graduates in the 1970s merely made the situation more pronounced.

Liberal arts instructors in most community colleges tried a variety of instructional innovations to increase their ability to affect student learning. Audio-tutorial instruction in biology, videotaped presentations in social sciences, computer-assisted language instruction, and taped and filmed sequences in the humanities and fine arts were all developed and used. However, the liberal arts courses still demanded that students be able to read and write effectively. Forms of the higher learning outside those modes of information reception and generation have been slow in coming. A generation of experience with electronic media has not yet yielded a pedagogy or a theory of learning that tends toward the transmittal of collegiate-level studies except through the written word. The same electronic revolution that yielded the audio cassette and the videodisc also brought forth the word processor and the electronic mailbox, both of which demand that the user decode printed language.

Other characteristics of the times have similarly effected changes in the curriculum. The sizable number of poorly prepared students made remedial studies in the liberal arts necessary. By 1980, one-third of the enrollment in mathematics classes was in courses at a level lower than that of algebra, and three out of eight students taking English classes were in remedial sections. Furthermore, most students attended part time, and few made regular progress through the curriculum. Ninety percent of the enrollment in liberal arts classes was in courses for which there was no prerequisite.

The strong occupational emphasis in community colleges also marked the liberal arts. Even though in most of the occupational programs students are required to take liberal arts courses if they wish to graduate with an associate degree, it is difficult to justify the claim that those courses are similar to freshman and sophomore studies in a university. A program designed to teach craft or paraprofessional skills succeeds to the extent that its graduates obtain employment and display competency in a related field. Therefore, the liberal arts classes that enroll large numbers of students seeking a short-term, job-related education shift emphasis. Instead of offering an introduction to the study of some academic discipline, they take on a general education form and emphasize the applicability of concepts. As they do, they become occupationally relevant to the extent that they assist prospective workers to understand what is going on around them, analyze communications, realize when something has gone wrong, interact with the public, maintain satisfactory relationships with fellow employees, and connect the tasks in which they are engaged with complementary activities elsewhere.

Merging Liberal Arts and General Education. Because of the necessity for balancing curriculum between university demands and the realities of the community college, a reconceptualization of the liberal arts has gradually been developing. At its best, this changed curriculum re-establishes the liberal arts in the form that they had before they were codified and segregated into academic departments in the universities. They become adisciplinary, integrated studies for people who want to understand their world and their place in it, who study concepts more directly related to civic action. Developing a sense of social responsibility in students is the general education ideal.

General education was the conversion of the liberal arts to something practical. Justified as education for action instead of for contemplation, it arose in the early twentieth century as a reaction against the highly specialized curriculum that had evolved in response to the free elective system. Those who favored general education as an integration of fields that had become highly specialized and a curriculum that had become parceled into a set of disparate courses contended that education should be an integrating experience. However, they inadvertently opened the system for occupational studies. To say that the liberal arts should be taught in interdisciplinary fashion because students become citizens who must use integrated knowledge for answering questions arising in their own lives or in the society of which they are a part certainly articulates a major purpose of higher education. But this conversion of the liberal arts to education that points to solutions suggests also an education that points toward direct application in a work setting. Alumni are not only citizens, family members, and homemakers, they are also workers. If their education must point up their responsibilities in any one of those areas, it can as well be justified as important for pointing up their responsibilities in the others. Coupled with the late-nineteenth-century development of the professional schools within the university setting, this conversion of the liberal arts to general education gave a strong impetus to all types of occupational studies. And indeed, throughout the decades, studies of alumni have repeatedly yielded responses indicating the value of their general studies as an aid to their obtaining employment and to their being promoted within their career lines (Solmon, Bisconti, and Ochsner, 1977). General education provided the bridge.

However, the development of a curriculum directed toward the students' general education occurs slowly and inconsistently. Enrollments in interdisciplinary courses have risen; requirements that students read and write have declined. There is less effort directed toward teaching participation in the polity, more toward stripping nuance and detail from courses introductory to disciplinary studies. Sequential study suffers as students drop in and out, but too few self-standing courses appear. Learning-laboratory support for students who are having difficulty with their studies is widespread in English and mathematics, rare in the social sciences and humanities.

Liberal arts instructors have continually tried different types of presentation and different arrangements of subject matter. A constant restlessness pervades the academy. The teaching of history swings from chronological to biographical to problem-solving to casual-connective to cliometric approaches and back again. Science courses center on terminology, explanatory or experimental methods, or the testing of theory. The humanities may be taught by direct experience centering on field trips to museums and galleries, by a chronological approach, or by examining aspects of the human condition. But nearly all the community college instructors have one thing in common: they were prepared in senior institutions and retain a respect for the way the courses are organized there. Furthermore, few students will bother with electives or courses that are not acceptable for transfer. Accordingly, new curriculum configurations, such as ethnic studies or women's studies, have made about the same progress in community colleges as they have in universities—not much.

The Path of Curricular Change. Problems in curriculum change little from era to era. How much course work shall be required, and how much shall be left to the students' free choice? Of all there is to know, what should be taught? What knowledge is of most worth? Which of the many purposes of higher education is primary? Within the colleges, the questions of curriculum appear in deliberations about core offerings. The issue of institutionally mandated requirements versus student choice is usually resolved by compromise: students are given a list of courses and allowed to pick a number from each category on the list. Even in colleges that have settled on the lists, questions of which courses shall remain on the list recur perennially. The question has never been resolved. A college that is moving toward free election is matched by one that is attempting to build integrated or interdisciplinary courses required for all students.

Whether or not courses are required, curriculum planners still must decide among offerings. No college exists in isolation; it is subject to pressures from legislatures, other colleges, accrediting commissions, and its own current and potential students and its staff. Curriculum is always made with an eye to the institutions to which the students transfer, the limitations imposed by accrediting agencies, the vagaries of meddling legislators, and the potential attractiveness to students. Furthermore, college leaders like to give the appearance of currency, and they continually make curriculum adjustments in response to real or imagined demands.

One strain of curriculum planners could be called romantic naturalists. They propose reducing course requirements and adding capstone tests or outcomes measures that would assess students periodically to determine what they have learned. The latest arguments for that form of curriculum planning are gathered under the heading "value added." Ideally, the students would pick their own way through the colleges' course offerings, taking what they wanted and being assessed to determine what they had learned from the time they entered. A variation of that would be assessment on specific competency measures, with students preparing to take tests in certain content areas. Within that form of curriculum planning, student competence takes precedence over which courses students have taken or the number of credits they have earned.

Course content or subject matter is another perennial problem. Whether or not courses are required, what shall be taught? The question frequently is posed in terms of integrated, interdisciplinary, or general education courses versus those that are more highly specialized or discipline based. For most people, the courses that they take in community colleges are their last exposure to patterns of thinking stemming from academic disciplines. Relatively few students transfer to senior institutions; for most students, any further education will not involve them with anthropology, psychology, or sociology. Therefore, the concepts stemming from many of the liberal arts disciplines should be woven together so that the relationships among the disciplines are put into a pattern useful to the students in their general functioning.

Arguments on behalf of the specialized courses suggest that the university faculty expect knowledge in an academic discipline of students transferring to their institutions. Nearly all universities require study in depth in one or another academic field. This area of major or concentration is usually highly specialized, and students are expected to have become familiar with the rudiments of the discipline in their freshman or sophomore work. The academic department–based university instructors typically take a dim view of having to teach core concepts, terminology, and introductory research techniques in their disciplines to students taking advanced courses in the junior and senior years.

Curriculum is also questioned for its relative rigor, the demands it places on the students. A curriculum is a set of courses, which by definition include specific learning objectives, media, and measurement of learning effected. How much can be demanded of the students? A course in history may or may not require that the student write a paper based on library research. A laboratory science course may require that the student repeat and write up any number of experiments. A composition course may demand more or less writing, a literature course more or less reading. Textbooks vary widely. Activities that are essentially spectator events, demanding no reading, writing, or student assessment, are also sometimes included under the rubric of liberal arts classes. There are no absolute standards.

Expectations for the magnitude and rigor of student work vary depending on the instructors' predilections and the students' abilities, which fluctuate between institutions and between class sections in the same institution. It is futile to demand a quantity of work that requires more time than most students are willing to commit to a class; they merely drop out or refuse to produce the required documents. Similarly, providing reading material or lectures cast in a language that most students do not understand yield bitter fruit. But some instructors persist in such activities, because they feel it their responsibility to use the class as a way of sorting students according to whether they are more or less able. The entire system of grade marking in higher education is based on that premise. Instructors who subscribe to it feel that if ten students of the thirty who began the term produce the papers and decode the tests, those ten deserve a passing grade, essentially an admissions ticket to the next rung on the curriculum ladder, and the instructor has done a proper job in determining which ten they are. Most instructors, however, take a middle position, attempting to do some prescreening of students, adjusting their materials and expectations to fit the dominant mode of the students who come into the class, beaming the instruction at the norm. They can take their responsibility as gatekeeper only so far.

The Associate Degree

Uses and Content. The liberal arts curriculum in community colleges has many uses, but it culminates in the associate degree, typically awarded to students who complete the equivalent of two years of full-time study. The associate degree has a long history in community colleges. Offered as early as 1900 by the fledgling junior colleges, it was modeled on a practice started by the University of Chicago, where the associate degree in arts, literature, and science was awarded to students at the completion of the sophomore year. By the 1940s, 40 percent of the colleges were awarding the degree. By 1980, nearly all institutions designated as community colleges were awarding the degree. In fact, the definition of a community college as "an institution accredited to award the associate degree as its highest degree" had become generally accepted. By the middle of the 1980s, more than 460,000 associate degrees per year were being awarded in the United States. Around 55,000 of those degrees were conferred by four-year colleges; the community colleges awarded the balance.

Several types of associate degrees have been awarded. The associate in arts (A.A.), associate in science (A.S.), and associate in applied science (A.A.S.), are the most widely used appellations, but as many as fifty more types of degrees are awarded. Most degrees other than the A.A., the A.S., and the A.A.S. include the names of particular programs, such as associate in business or associate in public service. The A.A. and A.S. degrees are used chiefly in transfer programs, and the A.A.S. is typically considered a nontransfer degree. In order to avoid the problems of degree proliferation, many colleges have settled on just those three degrees, in some cases adding the name of the student's major on the diploma.

Throughout its history, the associate degree has had three main purposes. The first was to offer an award, a terminal degree, to students who had completed two years at a community college and who might or might not intend to continue their studies. This proved a useful option, allowing students to leave the formal education system with a degree at the end of their fourteenth year of schooling. The second use of the degree was to signal the universities that students who were transferring were prepared in freshman and sophomore studies similar to those that the universities offered to native freshmen. And the third use, the one that has been least accepted, is to inform prospective employers that community college graduates have received a pattern of formal education suiting them for entry to the workplace.

In common with bachelor's degrees and all other types of degrees awarded in higher education, questions of content and competence have swirled around the associate degrees. The question of content is argued within the colleges as the proponents of one or another academic area contend for course requirements. Indeed, the content question often reaches outside the colleges as well, as state coordinating boards and other agencies attempt to bring uniformity into the requirements.

Well over half the states have some type of externally mandated or recommended course requirements for the degrees. A survey by the State Higher Education Executive Officers Association (Wittstruck, 1985) found thirty states with degree titles

and minimum requirements specified by state agencies and fourteen states and the District of Columbia without such specifications (six states did not respond). Rules sometimes differed according to whether the degrees were offered by community colleges, universities, or proprietary schools. Generally, sixty hours
of course work was the accepted minimum, with the general
education portion of those hours varying from around thirty to
forty-five hours for the A.A. degree to fifteen hours for the
A.A.S. degree. Ten states recommended the specific courses
that should comprise the general education component of the
degrees, usually a distribution among communications,
humanities, math and science, and social science.

Within the colleges, the pattern of course requirements
is varied. A survey conducted in 1983 by the Community College Humanities Association (Porter and others, 1983) found
that the number of humanities units required for the associate
degree ranged from zero to twenty. And a wide variety of courses
might be used to satisfy that humanities requirement, including
courses in composition, performing arts, speech, ornamental
horticulture, welding, journalism, and photography, among
others. These requirements usually were less stringent for the
A.A.S. degree, awarded to graduates of occupational programs,
where the general education distribution requirements might
more often be limited to only three or four courses.

Continuing Questions. What should be expected of a student who has completed a number of courses? Here the
arguments are similar to those raised regarding the baccalaureate
degree; competencies such as "the ability to think critically"
and "the ability to communicate orally and in writing" are easy
to list, harder to measure consistently. Should testing be imposed to determine competencies? Although there has been much
discussion of exit testing, few colleges have instituted such examinations. Should remedial courses be allowed to count toward
meeting associate degree requirements? During the 1970s, few
colleges were mandating entrance testing and curricular tracks,
but in the 1980s the notion that students should be held out of
degree programs until they had demonstrated some level of entry

skills was once again becoming prevalent. The difficulty with mandating such testing and placement was that for the poorly prepared entrants, the sixty or so units typically required for the associate degree might become seventy or eighty units as those students were directed toward remedial courses.

Are the students well prepared? Most receiving A.A. and A.S. degrees transfer to senior institutions. There, most studies show them proceeding toward the baccalaureate at about the same rate as comparable native students. Community college students who transfer without receiving the degrees tend to have lower grade point averages (GPAs). In an Illinois study, for example, transfers with the A.A. or A.S. degree had community college GPAs of 3.04, dropping to 2.55 in their first term at the university; those who transferred without the degree had GPAs of 2.87, dropping to 2.34 (Illinois Community College Board, 1986). However, the universities have been reluctant to demand the possession of an associate degree as a prerequisite for transfer students entering at the junior level. This is in contradistinction to their requiring the high school diploma of students entering as freshmen and suggests the relative lack of acceptance of the community college educational experience, perhaps because it competes with their own lower-division offerings.

Because numerous community college students begin with poor academic preparation and because a majority of the students attend part time, most take longer than two years to gain the degree. At Miami-Dade Community College, which awards far more associate degrees than any other institution in the nation, the median time to gain the degree is seven semesters, or three and a half years. In the Hawaii higher education system, the median time to complete the degree is around three years. Even though there are many moves toward structured programs and selective entry, few educators regard the length of time that students take in getting their degrees as a significant problem.

The question of program coherence is more of a problem. Should the community colleges devise associate degree programs that are self-contained, or, since most of the students who gain degrees will be transferring, should the degree be keyed to the expectations of the receiving institutions? Proponents of the self-contained degree contend that the students attending community colleges with the intention of concluding their formal education there and entering the work force should not be shortchanged. Those students should have a full program of general education studies that would assist them in taking their place as informed citizens. The educators who seek correspondence between associate degree studies and the lower-division efforts of senior institutions argue that, since most of the students who obtain degrees do transfer, the degrees should evidence a student's ability to enter upon junior-level studies.

Here again, the arguments are similar to questions raised by those who doubt the purpose of the bachelor's degree: Should it prepare students for specialization in graduate or professional school, or should it evidence some competencies useful for the person who will go no further in the formal education system? These issues by themselves have retarded the development of a single degree that is awarded at the culmination of a set of formal studies common to all students receiving either the associate or the bachelor's degree.

The Future of the Degree. Several groups have recently studied the associate degree and made recommendations regarding it. The National Task Force on the Redefinition of the Associate Degree of the American Association of Community and Junior Colleges (AACJC) recommended that associate degree requirements be strengthened and that mandatory testing be instituted before a student could embark on associate degree studies (Koltai, 1984). An ad hoc group of educators from several major community college districts, meeting at Miami-Dade Community College in 1983, recommended that the associate degree be defined in terms of student competence rather than credits earned (Lukenbill, 1984).

The AACJC's *Policy Statement on the Associate Degree* (American Association of Community and Junior Colleges, 1984, p. 1) recommended that the ''associate degree program should consist of a coherent and tightly knit sequence of courses capped by an evaluation process that measures the outcomes of the learning process, either at the course level, comprehensively, or both.'' The statement further recommended that the associate in arts and associate in science degrees be used primarily to designate students prepared to transfer, while the associate in applied science degree, which might have additional designations to denote special fields of study, be used for students planning to enter an occupation. And it urged that the names used for associate degrees be limited to those three titles. A separate AACJC-affiliated group recommended that the A.A.S. degree program include a minimum of 25 percent general education and 50 percent career and technical education courses (National Council for Occupational Education, 1985).

These efforts to bring order into the pattern of studies and competencies considered acceptable for the award of an associate degree seemed to be spreading and seemed also to be having a salutary effect on the acceptance of the associate degree as a legitimate designation. Efforts have been under way to have the degree accepted by universities at full faith. Nonetheless, recognition of the associate degree as an indication that its possessor has attained certain competencies is not widespread. According to a survey conducted by the AACJC task force, few employers granted associate degree holders any advantage over applicants who had comparable years of schooling but no degrees.

The trends in associate degree awards and in the development of standards for the degree seem positive. The reduction of titles has made headway; nearly all institutions awarding degrees offer the associate in arts degree, around three-fourths of them offer the associate in science degree, and just under half the associate in applied science degree. The associate in general studies degree is offered by only one in six, and all other degree titles are found but rarely. This reconciliation seems a useful step toward having the degree accepted by senior institutions and employers. Questions of content and requirements are also being settled as states mandate minimum and maximum hours and patterns of course distribution. However, the issue of which courses shall be required will continue raging as long as college staff members fail to agree on what knowledge is of most worth, an argument that will undoubtedly remain open as long as the colleges' doors do.

Questions of specific competencies to be gained seem similarly irreconcilable. Florida's College-Level Academic Skills Test, administered to all students before they receive an associate degree and/or before they enter the junior level at any of the state's universities, has been reviewed by officials in numerous other states, but it seems doubtful that it will spread. Exit testing within the colleges seems even less likely, as the educators find it impossible to agree on exactly which competencies should be measured. However, such testing might be introduced where the alternative of an externally administered examination looms, a concept explored in Chapter Six.

Attempts have been made many times to get the universities to agree that associate degree holders meet lower-division general education requirements. Even where such articulation agreements do exist, the universities often change their requirements. More often, they are subverted by the universities' academic departments, which demand that particular courses have been taken by students wishing to major in those departments. By demanding that students majoring in their own disciplines take additional preparatory courses, such departments, in effect, unilaterally modify the articulation agreements. They also reduce the students' incentive to obtain the associate degree, since the students anticipating transfer to such departments are more likely to take courses that the university departments require than courses that the community college requires for degree completion.

The issue of associate degrees for students in career programs is stabilizing as the associate in applied sciences degree becomes recognized as the suitable degree for such programs. However, many students in career programs transfer, and if the A.A.S. requirements do not include a substantial proportion of general education courses, they may find additional course work required at the senior institutions before a bachelor's degree will be awarded. This irreconcilable feature is endemic to community colleges, since sizable proportions of their students want to be prepared for careers but do not want to foreclose their options for further studies. It might be reconciled if the A.A.S. degree were to require a full complement of general education courses, but then the degree would entail considerably more than sixty units, because the career program managers and their advisory committees usually seek to fill the programs with particularized occupational courses.

The issue of awarding credit for remedial studies is tied to questions of mandatory competency examinations at entry. The trend seems to be in the direction of such testing and partitioning of the student body so that students must complete certain remedial work before they can enter the associate degree programs. But that has far to go and will undoubtedly be accompanied by many stops and starts as students demand the right to enroll in classes of their choice and as various political forces argue vigorously against the type of student segregation that entrance testing implies.

The four-year associate degree is on the horizon. Tried during the early years of the junior colleges, the program of study reaching from grades 11–14 was almost completely lost as the community colleges expanded in the 1950s and '60s and sought designation as postsecondary structures. However, the four-year degree has some merit. It connects the community colleges with their local secondary schools, mitigates the high dropout rate in grades 11 and 12 by making a natural stop point at the end of grade 10, and finesses the problem of degree credit for remedial work. By designating 120 or so hours of study for such a degree, the remedial studies and specialized occupational studies might be accommodated along with a full complement of general education requirements.

The AACJC's "Associate Degree Preferred" campaign (Parnell, 1985a), begun in 1984, was designed to encourage employers to seek degree holders. If the campaign succeeds in establishing the importance of the degree as a minimum entry requirement for many jobs, it will add to the degree's credibility. Students may become less likely to leave school without the degree merely because they are reluctant to complete requirements. And the college staff may be stimulated to enforce curricular prerequisites as more students opt for degrees.

Summary

The community college's role in connecting the lower school with the higher learning is carried predominantly by the liberal arts curriculum that it provides and by its students' tendencies to matriculate and, eventually, to transfer. The liberal arts curriculum was inherited from the universities, modified in the direction of general education, and further influenced by student abilities and the universities' shifting requirements. It culminates in the associate degree, which all community colleges (by definition) award but which few students receive.

If the universities had relinquished their freshman and sophomore classes, the liberal arts in the community colleges would have become and remained introductory to further, specialized study. But because they did not, and because the community colleges began emphasizing occupational studies (the two phenomena may be related), the liberal arts were modified. Further modifications have been occasioned by the poorly prepared students entering the colleges during the past twenty years. The result has been a curriculum emanating from the liberal arts but with a distinctiveness that identifies it uniquely with the community college. This curriculum is detailed in Chapter Two.

2

Forms and Functions
of the Arts and Sciences

The liberal arts curriculum is typically defined according to broad categories: science, social science, mathematics, humanities, composition, and fine or performing arts. Further subdivisions into academic disciplines are usually made. The sciences include agriculture, biology, chemistry, earth and space, engineering, and physics. Within the social sciences are economics, physical anthropology, psychology, and sociology. Computer science has been linked with mathematics, but it has grown so large recently that in some tabulations it is considered as a separate, occupational study. The humanities include art, music, and theater history and appreciation; cultural anthropology; foreign languages; literature; history; political science; philosophy; and religious studies. English composition is sometimes listed along with the humanities, though more often as a separate disciplinary area that includes English as a second language (although the latter is sometimes placed within the humanities along with the foreign languages). The fine arts include drama, studio art, dance, and music performance. And there are additional content categories within each discipline.

This traditional curriculum form, accounting for just over half of all credit-course enrollments, is buffeted by numerous conflicting forces: university transfer requirements, occupational program advisory committees and licensure examinations, college traditions, student abilities, and faculty desires. All these influence the patterns of courses offered. In this chapter, we trace influences on the liberal arts curriculum and present information on enrollment trends in each of the major academic disciplines that comprise it.

The University Influence

The requirements imposed by universities to which community college students transfer, worked out as agreements between the institutions or between sets of institutions, pose the dominant influence on the collegiate curriculum. An example of university pre-eminence is the case of foreign languages. When the language requirement for the baccalaureate degree is reduced or eliminated, the study of foreign languages in community colleges changes notably. This proved the case in the 1960s and 1970s and caused severe declines in the study of French and German. The overall figures on language study show little change, but that is because the slack in demand was picked up by offering English as a second language to the sizable number of non-native-English-speaking students. Within a few years, the bulk of language study in community colleges shifted to just Spanish and English as a second language, which together accounted for nearly three-fourths of the language enrollments in 1986.

However, the case of foreign languages is extreme. Other requirements have not changed much. To receive a bachelor's degree, a student typically needs an academic major and a set of classes distributed across fields of study to a total of between thirty-five and forty separate courses. Although most of the courses for the major are taken in the upper division, the introductory courses to fulfill the distribution requirement may be taken at the community college, just as they may be taken in the freshman and sophomore years at the university. Since university graduation requirements vary so little, little variance occurs in the pattern of courses presented in one or another community college as preparatory to university transfer. The history requirement may be Western civilization here, U.S. history there, but history it is.

Why is the university the dominant influence that it is? The answer lies in the forces brought to bear by accrediting agencies, the perception of the college as a college on the part of the public, the fact that most students do not want to foreclose their option for transfer at some time and are thus reluctant to take courses for which transfer credit will not be awarded, and the faculty's idea of a college course as one similar to those that they took at the university. The collegiate curriculum is expressed through courses designed to be as similar as possible to those offered to university students.

Within the art and sciences at the community college, most courses are presented as introductory to the concepts and terms of particular disciplines. Few courses have prerequisites; most are surveys of the field. This tendency toward the introductory has resulted because few students stay at the community college through the sophomore level and because the receiving universities frequently will not award transfer credit for courses that they themselves offer in the upper division as part of a major requirement. The disciplines that are in particular service to various occupational areas, such as sociology and biology; those that are offered particularly as part of a sequence on their own, such as engineering and agriculture; and those that are not part of a program but are directed more toward the students' own personal interest, such as religious studies, are less likely to be dominated by the introductory course. Other course divisions may be seen in the university parallel curriculum. Some of the disciplines, notably chemistry, physics, and biology, clearly distinguish between courses for majors and those for nonmajors, especially in community colleges that are large enough to support such separate courses. Further separations are made in courses directed toward differing student abilities. Mathematics and English stand out for their high proportion of remedial or below-college-level studies. Indeed, it is not unusual to find five or six levels of English in the catalogue, stratified according to students' ability to read or write.

Occupational Program Influences

The occupational programs impose a separate press on the curriculum. This influence comes through three areas: the application of concepts from the disciplines to specific occupational situations; courses built on concepts taken from branches of the discipline; and entire sets of courses from a discipline that form an occupational grouping of their own.

The application of concepts stemming from single disciplines to specific occupations appears in numerous courses. Foreign languages are offered for police and correctional workers, students in health and social service occupations, and those in programs preparing for business, particularly import, banking, and retail businesses that deal with overseas customers. Mathematics is offered for people planning to enter business; in fact, an entire area of mathematics known as business mathematics and business statistics has developed. Similarly, business English and technical English are offered within the pattern of courses applicable to specific occupational situations.

From the discipline of sociology come general and specific social problems for social workers: population density, crime, delinquency, alcohol and drug abuse. Sociology courses are also designed especially for people in correctional and health occupations. Physics has been cast for students in health areas, particularly radiological technologies, and for students in various engineering areas. Chemistry, too, is offered in special courses for students in health and engineering. Psychology concepts have been used in building courses in abnormal psychology for mental health and social workers, social and industrial psychology for students of business, and developmental psychology for students in education.

Courses built on concepts taken from branches of the various disciplines form an important part of the curriculum. Philosophy has yielded ethics, and courses in business ethics and medical ethics are frequently seen. Logic has also been derived from a branch of philosophy, and its concepts have been used as the foundation of courses for students in data processing. Music is taught not only as a performing art but also as a business, with special courses in composition, recording, and concert arranging for students who wish to work in the music industry. Economics has yielded portions of the overall discipline to form courses in money and banking for students planning to enter the brokerage or banking industries and courses in business economics for people planning to enter small businesses.

The liberal arts have also yielded entire sets of courses from particular disciplines to form occupational groupings. Agronomy, agriculture, and natural resources, now presented as separate programs, began as major subdivisions drawing concepts from biology, botany, and chemistry. Animal science, plant science, and soil science dominate the offerings in this occupational area. The courses have few prerequisites; they are presented as self-standing activities designed to lead people to practice in the particular industry.

Programs in the administration of justice arose as subdivisions of the social sciences, drawing concepts particularly from political science and sociology and, to a lesser extent, psychology. Students preparing for work in corrections, the courts, and the police departments study in this separately functioning academic area. Since in numerous districts the community colleges have taken over the preparation of police and corrections workers from such other publicly supported agencies as police academies, the administration of justice programs have moved into the collegiate arena and become an important source of students for the social sciences.

Other programs have drawn on the liberal arts to form separate occupational areas. Computer science grew out of logic and mathematics, and engineering technology is associated with mathematics and physics. Although the community colleges cannot claim full responsibility for forming these programs around the disciplines, the programs have become quite prominent in those institutions. Computer science alone accounts for 9 percent of the enrollment in all the science disciplines. Enrollments in electrical or electronic engineering classes dominate the engineering curriculum; 80 percent of the total engineering enrollment is students planning to enter occupations that do not demand the baccalaureate.

Student Interest

A third major influence on the liberal arts curriculum is revealed by the courses that have been developed for special student interest. This category is not nearly so large as the university parallel and occupational areas, but it still accounts for some of the more innovative and specialized curricula. Popular are foreign languages offered for travelers in the form of conversation classes and occasional specialized courses such as Italian for opera lovers or French for chefs. Some of the colleges have done imaginative work in history by engaging students' attention in oral-history projects or in local history. Anthropology is sometimes offered as special studies of the local community or of special cultures within it. Interdisciplinary natural science seeks to increase science literacy in general or knowledge of the environment in particular. The earth and space sciences have engaged the attention of students with planetary shows and with special studies of geography and geology of the region. Economics for consumers is sometimes offered. While continuing to draw students, these types of courses are rarely required for associate degrees or occupational certificates. They appear more often as general education options for nonmajors, in adult and continuing education programs, and as specialized electives brought forth by instructors with particular interest in developing innovative presentations.

Enrollment Patterns

Enrollments in the collegiate curriculum relate closely to the influences exerted by universities, occupations, and special interests of students. Here the university dominates, and most of the enrollment is in classes that carry university-transfer credits. Occupations also exert a major influence, with courses in service to the various occupational programs enrolling sizable proportions of the students. Courses for students' special interest claim a smaller share of the collegiate curriculum.

Obtaining precise data on enrollments, prerequisites, students for whom courses are intended, and related curricular information is difficult, because the data are not collected routinely on a nationwide basis. They are collected by agencies in some of the states, but between-state comparisons are precarious, because the definitions employed are extremely varied. For example, "academic transfer, basic education, and general education" and "occupational preparatory, supplemental, and home and family" constitute the curriculum categories reported by Washington's community colleges; "business, health, technology, baccalaureate-oriented, remedial, adult basic education—general education development—English as a second language, and general studies" are the breakdowns used in Illinois. Which courses go where?

According to counts made by the Center for the Study of Community Colleges, enrollments in the various disciplines show considerable stability. Overall, the liberal arts accounted for 51 percent of all credit-course enrollments in the large, urban districts in 1983 and 54 percent of all credit classes offered in public colleges nationwide in 1986. As shown in Table 1, five of the six broad categories within the liberal arts have similar proportions of the enrollment: the humanities and social sciences each account for 10 percent of the total enrollment, mathematics and composition each for 9 percent, the sciences for 8 percent, and the fine arts for 4 percent.

Variations in enrollments between districts and between disciplines within the liberal arts depend on the relative emphasis that the colleges place on offerings directed toward baccalaureate studies and curricula leading toward more immediate employment possibilities. The variation depends also on whether the district is responsible for adult basic education or whether that function belongs to the adult division of the lower schools in its region. Chicago is considerably below the mean in the proportion of its enrollments in the fine arts (1 percent) but well above in the number of students in composition classes (20 percent). Miami-Dade is high in humanities enrollments (14 percent); Los Angeles is low in composition enrollments (5 percent); St. Louis is well above the norm in mathematics (12 percent).

Table 1. Percentage of Total Course Enrollments in Liberal Arts Areas in Six College Districts, Fall 1983.

	Chicago	Dallas	Los Angeles	Maricopa	Miami-Dade	St. Louis	Six-District Weighted Average
Humanities	8%	13%	11%	9%	14%	8%	10%
Social science	11	12	9	9	12	9	10
Science	13	6	7	6	11	7	8
Mathematics	9	11	7	8	11	12	9
Composition	20	10	5	9	10	10	9
Fine arts	1	4	6	3	3	5	4
All liberal arts	63	56	45	44	61	50	51
All non-liberal arts	37	44	55	56	39	50	49

Within the districts, enrollments vary even more dramatically between colleges. The ratio of science enrollments depends
largely on the particular campus's emphasis on health-related
occupational programs. Science accounts for 21 percent of the
enrollment at the Medical Center Campus of Miami-Dade and
for 18 percent at Malcolm X College in Chicago. The colleges
without nursing and allied health programs have little science
enrollment; for example, 1 percent and 2 percent, respectively,
in the Maricopa district's Rio Salado and South Mountain
colleges.

Variation also occurs over time. Between 1980 and 1983,
enrollments in mathematics increased in all six of the large urban districts, while at the same time the sciences were down
in three of the districts, steady in two others. These enrollment
moves are related. Nearly all of the increase in mathematics was
in the remedial courses, which, in the six districts, accounted
for 60 percent of all mathematics enrollments. The relatively
low level of mathematics skills that students were bringing with
them to the community colleges created difficulty in their studying the physical and life sciences, thus decreasing enrollments
in those areas.

The enrollment data reflect the decline in students' reading ability as well. The low reading levels cause difficulty for
students in the social science and humanities classes. Between
1980 and 1983, the enrollment ratio in social sciences went down
in five of the six districts. Enrollments in the advanced or specialized classes in those areas also declined. Students still needed
the liberal arts to complete associate degree or transfer requirements, but they were taking only the minimum number of introductory classes. And the enrollment in remedial reading,
writing, and mathematics increased as the enrollment in advanced levels of science, social science, and humanities decreased.
Overall, courses without prerequisites accounted for 65 percent
of the science and 79 percent of the social science enrollment.
Only 25 percent of the mathematics enrollment was in introductory classes; 60 percent was in remedial classes (see Table 2).

These shifts toward remedial and introductory classes and
away from advanced or second-level studies were not confined

Table 2. Percentage of Total Enrollments in Liberal Arts Areas in Five College Districts by Course Level, Fall 1983.

	Maricopa	Dallas	Los Angeles	Miami-Dade	St. Louis	Five-District Weighted Average
Humanities						
Developmental	3%	0%	2%	0%	0%	1%
No prerequisites	88	65	80	78	97	80
Prerequisites	9	35	18	22	3	19
Social Science						
Developmental	0	0	1	0	0	1
No prerequisites	90	87	87	42	83	79
Prerequisites	10	13	12	58	17	20
Science						
Developmental	21	0	9	5	0	8
No prerequisites	55	53	71	67	59	64
Prerequisites	24	47	20	28	41	28
Mathematics						
Developmental	64	45	73	51	61	60
No prerequisites	20	38	15	39	24	26
Prerequisites	16	17	12	10	15	14
Composition						
Developmental	27	22	65	29	16	35
No prerequisites	50	54	28	51	62	47
Prerequisites	23	24	7	20	22	18
Fine arts						
Developmental	0	0	0	0	0	0
No prerequisites	48	54	52	62	73	55
Prerequisites	52	46	48	38	27	45

to the large urban districts nor to the period from 1980 to 1983. The center's nationwide curriculum counts begun in 1977–78 and updated in 1983 and 1986 revealed the trends. In 1977–78, introductory or survey courses for which there were no prerequisites in the same discipline accounted for 85 percent of the enrollment in anthropology, 89 percent in art history, 88 percent in history, 90 percent in music appreciation, and 84 percent in political science. The 1983 curriculum study showed enrollments deviating by only 1 or 2 percent from these figures (data on prerequisites were not tallied in 1986).

This feature of the curriculum as introductory to further study or as self-standing courses reflects its purpose. Overall, except for the fine arts courses offered to satisfy the students' personal interests, practically the entire liberal arts curriculum is in service to the university transfer function or to one or another occupational program. This has a limiting effect on what can be taught, submerging academic precepts in favor of practical applications and basic terminology and concepts. Breadth of knowledge, introduction to the field, a few principles dominate. But the reasons for these emphases are less to strengthen the students' general education or ability to apply principles to individual or societal problems than to enable them to perform well in a trade or to enter a more rigorous program if they transfer.

The Academic Disciplines

Data from the individual disciplines are illustrative of the trends and influences. Table 3 displays the percentage of colleges offering various science courses and the percentage of the science curriculum represented by each discipline in the sciences. Every college offers biology, psychology, mathematics, economics, and sociology. Separate classes for majors and nonmajors are offered wherever there are sufficient enrollments to support them. Biology and chemistry are prominent where the health professions are taught, physics where engineering technology programs are offered. Psychology is taught more as a social science than as a life science. Economics and sociology courses are presented primarily as introductions to the terminology and concepts of the disciplines for students preparing to transfer. The few classes in interdisciplinary natural or social sciences are designed for students who are not science majors but who need to fulfill a graduation requirement. They attempt to turn their students' attention to the impact of technology on science and the environment, to assist the students' ability to relate science to the world around them. In so doing, they come closest to reaching the promise of general education. Additional detailed information about each discipline is presented in the Appendix.

Foreign languages, history, political science, literature, and philosophy are the major disciplines on which community college courses in the humanities center. Nationwide, enrollments in the humanities have been stable, but there have been some shifts within the overall category in recent years. Interdisciplinary

Table 3. Science Instruction in the Two-Year Colleges.

	Percentage of Colleges Listing Course in Class Schedule		Percentage of All Science Courses Listed in Schedule	
	1978	1986	1978	1986
Agriculture and natural resources	61%	52%	6%	2%
Biology	100	98	13	11
Engineering	81	72	20	9
Mathematics and computer science	99	100	22	41
Chemistry	97	96	8	5
Earth and space	79	72	5	2
Physics	89	92	6	4
Physical anthropology and interdisciplinary social sciences	67	53	3	2
Psychology	99	100	6	12
Economics	99	97	4	5
Sociology	100	95	4	6

humanities has become a major new offering; jurisprudence has increased because of the colleges' involvement with corrections officer training; enrollments in English as a second language have exploded as the most recent wave of immigrants has entered the colleges; philosophy instructors have introduced specialized classes in ethics and logic for students in various occupational programs; the late 1970s' flurry of interest in ethnic and women's studies has subsided, and the content in those areas has been incorporated into history and literature courses.

Tables 4, 5, and 6 display the percentage of liberal arts class sections claimed by each subject area, the percentage of colleges offering the various types of humanities courses, and each discipline's share of the overall humanities curriculum. Summary information about each discipline is presented in the Appendix.

Studio art and the performing arts comprise the fine arts. Studio art includes classes in painting, drawing, photography, and ceramics. In the performing arts are classes in theater, music, and dance. The matriculation of adult students in studio art classes that are funded through the baccalaureate studies budget effects a continuing concern in assessing arts instruction. Courses in painting, jewelry fabrication, drawing, watercolor, and so on usually carry transfer credit. However, many people taking those classes already have degrees or have no intention

Table 4. Percentage of Class Sections in the Liberal Arts by Subject Area, 1986.

Agriculture	1.2%	Interdisciplinary	
Anthropology	0.6	social sciences	0.1
Art history	1.0	Interdisciplinary	
Biology	5.0	humanities	0.1
Chemistry	3.0	Literature	2.0
Earth and space	1.0	Mathematics	20.0
Economics	2.5	Music	
Engineering	5.0	appreciation	0.8
English	21.0	Philosophy	1.0
Environment	0.2	Physics	2.0
Fine and performing		Political science	2.0
arts	13.0	Psychology	6.0
Foreign languages	5.0	Sociology	3.0
History	4.0		

Table 5. Percentage of Community Colleges Offering
Humanities Courses During Spring Term, by Subject Area.

Humanities Subject Area	1975 (N = 156)	1977 (N = 178)	1983 (N = 173)	1986 (N = 95)
History	90%	92%	93%	92%
State and local	28	26	31	25
Western world	82	83	76	71
United States	87	88	85	83
Other world regions	28	23	26	25
Special groups	29	30	26	23
Social history	25	28	20	23
Political Science	89	94	90	86
American government	75	82	71	75
Local/city/state	40	40	35	40
Comparative	23	20	28	25
Tools and methods	26	26	15	3
Specialized (topical)	18	15	32	26
Jurisprudence	30	34	33	36
Literature	91	92	93	87
Introduction/survey	84	87	80	74
Genre	38	36	35	41
Authors	20	17	24	23
Group	24	22	22	22
Bible	6	6	12	6
Popular	15	16	11	9
Classics	10	9	10	3
Foreign languages	82	80	82	78
French	60	56	57	59
German	40	38	45	41
Italian	11	12	17	16
Russian	9	7	4	5
Spanish	70	68	72	68
Career-related Spanish	6	10	6	1
English as a second language	26	33	27	38
Classics	4	5	5	5
Other	8	11	15	15
Liberal arts/humanities	50	51	61	69
Interdisciplinary/survey	28	28	38	52
Theater	24	26	34	26
Film	12	16	21	17
Specialized	19	18	16	12
Philosophy	66	64	68	76
Introduction/history	56	56	54	58
Ethics	25	23	29	37
Logic	26	26	39	38
Religious	21	18	21	34
Specialized	15	19	20	13

Table 5. Percentage of Community Colleges Offering
Humanities Courses During Spring Term, by Subject Area. Cont'd.

Humanities Subject Area	1975 (N = 156)	1977 (N = 178)	1983 (N = 173)	1986 (N = 95)
Art history/appreciation	70	68	76	76
Introduction/history-appreciation	69	67	84	77
Specialized culture	3	6	6	13
Other specialized art	7	7	12	6
Music history/appreciation	74	70	69	63
Introduction/survey	73	68	75	62
Jazz	3	6	9	8
Specialized	7	7	4	13
Cultural anthropology	44	46	44	48
Introduction/survey	39	42	41	45
American Indian	4	5	8	7
Folklore/magic/mythology	1	2	1	NA
Other specialized	12	11	6	14
Social/ethnic studies	22	21	10	(Included
Ethnic	15	15	6	in
Women	3	3	4	history
Individual	1	1	2	and
Other	12	11	4	literature)
Religious Studies	26	28	24	
Introduction/survey	12	14	15	(Included
Specialized	10	11	8	in
Texts	16	17	12	philosophy)
Cultural geography	26	22	34	(Not
Introduction/survey	26	21	32	available)
Specialized/regional	3	1	5	

Table 6. Percentage of Total Humanities Class Sections by Subject Area.

Discipline	(N = 178 1977)	(N = 173 1983)	(N = 95 1986)
Cultural anthropology	3.2%	2.1%	2.7%
Art history/appreciation	3.8	4.2	5.7
Foreign languages	20.5	27.7	28.4
History	23.0	19.9	21.5
Interdisciplinary humanities	7.2	7.3	5.7
Literature	11.4	11.2	10.0
Music appreciation	3.3	3.4	4.8
Philosophy	6.4	6.2	7.8
Political science	16.6	14.7	13.5
Religious studies	1.5	1.4	(Included in philosophy)
Social and ethnic studies	3.1	1.9	(Included in history)

of transferring; they want the instruction, the association with peers, and access to the specialized facilities, all basic community college functions. Their attendance inflates the enrollment figures for the transfer courses and distorts the data on the number of community college students proceeding on to baccalaureate studies, offering a good example of why curriculum content and student intentions and behavior must be examined separately.

Mathematics is basic to the study of all the sciences, it is required for graduation in most programs, and it is integral to numerous occupations. It is a well-defined curriculum area and accounts for as high a percentage of community college effort as any other discipline. The nationwide curriculum studies by the Center for the Study of Community Colleges revealed that 97 percent of the colleges offered introductory and intermediate mathematics, 87 percent offered some advanced study, and 64 percent offered applied or technology-related mathematics, patterns consistent between 1978 and 1986. A sizable proportion of the enrollments were at the introductory or intermediate level, in courses in pre-algebra, introductory algebra, geometry, intermediate algebra and trigonometry, college algebra, and developmental or remedial classes. Computer science and technology showed notable gains just as mathematics designed for majors declined.

The literature indicates a split between instruction in remedial mathematics and college-level mathematics that is as great as the gulf between the teaching of English composition and that of English literature. The publications on remedial mathematics speak of laboratory experiences, tests, grades, auto-instructional programs, and ways of staffing the laboratories to make them more efficient. The articles on college-level mathematics discuss games, proofs, problem-solving strategies, theorems, and the unfortunately labeled concept "math anxiety." Other differences between remedial and college-level mathematics are found in the pattern of presentation (laboratory versus classroom) and in staffing (a lead instructor supervising a corps of aides versus a lone instructor in a classroom).

Mathematics instruction in the community colleges will remain concerned, for the next several years at least, with remedying the defects in the mathematics preparation of students graduating from high school. If recent curriculum reforms in the secondary schools have the desired effect, by the end of the decade the press for remedial studies in community colleges may have been lightened. At that time, the attention of the mathematics curriculum planners may turn increasingly to ways of merging the study of mathematics so that it becomes suited both for the liberally educated person and for the person seeking immediate employment. This seems logical, because most students coming to community colleges want to be prepared for immediate employment but, at the same time, do not want to forgo their options for continued study.

English composition is similar to mathematics in that most of the courses are in service to the transfer or occupational curricula, or to both. Nearly all transfer courses are based on reading, writing, decoding, and interpreting communication through language. Nearly all occupations demand reading; there are manuals to follow, memorandums to respond to, directives and instructions to consider; and many of the occupations include licensure examinations that are based on reading. In general, students could not proceed through any portion of the curriculum without being confronted with demands that they read and write. They must interpret the catalogues and the admissions and financial aid forms. They must watch for deadlines and opportunities that appear sporadically on bulletin boards and in flyers. And their ability to succeed in nearly all their classes is based in large measure on their ability to read the textbooks, write the papers, and read the questions on the examinations that do not demand freely written responses. The humanities may have lost their position at the center of the collegiate curriculum, but the need for the rudiments of literacy remains.

Remedial English accounts for more than one-third of all English instruction. In some colleges, graduation credit may be granted for completing a remedial class even though few senior institutions will grant transfer credit for the courses. In others, graduation credit is not awarded; the courses are seen as preparatory for students who would enter the college-level composition classes. There is no consistency in the pattern of credit awarded, just as there is no consistency in the way that remedial courses are funded. The teaching of remedial English has come to rely heavily on the learning laboratory, writing laboratory, or writing center, which students can use at unscheduled times. These patterns of instruction that involve programmed workbooks, tutors, and other aids are reviewed in Chapter Seven.

Many of the problems reported in the literature on English teaching are those of logistics or management. Who should do the selecting and placing of students in the various sections? Should nationally normed or teacher-made tests be used? Should there be departmentwide criteria and examinations, or should each instructor maintain individual standards? Who should select and manage the assistants and tutors? How much work-load credit should the instructors receive for managing the laboratory? Should students be given partial course credit for completing portions of courses in which problems in composition are treated separately? And, arching over all: Should all activity be directed toward instruction in the correctness of standard English? Or is the process of composing and of developing the students' own voice, regardless of form, the criterion toward which instruction should be directed? Is writing a skill learned through practice; or is it a creative art? Answers to these questions are derived through the political process on each campus, not through the findings of academic research.

Writing Across the Curriculum

Writing is a process of organizing thought and of communicating through the medium of language. As a tool for learning, the writing process itself is probably more important than its product. To learn to write, students must write. Most educators consider writing high on the list of what they are trying to teach, but many also know that the English composition classes alone cannot do enough. It takes an institutionwide effort to teach it.

Teachers in almost every field know about specialized writing. Chemistry teachers know best how their lab reports should read. Geographers know whether first-person narration is acceptable in professional geography publications. Regardless of whether they can diagram a sentence or remember the rules of grammar, most teachers can convey the style and form of written information in their professional disciplines. Teachers who prepare course materials are already practicing professional writers in their fields. Once they recognize that, they can more easily guide students toward acquiring those skills in their classes.

Keeping a journal or notebook can be a useful tool to enhance learning in a variety of disciplines. Following are examples of techniques that have proved useful: (1) An American history professor periodically interrupts her lectures to have students write for five minutes on their experiences related to a particular lecture point. This brief writing time effectively engages students more personally with the lecture topic. (2) A geography professor asks students to keep notebooks to stimulate their powers of observation. He finds that having to write down what they see causes students to look more carefully and begin to acquire the basic techniques of scientific observation. (3) A political science professor requires students to record frequently their opinions about current events. She also asks them to write short personal summaries of articles, thereby creating a record of what they have read during the term. (4) A music teacher asks his students to record their daily experiences listening to music, then uses the subjective content of these logs for class discussion.

Teachers generally find it easy to add writing to their classes by using journals, because they are an extremely versatile teaching tool. Their use does not take more teacher time, regardless of class size, and the writing can be spot-checked, skimmed, or read carefully, depending on the instructor's time and purpose. Journals serve as many functions as the ways in which they can be used. Five-minute writing periods in class can stimulate discussion, clarify hazy issues, start small-group activity, reinforce learning experience, and provoke student imagination. Asking students to free-associate while writing as fast as they can for five minutes is good for brainstorming new research projects or paper topics. It is also a good way to get students over the fear of the blank page. Topics can be anything from personal experiences or opinions to summaries of lecture and reading materials. Additionally, brief writing interludes in lectures allow the instructor time to monitor and evaluate the mood, progress, and problems of the class and to make revisions and adjustments in the course material where necessary. Advocates of writing across the curriculum contend that journal keeping encourages students to write frequently and take some risks, experimenting with form and style. Student anxiety about writing can be eased by the suggestion that the journal is a place to try new things without the worry of judgment and end product. The process matters more than the success or failure of the attempt.

Summary

This recapitulation of the academic disciplinary core of the collegiate curriculum has served to illustrate both changes and consistencies over time. The changes are that:

- Remedial English and mathematics have grown quite prominent, accounting for well over one-third of all offerings in those disciplines.
- All the disciplines have moved in the direction of service to students in occupational programs, most notably English, mathematics, chemistry, biology, and physics.
- Courses in the sciences have tended away from teaching research and experimental methodology and toward teaching terminology and concepts useful for understanding the effects of various treatments.
- Spanish and English as a second language (ESL) account for nearly three-fourths of all language study, with ESL showing a phenomenal increase in recent years.
- Courses without prerequisites dominate in all areas, although courses in sequence are often seen in chemistry, the engineering technologies, and the fine arts.
- Specialized courses for students with particular occupational or personal interests have been developed in philosophy, especially ethics, and in mathematics, where computer science and technology have grown rapidly.

- Ethnic studies declined precipitously after the political furor over that aspect of the curriculum subsided in the late 1970s.

The consistencies are that:

- A full complement of university lower-division general education requirements is offered in all community colleges except for the specially designated technical institutes and occupational training centers.
- Few specialized courses designed for majors in a discipline are presented.
- Political science has maintained high enrollments, although the students in the classes are less likely to be university bound, more likely to be studying for work as corrections officers.
- With the exception of interdisciplinary humanities, few courses in few colleges are designed especially for students who will never take another course in that field and who could benefit from instruction that fostered their own values and sense of social responsibility.
- Courses introductory to a discipline and courses in service to occupational studies dominate the collegiate curriculum.
- The liberal arts account for just over 50 percent of all credit-course enrollments.

These trends in the academic-credit curriculum are influenced by changes in university and occupational program requirements and by the college faculty and students. But not all the colleges' liberal arts–related presentations are subject to such forces. The noncredit classes touch nearly as many people, yet they are organized and sustained almost entirely within the colleges themselves. Part of the collegiate connection to the extent that they introduce the participants to the culture, these classes are described in Chapter Three.

3

Embedding
the Liberal Arts
in Noncredit Programs

Courses offered for academic credit account for most, but not all, of the community colleges' effort. Additional components, usually presented through divisions of continuing education or community services, are provided for people not on the degree-credit track. These activities are still part of the collegiate function to the extent that they are verifiably educative and socially useful. This rationale points community services away from activities benefiting individuals toward those having broader social impact. It directs the vision toward events enhancing social cohesion and a sense of shared values in the community. It leads toward the liberal arts.

This chapter considers liberal arts–related activities in the noncredit area. It reports on the magnitude of the arts and humanities presented through community services, details the difficulties in expanding these offerings and in integrating them with the credit curricula, and offers examples of liberal arts–related continuing education programs.

The Scope of Community Service

Community service is defined as college activities other than courses applicable to a degree or certificate that are undertaken on behalf of the surrounding community. Continuing education also centers on noncredit classes, but it is usually funded in part through state reimbursement, whereas community service tends more to be self-supporting. Community service is usually organized as a separate division, with its own director, budget, and advisory group, and supported by fees paid by the participants, extramural grants, or specially earmarked college funds. The separation, however, typically is not as complete as it is in the case of universities, whose extension divisions tend to be at arm's length from the regularly funded programs. The community college community service activity is more likely to be an integral part of the institution, with overlap in administrative costs, personnel, and facilities and with funding derived from a combination of internally and externally generated funds.

Community service activities are broad. They may include programs that do not fit the standard curriculum, such as short courses or courses devised especially for particular groups. New courses may be tried out in community service before they are proposed for the regular programs. Concerts, recitals, and other musical events, art exhibits, lectures, seminars, theatrical productions, and film series all find a home in the community service area. Other activities include health or book fairs, special days highlighting a particular ethnic group, tours of local cultural facilities, community-based forums, and historical celebrations.

Accurate figures on the number of people participating in community service programs are impossible to obtain because of vagaries in counting enrollment. A band concert presented in an open area on campus may attract an unknown number of observers. Opening the college's athletic facilities to community participants draws numbers difficult to count. The best estimate of community service enrollment is provided by the AACJC, which reports that in 1983–84 more than 3.7 million people were involved in "community education." However, these figures depend on self-reports from the institutions, and the compilers did not attempt to disaggregate the number of people who enrolled in noncredit classes from those who attended spectator events.

The major issues in community service relate to funding and the nature of programs offered. No community service office ever has enough resources to do everything that might be done for its constituents. The directors are obliged to extend whatever support they can derive from the college by seeking grants and by effecting joint arrangements with local social service agencies, civic clubs, and business-sponsored groups. Since there are few guidelines, formulas, or state rules regarding the magnitude of community service programs, there is wide variation. Some directors are exceedingly more vigorous than others.

What programs shall be offered? The charge to "serve the community" can be interpreted to mean anything. Community service directors tend not to be risk takers, typically avoiding areas that might be construed as controversial. The occasional forum on whether the local industrial plant should be obliged to install pollution-reduction equipment is outnumbered tenfold by travel talks and musical recitals. And most directors are reactors, not initiators. Rather than seek new ventures in areas of need, they are much more likely to wait for the managers of the local retirement home to ask that an arts and crafts program be set up for the residents.

Since the directors operate under their own rules, their programs differ. Some are designed primarily for the business community, with training courses for employees a feature. Others are more likely to be cultural and educative activities not otherwise readily available to the citizenry. According to the rationale behind the latter approach, it is appropriate for colleges in suburban and rural areas to bring in theater and dance troupes, but it might not be appropriate for metropolitan institutions to undertake this function. It would be inappropriate for a college located near one of the great museums of the world to offer slide shows on impressionist art where such services are available at a reasonable fee for the people whom the college typically serves. Nor would the community service division of a college located in a city that enjoys an extensive network of parks and a vigorous parks and recreation department offer recreational softball, picnicking, or horsehoe pitching. However, opportunism prevails more often than rationalism.

Liberal Arts Offerings

Although the liberal arts rarely have been a central feature of community services, there is reason for optimism. For one thing, in an era of reduced budgets, funds for liberal arts–related programs have become easier to obtain as the National Endowment for the Humanities and several private philanthropic foundations have turned their attention to the community colleges. For another, the budget reductions have caused closer scrutiny of all types of college offerings, credit and noncredit. The liberal arts thrive in such a climate, because they can be readily defended as essential both to the collegiate character of the institution and to the well-being of the broader community. (Of course, this conception of the liberal arts centers on those experiences that seek to make people reflective and responsible, to connect them with their heritage and with the world around them; it does not include the ill-starred basket weaving and belly dancing that are occasionally and mistakenly forced into the rubric.)

But the connections between the liberal arts and community services still are tenuous. Some data gathered in a 1982 survey of community service directors in 139 colleges across the nation point to the achievements and to the problems (Brawer, 1984). The directors were asked about their offerings in arts and humanities, whether they had expanded in the preceding five years, which community agencies were involved in planning or presenting those activities, how the activities were funded, and whether the regular instructors took part. The findings: Over the five years prior to 1982, the number of arts and humanities activities offered through community services increased in more than one-half of the colleges, remained the same at about one-third of them, and decreased at only 13 percent of them. In nearly all cases where arts and humanities were presented through community service divisions, members of musical groups, art councils, libraries, local radio or television stations, civic organizations, or senior citizens' centers participated in planning or presentation. The humanities instructors at the colleges were involved in planning or performing in about one-third of the activities. This involvement may have consisted only of pro forma approval of a planned presentation, one reason why liberal arts community service offerings are rarely integrated with the credit courses.

The community service directors were definitely in charge of their offerings. In nearly three out of five colleges, the directors had full authority to plan and present humanities- and arts-related activities to the community. The dean of instruction was involved in the approval process in around three out of eight colleges; in 13 percent of the institutions, the approval had to be gained from a collegewide committee.

Arts- and humanities-related activities in the 139 colleges were supported by a combination of college funds (63 percent), participant fees (24 percent), and external grants (13 percent). The proportion of support for the activities from college funds ranged from 76 percent for presentations highlighting a particular ethnic group down to 43 percent for community-based forums on humanities-related issues. This latter set of activities was most likely to receive external grants; 27 percent of the funding for the forums was received from the outside, usually from the National Endowment for the Humanities. Participant fees were most likely to support tours of local cultural facilities (42 percent) and theatrical productions (31 percent). The types of activities and presentations ranged from concerts, recitals, and other musical events, offered in 90 percent of the colleges, to historical or period celebrations, offered in 41 percent (see Table 7).

Other studies have confirmed these characteristics of the programs. An analysis of the humanities in community service programs in Southern California community colleges revealed not only their scope but also the way that they are introduced and maintained. Fay (1982) found the humanities represented in cultural programs, avocational classes, arts and crafts activities, films, lectures, activities involving the performing arts, and travel packages with emphasis on visiting sites of cultural and historical interest. She found the community service directors to be acting as deans with authority over the programs. They tended to be influenced more by what was being offered by colleges in neighboring districts than by initiatives coming from their own communities. Their community influence came from informal contacts; they rarely conducted needs assessment studies. Some of them had advisory committees, but these com-

Table 7. Liberal Arts–Related Activities Offered
on or off Campus in 1981–82 (139 Colleges).

	Percentage of Colleges Offering Activity	Average Number of Activities Per Year	Percentage of Total Cost of Event Funded by:		
			Participants[a]	College Funds[b]	External Grants[c]
Concerts, recitals, other musical events	90%	11	18%	70%	10%
Art exhibits	85	5	15	71	8
Lectures, seminars	82	7	16	64	16
Theatrical productions	77	3	31	63	5
Film series	65	4	18	65	16
Activities highlighting a particular ethnic group (for example, Black Culture Week, Asian Cultural Week)	58	1	14	76	9
Tour of local cultural facilities (for example, architectural or historical sites)	56	3	42	55	3
Community-based forums on humanities-related issues	46	1	22	43	27
Historical celebrations (for example, Renaissance Fair, County Centennial)	41	1	26	58	12
Other	27	<1	—	—	—

[a]Fees paid by the people attending the event.
[b]Regularly budgeted and scheduled funds.
[c]Special project funds.

mittees tended to be honorific. The main community participation seemed to be attendance at classes and events; the community voted for cultural activities with its feet.

This tendency to use attendance as the mark of value was justified by the fact that the community service activities were in the main self-supporting. An offering that the community showed up and paid for was considered a good one. The educative value of the offering was rarely considered; the programs depended more on marketing and responding to clients who could and would pay for their attendance. Only four of the eight institutions that Fay studied had humanities forums, but all of them were involved in presenting fine arts performances and trips or excursions. In one college, the program emphasis was almost exclusively on concerts, dance programs, travel films, and attendant lectures; in another, it was on travel and travel films. Fay's classification scheme revealed that among all the community service classes offered, the liberal arts accounted for about 70 percent of the total if the definition included personal enrichment, problem solving, and arts and crafts activities. The latter finding confirmed the conclusion reached by Karvelis (1978) in his study of community services in California community colleges.

Prior studies of twenty colleges in fourteen states had yielded similar information (Center for the Study of Community Colleges, 1978). The pervasiveness and types of offerings ranged from no programs in most of the private colleges to an open campus for community education at one large comprehensive college. Most colleges combined the continuing education and community service functions and offered both credit and noncredit courses, speakers, and special programs and events on campus in the evenings and in outreach centers. One such program claimed to serve over 60,000 people in a single year by offering free activities. Estimates on the percentage of total offerings in the humanities were never higher than 20 percent, and most were around 5 percent. Several directors noted that humanities-related courses were most frequently requested by senior citizens.

Does community service stimulate interest in other college offerings? Of the several people on each campus who were asked whether subsequent enrollments in credit courses increased, the community service directors were most likely to believe that they did. Some directors and counselors suggested that adults sometimes "tested the water" by returning to school through ungraded classes. On the other hand, deans of instruction and department chairpersons were less likely to believe that the presentations stimulated their enrollments. Few special efforts to increase liberal arts offerings were mentioned, and although several colleges sponsored cultural events series such as art shows, musical performances, and plays, either through community services or through student activities, there was practically no relationship between them and the credit-course program.

Connecting the Services

Although the enrollment-stimulating effect of community service offerings is arguable, there is a distinct problem in connecting community services with the academic credit program. This centers on the practicalities of bringing the regular faculty into active participation. The results of several large-scale surveys of faculty members illustrate the point. In a survey of 1,493 instructors of the humanities in two-year colleges nationwide, the group revealed their concern for community services at the same time that they indicated their own lack of involvement with it (Cohen and Brawer, 1977). One question asked the faculty to indicate their level of agreement or disagreement with a number of statements about community colleges and about their own work. The statement "This college should be actively engaged in community services" drew more than 90 percent agreement, higher than that for all but two of the other statements in the entire list of thirty-four. Yet in that same survey, when asked how many hours they had devoted to various activities on their most recent working day, these same instructors indicated that they spent less time in community services than in any other activity except professional association work or their own graduate education; eight other activities occupied more of their time. Nor were they particularly interested in spending more of their own time in community services. When asked, if they had free choice in the matter, how much time they would give to a variety of activities, 31 percent of them said that they would give "more than now" to community service. The only choices to receive a *lower* percentage were administrative activities, professional association work, classroom work, and reading student papers.

A survey of humanities instructors in the Washington community colleges yielded comparable information. There, the instructors seemed to be involved with extracurricular activities in the humanities, but it appeared that they were doing so on their own. Whereas 43 percent said that in the past two years they had "developed and/or presented an extracurricular offering in the humanities (forum, exhibition, lecture)," only 15 percent said that they had "met with community leaders to see how the college could enrich the cultural life of the town." Similarly, few of them felt that the humanities programs at their colleges could be bolstered by "working more closely with the continuing education/community service division to present humanities offerings" or by "offering humanities through forms other than course-related presentations (lectures, exhibits, colloquia)." The instructors were inclined to think that "community service activities in the humanities tend to increase enrollment in humanities credit courses" and "an effective way of increasing humanities participation in the community would be to offer more community services (for example, plays, museum events, lectures, films)." But they placed "engaging in humanities-related community service activities" last on their list of ways of enhancing the humanities at their colleges.

The weakest link in connecting the liberal arts with the community is mutual desire to do so on the part of both community service directors and the faculty. Cooperation between faculty and community service directors has been effected on a few campuses, but in the vast majority of institutions, the two rarely meet. Where the community service directors do establish liberal arts–related programs, they tend to involve lay people on an *ad hoc* basis. Where the faculty arrange to offer lecture or film series, meetings, and forums, they tend to do so through the colleges' instructional divisions. Getting the two together seems a reasonable goal, and it is certainly feasible; the wonder is that it is not done more often. One or the other side must take the initiative. An error typically made by community service directors is relying exclusively on outsiders to conduct their liberal arts–related programs. This serves only to build resentment among the regular faculty, who feel that they are not consulted regarding program content, or involved in program presentation.

The problem is not one of funding. Costs in liberal arts–related community service presentations are typically modest. Special equipment or facilities are rarely needed, and for modest sums the faculty can usually be enticed to participate in planning a presentation. Many of them are concerned about enrollments in their own courses, and it takes little to convince them that a well-designed and -publicized community service program centered on the liberal arts can serve as an aid to student recruitment.

The faculty are not the only group influencing college offerings. Because community service is not prominent among faculty concerns, the community service director has a free hand, and programs in that area will reflect the director's tendencies. Curriculum in continuing education moves closer to faculty oversight, because, even though the courses do not carry graduation credit, the faculty usually retain teaching rights. The credit classes in both liberal arts and occupational education are totally within the purview of the faculty; hence, it is there that the faculty influence is most pronounced.

Institutional funding follows a similar channel. Community service is least likely to attract state monies and, accordingly, least likely to be a concern of accrediting agencies, state boards, or state administrative departments. Continuing education derives some funding, although usually at a lower rate, and thus receives some scrutiny. Occupational certificate programs are next in the order of external reimbursement. The regular faculty may be involved in them, but they usually include also a cohort of part-timers and have firm links with employer groups and trade unions in the area. The courses that carry graduation and transfer credit are the ones that are totally under faculty domination, with rules of behavior, teaching rights, class size, and related curricular influences most carefully watched by the faculty.

This pattern from lowest to highest level of extramural funding, matched by the pattern of lowest to highest faculty domination, poses a dilemma for institutional managers. It is within the interest of the administrators to have courses and programs move along the continuum in the direction of credit for which full cost reimbursement may be received. But increased external funding brings with it an increased measure of faculty control over the curriculum.

The continuum from participant-supported community service to fully reimbursed credit classes matches also a continuum of prestige. The courses that carry transfer credit carry the highest prestige within and outside the institution. The liberal arts were the main occupants of that high-prestige domain before the occupational programs became prominent. The hierarchy of prestige is now in transition, with the liberal arts falling lower as ever more students from occupational programs transfer to senior institutions.

The Liberal Arts in Continuing Education

Programs of continuing education are in the middle ground between community service and academic credit. The liberal arts have been maintained reasonably well in continuing education because of popular interest in self-help and job upgrading that demands attention to concepts stemming from psychology, communications, language, and political science. Several institutions have developed special programs in continuing education for adults that carry sizable portions of the liberal arts within them, and open-circuit television courses offered by many districts often include liberal arts classes. As elements in continuing education, they fall under state rules and must be approved for funding. This means that course outlines must be prepared and students must take tests or show other evidence of learning. Some of the more popular televised courses in the liberal arts have been in history and interdisciplinary humanities.

A useful linkage could be made between the noncredit presentations in the liberal arts and the regular academic program. The continuing education directors might be encouraged to give first priority to the regular faculty in selecting staff. Faculty could be encouraged to prepare courses and presentations to be offered through the community service divisions. Necessary budget links could be forged by the administrators. But the few attempts that have been made to divert a portion of every instructor's work load to community services have met mixed success, because they have asked instructors to split tasks, loyalties, and schedules and to think differently about curriculum construction. The concept is unpopular also because of the greater costs associated with assigning regular faculty to an area that has depended traditionally on volunteer and hourly rate personnel.

Where such mergers have been attempted, some notable successes have resulted. The College of DuPage (Illinois) involved instructors in art, history, philosophy, religion, and social values in presenting a series of film forums and discussion groups in several off-campus locations (Peterson, 1975). The program was funded by the National Endowment for the Humanities; the program operators estimated that it would have cost about $70 to $80 per session if the college had had to support it itself. On the basis of attendance, they felt that fees of from $2 to $5 per person per six-session unit would cover those costs. This estimate was based on 1975 dollars, but even today the costs would still be relatively modest. Most important, the regular faculty would be involved in doing what they liked for overload pay, and the community would be connected with the college's humanities program.

The St. Louis district has had a very well-organized, highly integrated adult program in the liberal arts, offering an associate degree in liberal arts studies designed particularly for working adults, who attend one night a week plus Saturdays. The program was based on a sequence of courses taught by the regular faculty. It was so successful that it now operates on all three campuses, each with a liberal arts coordinator. Upon completing this program, students receive the associate of arts in liberal arts study degree.

The American Association of Community and Junior Colleges sponsored a program in which eleven colleges designed and conducted community forums in the liberal arts. This series was based on articles and supplementary materials prepared by distinguished humanists for courses by newspaper, readings carried by local newspapers with attendant test questions to be sent in for review by college instructors. The Community Forum Demonstration Program added the additional dimension of using lectures, panels, debates, dramatizations, films, or radio broadcasts to provide information for open discussion. The humanities instructors were involved in all aspects of the program, serving on advisory committees and as resource people, speakers, moderators, discussion leaders, and compilers of materials.

Another liberal arts–based program that bridges community and college was designed in Kishwaukee College in Illinois (Gober and Wiseman, 1979). Community leaders from three rural areas sought the college's assistance in developing educational, recreational, and cultural programs. The college staff arranged for funding through the Illinois Community College Board, a philanthropic foundation, and a university branch. Together, the group arranged for drama productions, dance lessons, state park tours, astronomical observations, and crafts. This program, which involved over 4,000 participants annually, affords an example of what can be done when a coordinator with imagination and knowledge of funding sources gets involved.

Miami-Dade Community College reaches out for junior high and high school students through an arts program. The students participate in after-school and weekend dance, art, and music activities. The college also sponsors a social science visiting speakers' group, bringing in social psychologists and political scientists to discuss controversial issues with the public. Since 1984, the Downtown Campus of Miami-Dade has sponsored an annual extraordinarily successful book fair. With support from the public library system and funds contributed by city and county governments and corporate donors, the college offers the fair as a public service. College staff, local bookstore owners, and community volunteers organize and promote the events, which include street performers, autograph parties, book stalls, and lectures by notable authors, all open free to the public during the course of a week. Over 100,000 people attend each year.

Summary and Prognosis

These few examples of liberal arts–related community service and continuing education efforts include some organized exclusively by program directors and others where administrators, faculty, or community groups have taken the initiative. Regardless of the pattern, some person or group must act. In the majority of colleges, such actors are scarce. More often, the community service directors take the easier path of imitating activities in other colleges or of waiting for the college president or a concerned citizen to suggest ventures. As one director noted in an interview, "We don't consciously say we want to offer liberal arts courses. We go by the needs expressed by the community or an instructor bringing in an outline."

Similarly, few instructors take responsibility for coordinating community-based programs. Most prefer that someone else solicit funds and permissions, advertise the events, and arrange for date, time, and space, they themselves then giving the lecture, demonstration, reading, or recital. Coordinating an entire program lies outside their role definition. And only in the rarest instances do students organize community-related efforts on their own.

In some colleges, concerned staff members have mitigated these problems by forming advisory committees composed of interested lay people, instructors, and administrators. The use of advisory committees in connecting community college occupational programs to their constituent groups has a lengthy history. More recent is the realization that such committees could also be used in strengthening and promoting the liberal arts. In the past few years, such committees have been formed in around 15 percent of the colleges nationwide (if community arts councils are included in the definition). This involves the college staff in obtaining preliminary informal approval from their administration, designing the committee's working procedures, gaining formal approval from the board of trustees, generating support for the committee from among the faculty at large, selecting the committee, and convening the group. Where the formation of such committees has been done successfully, the members have been chosen from among influential community people who have been willing to support the colleges' liberal arts programs and to offer a direct connection to the community. In many of these efforts, the faculty have circumvented the community service director and gone directly to the lay citizenry as a way of gaining the needed community connection. The most successful efforts have been led by faculty members who have experience with the politics of their institutions and who have the tenacity to follow their ideas to a conclusion (see, for example, Berger, 1982).

In sum, in all cases where the community served by the college does not enjoy a surfeit of liberal arts offerings, and that applies probably to every district, the concerned community service directors could strengthen that aspect of their programs by involving the faculty and assisting in creating lay advisory committees to the liberal arts program on campus. The understanding and application of liberal arts concepts are essential for enhancing community cohesion through shared values. If this is not done by our institutions of higher education, then who shall do it? Unfortunately, in most communities, the ground has been surrendered to other groups without a struggle.

The historical function of higher education is a graded school for the young and a stepping-stone to the professions. Institutional funding and public perception rest on those two foundations. Hence, community service would have a low priority in the best of times. The idea of lifelong learning has not fully run its course, but there has been a retreat from it. In 1978, passage of the ballot measure known as Proposition 13, which cut property taxes in California, reduced the amount of local tax funds available to that state's community colleges for the support of community services. In 1986, the California Master Plan commission issued a report indicating a hierarchy of priorities for the colleges, with transfer and vocational education as primary functions and remedial education an important secondary function; noncredit adult education and fee-based community services were considered "authorized" functions. Similar moves to restrict the colleges' offerings in continuing education were made in other states, occasioned by opposition to the use of public funds to support students who attend college without definitive goals. The colleges were to be brought back into the mainstream of graded education, offering freshman and sophomore studies, education leading people to gain better jobs, and remedial work that would correct the deficiencies of the lower schools whose students graduated without learning basic reading, writing, and arithmetic. All else was to be put on a self-supporting basis; the colleges could offer it, but the participants themselves had to pay the cost.

Ideally, providing liberal arts education for the community would give the colleges a more direct role in enhancing public awareness of societal issues. But this is not likely to happen. Prime among the reasons is that higher education's role as social critic fell into disrepute because of the excesses of the 1960s campus activities against the Vietnam War and the corporate state and in favor of civil rights for minorities. Although the community colleges were decidedly less involved in those activities, by the 1980s, most collegiate institutions had withdrawn from the field of direct social involvement. The justification for this withdrawal is that attempting to educate the public on social issues is a dangerous, potentially divisive activity. It might be a useful function if people used the ballot box, town meetings, and the legislative process as their major channels for redressing grievances. But the tendency is more for them to band together in voluntary associations and to use the courts. The community colleges have never become involved in assisting people to form associations that would deal with one or another social problem. That avenue of community service is completely alien to their traditions.

For the community college to attempt to open dialogue on rent control, nuclear weaponry, toxic waste disposal, fetal rights, or any of a score of other social issues would tend away from its self-ordained role as guardian of the status quo. The liberal arts may make inroads in community service areas, but they will not be along the dimension of concern for societal issues; they will be toward offering courses that satisfy individual interests and presentations that attempt to elevate a cultural tone.

If the faculty were more inclined to participate in noncredit presentations, a greater emphasis on liberal arts concepts in community service programs would probably result. The faculty teaching the humanities, arts, sciences, and social sciences represent a constant, an institutional memory of the liberal arts. They could connect programs for the community with degree-credit classes, to the benefit of both. The reasons why they tend not to be so involved are detailed in Chapter Four, along with commentary on other dimensions of faculty functioning.

4

Faculty Roles in
Shaping the Curriculum

The faculty are the arbiters of the collegiate curriculum. The universities and state agencies change requirements, the students seek out or avoid certain programs, but the faculty transmit the concepts and ideas. They decide on course content and level, select the textbooks, determine classroom activity patterns, write and mark the examinations, and, in general, structure the conditions of learning. No aspect of the curriculum can be understood without considering the faculty.

Many characteristics of the faculty affect their work. The instructors' age relates to their concern for their students. Their level of graduate school preparation is related to their depth of interest in an academic discipline. The length of time that the instructors have spent in a single college is associated with their power to control the curriculum. The level of professionalization of the faculty as a whole affects the way they transmit the liberal arts, from the class size they prefer to their political activities on behalf of the curricula they espouse. In this chapter, we review faculty demographics, attitudes, activities, and level of professionalization as they affect the collegiate function.

Demographic Factors

Age and Experience. Except for an increase in age and length of teaching experience, the demographics of the faculty teaching in community colleges have been notably consistent in recent years. Several surveys conducted by the Center for the Study of Community Colleges (CSCC) between 1975 and 1984 reveal the patterns. Data from some of these surveys are reported here (the 1979 survey was limited to Washington; all others were applied to nationwide samples). Table 8 shows the number of

Table 8. Numbers of Faculty and Colleges
Surveyed in CSCC Instructor Surveys.

Year	Faculty Group	Number of Colleges	Number of Respondents
1975	Humanities	156	1,493
1977	Humanities	178	860
1978	Science, social science	175	1,275
1979	Humanities	27	1,160
1983	Humanities	159	1,467
1983	Liberal arts	38	403
1984	Humanities, social science, professional (for example, nursing)	24	347

colleges surveyed and the number of faculty responding. Samples of both full-time and part-time instructors were drawn by sampling every *N*th section from the college's class schedule and addressing the survey form to the instructor of that class. This method of sampling yields data that represent the faculty in terms of proportionate number of classes taught, not by head count; therefore, the sample is biased in favor of the full-time instructors. Response rates ranged from 79 to 84 percent of the deliverable surveys.

Although full-time instructors account for fewer than half the faculty by head count, three-fourths of the class sections are taught by the full-timers. Their typical teaching load is between twelve and sixteen hours per week. Their modal age is in the mid forties. The CSCC 1975 survey had shown a mean age in the high thirties, but few new young instructors were employed during the ensuing decade; hence, the mean age and tenure of the existing staff increased in the 1980s (see Table 9). The shift in length of experience over the same period reflects the advancing age (see Table 10).

Table 9. Age of Humanities Faculty.

Age	1975 (N = 1,493)	1983 (N = 1,467)
25 and under	1%	1%
26-30	12	3
31-35	20	11
36-40	16	21
41-45	13	19
46-50	14	14
51-55	10	13
56-60	8	8
61 and older	6	11

Table 10. Length of Time Humanities
Faculty Have Taught at Present Institution

Years	1975 (N = 1,493)	1983 (N = 1,467)
Less than one year	10%	7%
1-2 years	14	6
3-4 years	17	8
5-10 years	42	25
11-20 years	15	48
Over 20 years	2	6

Surveys administered in individual college districts corroborate the findings of the nationwide surveys (see Table 11). The greatest variability in the demographic figures for the faculty teaching collegiate courses shows up in age. This is especially so in the case of colleges that have had static enrollments for a number of years. For example, in the Los Angeles Community College District in 1983, 20 percent of the faculty were sixty-one years of age or older, as compared with a nationwide average of around 10 percent. This advance in age and the corollary

Table 11. Faculty Age in Six Districts, 1983.

	Total	Chi-cago	Dallas	Los Angeles	Mari-copa	Miami-Dade	St. Louis
0–30 years	3%	1%	7%	2%	0%	8%	7%
31–40 years	25	13	40	19	24	32	34
41–50 years	37	42	37	37	44	42	35
51–60 years	23	31	13	28	26	14	10
61 years +	12	14	3	20	7	5	14

increase in years of experience in a college have several implications for the collegiate connection. The survey reported in detail in *The Two-Year College Instructor Today* (Cohen and Brawer, 1977) revealed that the younger instructors had a greater concern for students, defined as spending more time in interaction with students outside class and being more conscious of qualities that they would want their students to gain. Instructors who were high in this construct generally tended to be involved practitioners who were also high in functional potential, a trait measuring self-integration. The older instructors tended more to be involved with the managerial aspects of their work: committee service, community relations, professional association activities, research on teaching, and similar extraclassroom responsibilities.

This suggests that the older faculty group may be in better position to promote policies that affect student transfer and to ensure that the liberal arts retain a prominent place in the curriculum. They may be able to influence other college staff members to join in organizing transfer-related activities, modifying curriculum and course entry requirements to maximize student success, and maintaining liberal arts graduation requirements. The instructors with the longest period of service, naturally a correlate of age, seem most likely to be involved in these essential components of the collegiate connection.

Other Factors. Approximately three-fourths of the collegiate instructors hold the master's degree as their highest degree, and around one-fourth hold the doctorate. Some change has occurred in these figures; as the influx of new instructors without doctoral degrees tapered off in the 1970s, the percentage of staff with the degree increased. The reason is that sizable numbers of faculty tend to earn the degree after they have been hired: in 1975, one-fourth of the instructors were working on a higher degree, a figure that had dropped to 18 percent by 1983.

Demographic variability shows up when faculty in private and public institutions are compared, with the private colleges having a higher percentage of female instructors. Overall, women are still more likely to be part-time instructors and less likely to hold the doctorate. Exactly two-thirds of the faculty are men. Fewer than 10 percent are members of ethnic minorities. The consistency of these ratios over the past decade suggests that affirmative action has been more form than substance. Perhaps if more new faculty had been employed during the period, the figures would have shifted.

The data on sex and ethnicity are useful for rounding off a general picture of the faculty, but they do not seem to be related to the way the instructors approach their work. Male and female instructors appear to be equally involved with their teaching and professional activities; that which propels them to be more or less concerned for curriculum or student flow is not directly gender related. Similarly, ethnicity is not important in determining the instructor's relationship to the collegiate function, although there might be an indirect association with student transfer in the form of role modeling.

Data on degrees do relate to professional functioning. The instructors seeking the doctorate are more concerned than others with research, a natural consequence of their association with a graduate school. Those who have the doctorate are more likely to be active members of professional associations and to read and to write for professional journals. They are slightly less concerned about their students, somewhat more involved in administrative activities. However, on such key components as concern for the liberal arts curriculum or for the number of students transferring, they are not different from the non–degree holders. See Table 12 for a summary of faculty demographic patterns.

Table 12. Faculty Demographics.

	1975 Humanities (N = 1,493)	1983 Humanities (N = 1,467)	1983 Liberal Arts (N = 403)
Ethnicity			
Black	3%	4%	6%
Hispanic	2	5	6
Asian	1	1	2
White/Anglo	91	87	85
Sex			
Male	67	68	69
Female	33	32	31
Highest degree			
Master's	73	73	71
Doctorate	16	23	27
Working toward doctoral degree	24	18	16

Professionalization

When we began our studies of the collegiate function in community colleges in 1974, we considered the faculty as a professional group and attempted to trace their level of professionalization. A profession is an occupational group that has taken on certain characteristics, including controlling entry to the group, a long period of training before a person may be allowed to enter, peer judgment or self-policing, ministering to a client population, possession of a body of specialized knowledge not readily available to lay persons, formal organization, and a code of ethics. An occupational group is not simply either professional or nonprofessional; there is a continuum of professionalization, and a group's position on that continuum is measured by the extent to which it exhibits those characteristics.

With only a few exceptions, further studies have confirmed many of the characteristics of the faculty that we found in our first survey, done in 1975. No change has occurred in the faculty's tendencies to control entry to their ranks. Certification requirements set at the state level with only minor modification in local college districts, typically include a master's degree in an academic subject area and, in some cases, a stint as a teaching intern. Although statewide faculty associations make input to these policies, with only subtle variations they are constant and consistent between states. The only control by the local faculty is exercised by their participating in the selection process; in most institutions, a faculty committee is involved in the prescreening and interviewing of candidates for vacancies. In the case of a part-time instructor employed without expectation of continuing employment, the process may be exceedingly casual, with a department chair taking major responsibility for the decision. Appointments to a full-time position may be initiated by a committee, but final approval usually goes through administrator ranks to a governing board.

The long period of training prior to entry is, if anything, getting longer. The master's degree may be the minimum requirement, but increasing numbers of instructors are obtaining doctoral degrees prior to employment or soon thereafter. As shown in Table 12, 16 percent of all instructors teaching courses in the humanities in 1975 held doctorates. By 1983, that percentage had increased to 23 and, among instructors in all the liberal arts, to 27. At the same time, the number of instructors working toward doctoral degrees decreased from 24 percent to 18 percent. The ratio of people holding the doctorate will probably increase slightly over the next several years until the teacher shortage anticipated for the 1990s brings in a sizable cohort of new instructors without the highest degrees. At that time, the ratio will stabilize at between 28 and 30 percent and remain at that or a slightly lower level until after the end of the century.

The faculty as a group exhibit a modest form of self-policing. They have been successful in warding off most attempts made by legislators, governing board members, and administrators to make judgments about who should be dismissed. And even though the ultimate power for employing and retaining instructors remains with the governing board, the faculty associations typically protect their members. The faculty have not developed succinct, reliable, readily understood guidelines for peer review, and it is unlikely that they will do so. Most sets of evaluation procedures call for faculty review committees to consult with the instructors under review and to make every effort to assist the instructors to better their performance within and outside the classroom, according to vague standards of professional conduct.

Cases where a faculty committee has recommended that a member of the staff be dismissed are indeed rare. That is not surprising; a professional group tends to protect its members. The faculty should and, in most instances, do assist all their members in attaining a level of practice in accordance with the highest standards of the group. But faculty have not developed codes pertaining to their primary function, that of causing student learning. Therefore, as a group, they have no basis for recommending dismissal short of extremely aberrant personal behavior. Unless the group as a whole has distinct guidelines for professional practice, including a vision of the expected outcomes of instruction, any other peer review would probably take the form of periodic witch-hunts.

The research universities do not reward undergraduate teaching; the community colleges do not reward disciplinary research. The ascendancy of the academic disciplines led to a set of standards in universities that precluded giving much reward for classroom teaching. The model of independent scholarship remains as strong as it ever was. The community colleges do not reward academic research, but neither do they find it easy to recognize and reward teaching. The faculty promotion systems rest securely on the extent of formal preparation and years in service. "Good teaching" may be given an occasional nod, but it is given about as much emphasis as it is in the universities.

The faculty do minister to clients. By definition, instructors teach, work with students individually and in groups, prepare instructional materials, make decisions on curricular modifications, and judge their clients' progress through the use of periodic measures of student learning. This is the foundation of their professional life, the element that brings them the most satisfaction, that by which they define themselves.

To most instructors, the dynamics of the classroom are the essence of their work. They value their interaction with students and scorn the reproducible media that remove them from direct association. But the idea of a student-centered institution creates stress. It blurs the faculty role as subject specialists and induces a sense of personal responsibility for matters beyond their control. Some students expect their instructors to act as therapists, and that imposes additional demands on the instructors' time and attention. The instructors are supposed to be accessible to students, who often feel that they can wander in to talk at any time. But the faculty may despair of the commuting students who do not take time to visit. The full-time instructors who see 100 to 200 different students in class each week have little time for informal interaction with them. Yet, when asked specifically about their students, faculty members usually give high marks both to their students' enthusiasm for learning and to their own relations with the students. If they could have "free choice in the matter," half would give more time to student interaction outside class than the one hour or less per day typically accounted for by that activity.

Much faculty disaffection results from their lack of control over the types of clients they serve. Seidman (1985) interviewed seventy-six instructors and counselors in colleges on the two coasts and noted the despair of faculty members who saw the community college as a partner in the welfare, parole, and mental health services of the state. They resented the fact that their colleges were viewed as just another of those agencies, with prison and welfare clients being dumped into the colleges. Seidman's interviewees also deplored the quality of their students' preparation levels and intellectual abilities. Students who were poor readers and writers were those least asked to read and write and were able to skirt those courses that made reading and writing demands on them. The faculty were frustrated by marginal students who were uncomfortable with and tended to avoid the arts yet who were not disqualified from collegiate studies by virtue of their lack of ability.

Overall, both the CSCC surveys and Seidman identified a pattern of professional loneliness. The faculty feel powerless to change the conditions of their work, a finding similar to that reported as long ago as 1967 by Garrison, who commented on faculty dismay at their inability to set standards for the types of students entering their classes and at the time it took to reach the large numbers with whom they were faced (Garrison, 1967).

Of course, there are individual exceptions, instructors who come alive in the face of large audiences. And in some colleges, small groups of instructors have banded together to differentiate their responsibilities, thus changing the pattern of their activities. In the 1970s, the staff of the humanities division at Valencia Community College (Florida) coalesced around a chairperson and began working together as an instructionally and politically active unit. They wrote many of their own texts. They coordinated an interdisciplinary program that included mathematics, sciences, social sciences, and humanities. They were involved in student recruiting and in student placement. They were so effective on the college's curriculum committee that a humanities course became part of every occupational certificate program's requirements. As a more recent example, in the San Diego district in 1985, the faculty obtained funds from the board of trustees to begin "Project Success," a districtwide, faculty-initiated and -managed program to impose standards for curricular entry and exit.

Do the faculty have a body of specialized knowledge not readily available to lay persons? They are knowledgeable about their academic field; the faculty teaching the liberal arts usually have earned at least a master's degree in the subjects they teach. Some remain current in their field; others do not. Three-fourths indicate that they occasionally attend conferences or symposiums related to their teaching. Around one-third have written articles for publication; around one-fifth have authored or coauthored a published book. One-fourth of the faculty have applied for grants to study problems in their field or related to their teaching. More than half are members of disciplinary associations, such as the American Sociological Association; fewer than half attend the meetings; around 15 percent present papers. Three-fourths read discipline-related journals; three-eighths read journals in professional education.

The type of specialized knowledge that these figures suggest is certainly not possessed by lay persons. Compared with faculty in senior institutions, the figures are low; compared with faculty in secondary schools, they are high. A more useful mode of comparison is to review the community college group's progress over time. Here, the percentage of instructors publishing papers and receiving grants shows marked increase between 1975 and 1983. Much of the increase is due to the National Endowment for the Humanities' expanding the availability of grants for community college staff members. It suggests that when opportunities are there, the faculty will take advantage of them. These and other aspects of the faculty role are reported in Tables 13 and 14.

The faculty are tending more toward affiliation with professional organizations. Laws allowing them to bargain collectively have stimulated membership in state and national faculty organizations, including the American Federation of Teachers and the National Education Association. More than half the faculty belong to those groups. The contract negotiations show marked concern for faculty welfare: salaries, fringe benefits, and rules governing class size and working conditions. Most of the contracts specify the number of students that an instructor shall meet. Even though the number of class hours taught is not

Table 13. Professional Activities of Community College Faculty.

Percentage Who Have:	1975 Humanities Instructors (N = 1,493)	1983 Humanities Instructors (N = 1,467)	1983 Liberal Arts Instructors (N = 403)
Received a formal award for outstanding teaching	21%	24%	26%
Taught courses with faculty members outside their department	27	37	33
Had an article published	29	35	36
Attended a conference or symposium related to teaching	76	79	74
Authored or coauthored a book	13	20	19
Applied to an outside agency for a grant	25	27	25
Received a grant from their own college	4	10	10
Received a stipend from a private foundation	7	13	12
Received a grant from a federal/state agency	6	27	29

associated with faculty satisfaction, this is still one of the most important negotiating points in collective bargaining. Instructors in one of the largest community college districts in the country are responsible for twelve weekly hours of teaching instead of the usual fifteen hours. In exchange for this reduced load, they have forgone sabbatical leaves, instructional development grants, and funds for travel to conferences.

The community college faculty subscribe to the codes of ethics held by teachers at all levels of education; they strive to teach as best they can and hope their students learn. They exhibit honesty in their teaching, espousing truth and a sense of dispassionate inquiry. They are there to elevate their students' level of learning. They differ primarily from their counterparts elsewhere in their persistent quest for new ways to instruct. Faced with a remarkable heterogeneity of student abilities, they attempt

Table 14. Educational Preferences of Community College Faculty.

	1977 Humanities Instructors (N = 860)	1983 Humanities Instructors (N = 1,467)	1983 Liberal Arts Instructors (N = 403)
More freedom to choose materials	10%	9%	8%
More interaction with colleagues or administrators	21	20	15
Less interference from colleagues or administrators	5	4	6
Larger class (more students)	13	14	7
Smaller class	27	25	32
More reader/paraprofessional aides	12	13	21
More clerical assistance	19	17	21
More media or instructional materials	43	39	31
Stricter prerequisites for admission to class	22	22	35
Fewer or no prerequisites for admission to class	1	1	2
Instructor release time to develop course and/or materials	38	38	36
Special assistance for under-prepared students	N/A	45	56
Professional development opportunities for instructors	36	39	31

to teach all, but they know that their success is limited. Accordingly, they constantly seek new approaches. They search for new media, reaching for a variety of stratagems so that as many of their students as possible will achieve. But at the same time, they guard their isolation. They want little to do with their colleagues or administrators, feeling that they above all know best how to teach the students with whom they are confronted.

The determination with which instructors cling to the privacy of their work space was traced by Purdy (1973), who found the faculty in one community college selecting or rejecting technological or other innovations in instruction according to the degree that they intruded on their "psychological and physical work domain." Belief in autonomy was the basis of the faculty subculture and of the informal organizations that they used to protect their work space from peer or administrative interference. Whether or not an instructor changed teaching patterns depended less on the availability of funds or expert assistance than it did on the degree of autonomy that had to be surrendered if the innovation were adopted. The faculty's desire to teach well is a code of ethics. Their wanting to teach independently is a norm of behavior based on egocentrism.

To summarize the professionalization of the faculty, they are teachers first, members of a teaching profession second. Few of them perceive aides, readers, or assistants to be of value in extending their influence on student learning. They use their collective bargaining rights first for self-interest and, in successive contract iterations, to expand their power over the curriculum. They tend to be modestly connected with their academic field, and the longer they stay in the colleges, the weaker that connection becomes. They are concerned more with their own and their students' personal development than with the societal implications of their efforts. They deplore their institutions' ungenerous sabbatical leave and travel funds policies, but when offered the choice, they may choose reduced teaching loads over perquisites, even while demanding first refusal of overload classes for extra pay. Above all, they view teaching as a solo performance, guarding unstintingly their right to the closed classroom door.

Community college instructors are relatively highly professionalized, certainly so in comparison with secondary school teachers, probably less so than university professors. The instructors meet many members of the lay public who attend as adult students, and that group have much concern about their professional integrity. Few instructors despair of their image in the eyes of the public. Few interact regularly with their counterparts in other colleges. Most are concerned almost exclusively with their relationship with the institutions in which they work.

Disciplinary Differences

A few detailed differences in the way the instructors approach their work may be discerned by aggregating data on the instructors teaching each of the various subjects. Differences appear in the literature about the teaching practices in the various fields and in the data obtained from the surveys. Trends are as follow:

- The foreign language instructors seem to prefer classes in which all communication, explanation, reading, discussion, and testing are done in the target language.
- The literature instructors have been tending away from the chronological toward the thematic approach.
- Less memorization of factual information is being required in history and philosophy.
- Geography is being taught more as a science than as a social science, just as psychology is moving in the opposite direction.
- Psychology instructors are more nearly like the social science instructors in the outcomes they desire for their students than they are like the instructors in the other sciences. They want their students to become acquainted with the concepts of the discipline, and they feel that students' recall of specific information is very important.
- New classes are frequently introduced in all fields, especially by the faculty members with the fewest years of experience. Specialized courses are initiated when they are not considered competitive with those traditionally offered at the four-year college level. Among the motivations for developing new courses are attracting students to departments with declining enrollments, instructor interest in teaching advanced-level courses in their subject area, and addressing the remedial students in math or English or the advanced students in math, foreign language, and music.
- Many instructors skirt the time-consuming approval process for new courses by offering the new class or approach under an old course name.
- The science instructors prefer integrated lecture and laboratory sections, with the same instructor teaching both sections.

- The proliferation of regional and ethnic studies courses in history, anthropology, sociology, child development, and religion offered in the late 1960s has been curtailed in favor of integrating new course content into introductory-level classes.
- Instructors are much more concerned with the textbooks used in their course than they are with the syllabi, course objectives, or texts. In some fields, they review thirty or forty books a year for possible use in the next term's classes. Criteria used by instructors in text selection are as varied as the books themselves, but some consistent standards transcend disciplinary boundaries: texts that offer a sophisticated approach to problem solving or that present information, examples, and questions at the highest level that students could understand are preferred. Most instructors shun texts that offer an encyclopedic presentation of material as too intimidating for students.
- In dynamically changing fields, such as economics, astronomy, and physical anthropology, instructors select texts with the most recent publication date, while teachers of skill courses, such as speech and music theory, are often wary of changing texts. Teachers in the social sciences, psychology, sociology, and cultural anthropology tend to select works that avoid sexist, racist, or ethnocentric language, selecting instead books that incorporate cross-cultural comparisons with non-Western societies.
- The instructors especially seek instructional materials that are appropriate for the diverse backgrounds of the students taking their courses. They want topical coverage similar to that in parallel courses at the four-year colleges and universities but with a less intense level or depth of treatment.
- In most classes, all the students study the same material at the same time. Outside of the learning laboratory–based remedial sections, very few classes are self-paced.
- Although instructors often rate the abilities of their students as less than desirable, half the science teachers whom we surveyed felt that their students could summarize at least the major points in the class reading assignments, work on laboratory exercises by following sets of written directions, work on problems requiring arithmetic, and understand the texts.

Other discipline-associated differences relate to the instructors' goals for their students and their opinions of their students' abilities. The humanities instructors want their students to learn to think critically. They also would like to help their students to develop esthetic appreciation and their own values and to gain the ability to study further in the field, respect for tradition and heritage, and the ability to understand self. Esthetic appreciation is held as the primary goal by music and art instructors, while language and literature instructors rank first the development of language sensitivity and skill. Instructors in anthropology and history emphasize students' understanding of their own and other cultures, and philosophy instructors consider most important the development of values.

The science instructors hold other goals for their students. The main goals for general education science courses are for students to understand and appreciate the interrelationships of science and technology and to relate classroom-acquired knowledge to real-world systems and problems. The main goals of courses for science majors, on the other hand, are to apply scientific principles to solve qualitative and/or quantitative problems and to understand the discipline's principles, concepts, and terminology. As with the humanities faculty, differences in course goals among the various disciplines are substantial.

When instructors were asked to rate their students' abilities, over half the social science faculty felt that most students were able to adequately summarize major points in class readings, express themselves when speaking, and understand reading assignments. Fewer than 40 percent of the science faculty felt that the majority of their students were able to study for a concentrated time period, learn independently, complete course assignments, integrate various parts of the course, express themselves in writing (merely 17 percent), and identify biases that might possibly influence research findings.

From a list of sixteen items, any or all of which could be selected, the overwhelming first choice (53 percent) for what science instructors thought would make their class better was "students better prepared to handle course requirements." When instructors in Los Angeles were asked why women, members of ethnic minorities, and the handicapped tended to be underrepresented in science courses, programs, and careers, one-third reported that women lack knowledge about science careers, and 29 percent said that women have poor mathematics backgrounds. Over 40 percent stated that minority students have inadequate backgrounds in the sciences, poor backgrounds in mathematics, and limited preparation to comprehend course material. Physical barriers were cited by one-third of the respondents as deterrents for the handicapped.

But science and social science instructors also felt that mathematical and/or statistical ability, writing papers, doing laboratory exercises, and identifying research biases were less important for student success than the ability to summarize readings, the necessary time to complete course assignments, and the ability to use arithmetic to solve problems. And although these same science instructors felt that their students should take time to study, do mathematics, and understand their readings, significantly fewer instructors believed that their students could do these tasks adequately. Generally, if an activity were considered very important by the instructors, they believed only half their students able to do it adequately. Science instructors tended to perceive students' abilities as lower than did nonscience instructors.

Attitudes toward specific job-related issues may vary depending on the situation. During the 1970s, the decline in humanities enrollments in community colleges distinctly affected the way that faculty viewed their work. Increasing numbers felt that their colleges' humanities curriculum should be modified, even though few were able to consider humanities instruction through approaches other than the university parallel course format. Requiring courses for students enrolled in occupational programs and/or developing and implementing interdisciplinary courses seemed appropriate and feasible, although some instructors argued that the integrated courses cannibalized the specific courses.

The discipline-related differences are not as pronounced as those found among the universities' academic departments, and they are considerably less distinct than the differences between the liberal arts instructors as a whole and the instructors in occupational programs. As an example, the idea of recruiting

students from high schools in order to compensate for enrollment declines seems generally unappealing to most faculty members in the liberal arts. By self-report, only one in eight instructors had ever gone into a high school seeking students or even
talking about comparable classes with the high school teachers.
Most, in community colleges and universities alike, seem to feel
that that is outside their area of responsibility. By contrast, the
occupational program faculty typically coordinate curriculum
with secondary schools, recruit students, and often organize their
own follow-up studies to see where the students obtain jobs.

Seidman (1985) reported a split in satisfaction between
instructors in career and collegiate programs, with the latter
seeming less content. The faculty frustrations include the peck-
ing order of higher education, with the community colleges on
the lower end; the sentiment that these colleges perform the most
difficult jobs in higher education; the administratively maintained lines of separation between programs; a sense of professional loneliness defined by little interaction with colleagues on
intellectual matters; and the idea of the community college as
less a college than a member of a postsecondary movement.

The liberal arts faculty sometimes band together to relieve
their frustrations. At Richland College (Texas), many of them
meet regularly to discuss books and ideas. Their goal is to
develop what they call an "intellectual community." In the
Maricopa district (Arizona), staff development activities are
coordinated on each campus, and travel money is readily available. Many preretirement programs, incentives, leave policies,
and quality-control hiring procedures have been designed by
the campus faculty and implemented by the district. And in the
Los Angeles district, which requires 450 weekly student contact hours, faculty are able to teach small classes if they can
balance their load with large classes. Funds for professional
development, sabbaticals, and student assistants are available.

Effect on the Collegiate Connection

Faculty attitudes toward the collegiate connection tend
to mirror their feelings toward their work and the place of their

Table 15. Faculty Responses to Selected
Transfer Function Attitudinal Items.

Items	Faculty Responses (N = 340)		
	Agreement	Neutral	Disagreement
The primary function of the community college should be to prepare students for transfer to four-year colleges or universities.	19%	23%	58%
First-time freshmen in community colleges should be encouraged to earn, at the very least, the baccalaureate degree.	34	29	38
Transfer education should be this college's most important function.	16	20	64
Community colleges that place too much emphasis on the transfer program create unrealistic expectations for their students.	36	18	46
The best indicator of a community college's effectiveness is the proportion of its freshmen who go on to earn a baccalaureate.	19	20	61
Community college students will feel a greater sense of accomplishment if they earn a baccalaureate degree.	53	29	18
A community college that emphasizes transfer education will lose community support.	6	11	82
To strengthen the transfer function, community colleges would have to deemphasize some of their other functions.	22	14	65
The expansion of community and continuing education programs threatens the vitality of the transfer function.	9	15	77

Table 15. Faculty Responses to Selected
Transfer Function Attitudinal Items, Cont'd.

Items	Faculty Responses (N = 340)		
	Agreement	Neutral	Disagreement
Excessive emphasis on community service education downgrades the transfer function of the community college.	30	24	46
Community education enhances the transfer function because it attracts more students to the college.	60	25	14

institution in the American educational scheme. Table 15 shows the attitudes of the faculty in the twenty-four Urban Community College Transfer Opportunities Program (UCCTOP) colleges. Generally, there are at least two ways in which faculty contribute to the support and maintenance of transfer function goals. First, in their teaching role, they assume the responsibility for the academic development of students who hope to transfer to senior institutions. This requires that faculty be sensitive to equipping students with the skills needed to compete effectively in senior institutions. However, although a large proportion of the faculty compare course content (syllabi and textbooks) with equivalent senior college courses, a much smaller proportion attempt to determine comparability of course requirements (exams and assignments). This suggests the faculty's greater concern for the form than for the substance of collegiate studies.

The second way in which faculty contribute to the support of the transfer function is less easily definable, for it encompasses a variety of activities. Some of these are associated with but not directly related to teaching functions, while others reflect faculty attitudes and commitment as exemplified in actions, beliefs, or values. Faculty advise students on course selection and meet students during office hours to discuss assignments or suggest ways of improving performance. Most of the faculty are involved in these types of activities, because in most institutions faculty are expected to commit a certain amount of time to office hours. In contrast, few instructors involve themselves in voluntary activities of either a formal or an informal nature; for example, student orientation sessions.

Little or no faculty participation in activities that increase their interaction with students and with other domains of the institution may indicate that faculty influence vis-à-vis the transfer mission does not extend beyond the boundaries of the curriculum. Exposure to a sequence of transferable courses alone is not likely to increase most students' chances of transfer. But the faculty tend to perceive transfer education, policy, and special efforts as being primarily an administrative function controlled by student services personnel. Most of them do not even agree that the colleges' primary or most important function should be activities that enhance transfer rates. More of them feel that lifelong education or occupational studies supersede transfer in importance. Few would accept the premise that the best indicator of a community college's effectiveness is the proportion of its freshmen who go on to earn the baccalaureate. Evidently, the majority of the faculty share the philosophy espoused by advocates of the community college movement who contend that the character of the colleges precludes programmatic priorities as well as measures of effectiveness based on graduation and transfer rates.

Faculty attitudes toward their work and their institutions also affect their involvement with the essentials of curriculum coordination, measures of student learning, and, in general, the promotion of the liberal arts. While granting the numerous exceptions, as a group the instructors exhibit the tendencies of individuals practicing a craft in isolation. They want fewer students, better prepared students, released time for themselves, less scrutiny by their colleagues. They want to be left alone to ply their craft in their own individually tailored way. And, like teachers elsewhere, they are ahistorical; an instructor with twenty years of experience has little to offer a neophyte except for a few tips on classroom or college routines. They have no language through which communication on effecting human learning can occur, no tools, no criteria for success. Most teachers perform idiosyncratically, discover their own favored mode of procedure, establish their own standards.

Instructors will argue at length over content: adding an author, changing a text, introducing a different concept. The process dominates; the product is unknown (and to them, unknowable). They teach self; it is their stock in trade. They value change in self as expressed by the students. That is why they ascribe more validity to the sentiments expressed by the occasional student who returns to say, "You changed my life," than to the test scores made by the hundreds of students whom they contact annually.

Similarly, they believe that one cannot teach what one is not. (Here they betray their ignorance of theater.) One of the results of this belief system is the faculty's often subtle but sometimes overt rejection of the people who manage the learning laboratories. To the faculty at large, the only true teaching situation is one in which an instructor is in a classroom with a small group of students. Those instructors who have stepped out of that role to become managers of learning centers or media laboratories have separated themselves from the dominant faculty view in two ways: they are not in the classroom with the door closed, lecturing to or conducting discussions with small groups of students; and they have reduced their disciplinary connection, because instead of teaching mathematics or English, they are assisting students to learn mathematics and English. The faculty have never accepted the definition of teaching as "causing learning"; hence, the instructors in the learning centers have become a caste apart. Those staff members may be quite expert at effecting student learning through the use of tutorials, programmed materials, small-group interaction, and so on, but they are perceived as having denied their academic connections. They no longer teach content or self; all they do is teach students.

The belief in process and self spills over also into controversies among varying views of curriculum. The proponents of curricular structuralism (perennialism, rationalism) can accept the intellectualization that dominates the collegiate form. But the antagonists to a content-centered curriculum typically deny a canon and act as student-centered general educationists. Women's and ethnic studies instructors, for example, usually line up on the side of a pragmatic approach to instruction, acknowledging the consciousness-raising efforts that, they allege, are not a part of the broader curriculum.

The faculty realize that community colleges have to do the most difficult jobs in higher education, and they are ambiguous regarding the standards that they hold for their students. They want to think that their courses are just like those offered in the four-year institutions, but they know that they are dealing with a less qualified student body, and they feel that they must help the students that they have. They long for better prepared students but realize that they are not likely to see such a group in all their classes. That is why they cherish the chance to teach an honors, advanced, specialized, or second-level course in their field.

The instructors tend to be uncomfortable with the structure, bureaucracy, and layers of authority in their institutions. They have little control over anything outside their classrooms. They are able to gain power as individuals only by becoming administrators, program coordinators, managers—all roles that they see as removing them from their students and their classrooms. They find the false dichotomy between career and academic instruction harmful and debilitating. And, above all, they deplore the relatively heavy work loads: four or five classes per week with a total of 150–200 students.

The institution takes its toll in yet other ways. The faculty chafe under the forced separation of research in academic disciplines from teaching. They may be ambivalent toward the possession of a doctorate, feeling that if they have the degree, which is supposed to evidence the ability to do research, they are not living up to their potential. The colleges provide no intellectual rewards for publishing, no recognition for scholarship. Among the faculty as a group, there may be suspicion of those who do research in an academic field, with colleagues wondering why an instructor is doing research when he or she does not have to and when the institution does not reward it. Granted that there are exceptions. Montgomery Community College (Maryland), for example, has made funds available for faculty to engage in research in their academic disciplines; in 1985–86, thirty-four instructors from twelve different departments were pursuing such research (Parilla, 1986). However, the faculty in most colleges see their institutions as, if not anti-intellectual, at least a-intellectual. Clark (1987) sums up some of the feelings about the doctorate for community college instructors. In *Academic Life in America: Small Worlds, Different Worlds,* he writes, "Long noted by academics who move into teaching careers, a disjuncture exists between the intense specialization of graduate school preparation and the generalist performance demanded in job assignment. The wish to lessen this gap is one reason why, historically, community colleges have sought academics who terminate their studies with the master's degree. The Ph.D.'s are 'overeducated'" (p. 33).

The isolation of the community college instructors makes it difficult for them to maintain awareness of new ideas coming into their teaching field. A faculty that does not participate in academic research tends not to maintain current awareness of the products of research conducted elsewhere. A faculty that is little aware of patterns of curriculum and instruction in neighboring institutions must devise for itself any change in teaching or curricular strategies. A faculty unaware of its own outcomes finds difficulty in defending its belief in the liberal arts. A faculty unaware of trends in the liberal arts can sustain its own commitments only by appealing to tradition.

Toward Greater Involvement

The collegiate connection might well be enhanced by various trends now under way and by others that might be supported. The faculty could move toward a greater affiliation with their academic disciplines, essential if the instructors are themselves to reconceptualize those disciplines to fit the realities of the institutions in which they work. The community college instructors cannot depend on university professors or on administrators in their own institutions for leadership in this essential reconstruction. As codified by university professors, the liberal arts have tended toward esoterica and reductionism. By translating knowledge stemming from the disciplines into forms usable by lay persons, the community college faculty would make a real contribution. However, that takes stimulation from peers, attendance to proselytizers and innovators, and, above all, the application of thought about the core principles in each discipline as they pertain to teaching the students with whom the faculty are faced and to whom they are committed.

The National Institute of Education's (1984) report *Involvement in Learning* made many recommendations applicable to community college instructors. The report stated that keeping current in one's field is vital to good teaching and that professors at all levels should accept a broader definition of scholarship. It called for research in the teaching of the liberal arts as opposed to research in disciplinary arcana. It recommended cross-faculty perusal of course syllabi and examinations; peer review by faculty who are knowledgeable about good teaching; the use of student evaluations as a learning device for faculty members, not as input to personnel decisions; and the rewarding of faculty members for their contributions to the literature on college instruction and student development and for the preparation of new instructional materials and courses. It suggested further the consolidation of as many part-time teaching lines into full-time positions as possible, arguing that faculty identification with the institution and involvement with students require a primary commitment not often seen among part-timers.

Professional consciousness develops slowly, but the chances for an accelerated move toward a higher order of involvement with the collegiate function are greater now than they have ever before been in the history of the community college. External agencies have begun making extramural funds available for study grants; the National Endowment for the Humanities has moved decidedly in that direction. Static enrollment in the colleges has allowed the faculty to become more concerned with the students that they have, as opposed to their prior frenetic rush to accommodate ever increasing numbers. There has been a relative increase in faculty salaries, making it less necessary for instructors to take second jobs outside the institution. Professional and disciplinary associations have sprung up; the Community College Humanities Association and the Community College Social Science Association are active in engaging their members' concern with teaching in those disciplines. And among the institutions themselves, there is a trend away from the concept of access at all costs and undifferentiated service to the community and toward the traditional mainstream activities of teaching general education, career education, and the liberal arts.

The faculty might seek ways of taking the liberal arts into the occupational areas through the introduction of segments of courses pertaining to particular career fields. They could find materials suitable for presentation to students whose main mode of information reception is through other-than-print media. They could work with community service directors in presenting short courses, lectures, and instruction in other formats to the community at large. And they could argue for changed modes of faculty work-load accounting so that such innovative presentations would become a normal part of every instructor's work.

By accentuating the collegiate connection, not from a posture of defensiveness but from an understanding that collegiate programs must be maintained if the institution is going to continue its claim to comprehensiveness, the faculty would further their own work. They could support studies not only of their college's effect on individual students but also on its total community. They could espouse arguments favoring the liberal arts as an essential component of acculturation for immigrants to American society, native as well as foreign born, using indigenously generated data to support their contentions. And they could help their college's research directors design and conduct studies of student flow through the institution, an essential component of the collegiate connection.

5

The Transfer Function: Making the Connection to Four-Year Institutions

The two essential aspects of the collegiate connection are the higher learning provided through the liberal arts and the transfer of students from community colleges to four-year colleges and universities. In colleges where both are pursued with equal vigor, the collegiate connection thrives; if either is weakened, it suffers. If the colleges did not offer grades 13 and 14 in an articulated educational system or if they did not teach qualities of literacy and rationality, there would be no collegiate connection.

However, these two components differ. Transfer is an *intention* expressed by some students who take community college classes and a *behavior* manifested by those who eventually matriculate at a four-year college or university. The liberal arts, on the other hand, are a way of categorizing and organizing the curriculum. Universities usually award credit toward the baccalaureate to students who have taken liberal arts classes in community colleges, but they also award credit for many classes that are not organized around the liberal arts. And not all, or even a majority, of the students in liberal arts classes transfer. Even though most students preparing for transfer take some liberal arts courses, and most of the students in the community college liberal arts classes aspire to transfer, the content of the curriculum must be examined one way and the intentions and behavior of the students another, a concept we explore more fully in Chapter Nine.

In the preceding chapters, we focused on the structure and purposes of the liberal arts curriculum. Here we examine the transfer function, the flow of students through the institution, with particular attention to the perennial questions raised in any discussion of transfer: How many students transfer? How many want to transfer? Why do more students not transfer? How well do students do when they get to universities?

How Many Students Transfer?

Data revealing the number of students who transfer are essential for answering questions of the community colleges' place in the fabric of American education. Do the colleges pass students through smoothly, or do they represent an eddy in the flow of students from one grade level to another? The question of how many students transfer appears simple, but the answer is that no one knows. There are no reliable, uniformly collected national data sets that can provide answers. The data are scanty even within the states and within separate college and university systems.

The major difficulty in collecting data is that the concept *transfer* is variously defined. Some students begin their collegiate studies at a community college and transfer to a university after earning an associate degree; many transfer after only one or two semesters. Others begin at the university, drop out and take courses at a community college, and then return to the university. Some students concurrently take courses at both a local community college and a university. Some start at a community college and stop out for a period of years before entering the university. Some disappear from the record when they transfer to universities in other states. All these permutations affect the data sets.

Even in individual college systems, there are gaps in the data. A state university system may ask each of its campuses to report the number of students transferring in. The campus admissions officers may generate the data by reviewing the students' responses to the item "college last attended" on the application form. A student who spent a year or more at a community college and then took one course at a private institution may name the latter as "college last attended" and thus not be credited as a transfer from a community college. Some of the data compilers may accord the students transfer status if they took but one summer class at a local community college, while others would require that the student had had twelve or fifteen units there. Consistency across the system is difficult to monitor.

The data on transfers that are collected by state agencies similarly contain gaps. They often omit students who transfer out of state or who transfer to private universities within states. They never resolve the issue of reverse transfers, those who begin at the university, take classes at a community college, and eventually complete their studies at the university. And in all cases where the data sets rely on student completion of forms, missing and inaccurate data are a certainty.

Individual community colleges suffer also from a lack of information about students who transfer. Some count as transfers all those students who request that transcripts of their community college work be sent to a senior institution. Others do periodic follow-up surveys of samples of their former students. Most rely on information sent by various senior colleges and universities within their state. None have reliable data.

There are efforts toward consistency. In Florida, the state university system and the department of commerce prepare a tape each year that contains the social security number of each student who has entered the university or obtained employment. The community colleges can check their own records against the tape and gain an estimate of the number of their former students who have transferred or gone to work. And while the tape is incomplete in that it does not include students who have transferred to private or out-of-state universities, it does offer a step in the right direction.

Figures from some of the states where data are collected show that around 5,000 students per year transfer from community colleges to state colleges and universities in Washington, 35,500 from California community colleges to the University of California and the California State University System, slightly more than 10,000 from two-year colleges to both public and private senior colleges and universities in Illinois, and slightly fewer than 5,000 in Maryland. (Head-count enrollment in the community colleges of those four states exceeds 1.5 million.) It is quite unuseful to attempt to extrapolate these data to arrive at a nationwide figure because of the vagaries in counting between states and the aforementioned definitional difficulties. However, it is likely that any numbers that are used understate the magnitude of transfer because of the data that are missing.

Why are the data as incomplete as they are? The answer is that, in addition to their being difficult to collect, they are relatively unimportant to the college staff members. The colleges' funding is awarded on the basis of the number of students taking classes or enrolled in certain programs; it is not dependent on where the students go when they leave. State funds may be allocated on the basis of the number of students enrolled in various categories of classes—for example, academic, occupational, adult, business, remedial, noncredit, and so on—but never according to the number of students who go on to universities. On the receiving end, the universities similarly have little incentive for collecting the data. Upperclassmen are upperclassmen, regardless of where they were freshmen. The number of students transferring in or out has minuscule effect on the activities of staff members on either side.

Each community college gathers figures on the number of students enrolled in each of its classes and has good data on the number of degrees it awards. But there it stops. There are no incentives for spending the effort and dollars that it costs to collect data on student flow between institutions. Any such data that are collected reliably are collected at the program level, where managers of programs that are closely articulated with programs at senior institutions often maintain their own data files. But it is impossible to get from there to any general numbers.

One way of estimating transfer rates is to count the number of university students whose transcripts show courses taken at community colleges. In states with well-articulated community colleges and public university systems, the community colleges provide significant proportions of the universities' undergraduates; 42 percent of all undergraduate students in Florida's public universities previously attended community colleges in that state. However, in states where the community colleges serve a different function or where the universities have clung vigorously to their freshman enrollments, the proportion is much lower; only 17 percent of the undergraduates in state universities in Kansas are transfers. There is much variation also among institutions in the same state: the nine campuses of the University of California receive one-tenth as many transfers as do the eighteen campuses of the California State College and University. Where the universities work closely with community colleges in their immediate area, they may have more transfers than native freshmen; Arizona State University and the University of Massachusetts at Boston are examples of that type of institution.

Probably the only accurate way of determining how many community college students transfer would be to analyze the transcripts of all students who are enrolled in the universities and to accept a certain number of community college classes as evidence that the student has met the definition of one who has transferred in. But this form of transcript analysis demands fully computerized student transcripts, uniformly maintained for all the students in all of a state's institutions. And although higher education systems in some states are building such systems, nationwide we are a long way from any such data file. The data are expensive to collect. Maintaining the accuracy and currency of data files takes staff time. Some state agencies do it because their legislatures demand updated figures on the condition of the state's public colleges and universities. But in most states, providing such data is either a voluntary act on the part of the colleges or something requested of them (with no funds for complying or penalty for refusing) by their state board or by a coordinating agency.

An educated guess based on incomplete data would be that, nationwide, around 250,000 students per year complete two years at a community college and then transfer immediately to a university. Probably another 300,000 to 400,000 transfer without having completed a two-year program. Those figures may seem low when put against the 4.7 million students enrolled, but considering the number of students in current interest courses, courses for people who already have degrees, occupational programs, remedial courses, and noncredit educational activities, all of which are summed together to arrive at the community college enrollment figures, it is a wonder that the figures are as high as they are.

How Many Want to Transfer?

The question of the number of students who want to transfer is equally difficult to answer. Not only are the data incomplete, but any student's intentions may be interpreted variously depending on how or when the question was asked. Studies done over the years usually have suggested that around three-quarters of the students beginning college in a community college intend eventually to obtain the baccalaureate or a higher degree. In 1929, 80 percent of the students in California junior colleges declared intentions of transferring to a senior institution. Nationally, between 1940 and 1960, the number of those who declared transfer intent hovered at between two-thirds and three-fourths of the student body. In 1983, a survey of students taking classes in twenty-four urban community colleges found 74 percent of them declaring transfer intent, and in 1984, the Cooperative Institutional Research Program (CIRP) found 76 percent declaring intentions of obtaining a baccalaureate or better (Astin, Green, Korn, and Maier, 1984). The usefulness of these data is limited by the fact that they were obtained from samples of younger students. The CIRP surveys first-time-in-college, full-time freshmen, 90 percent of whom are aged nineteen or younger. The samples in other studies are not as extremely biased, but they usually draw students only from among those taking credit courses and often use the class itself as the unit of sampling, thus skewing the sample in the direction of full-time students.

The form of the question asking transfer intentions also biases the answers. The question is usually asked as "What is the highest academic degree you intend to obtain?" That suggests a goal to be reached sometime during the person's life. Few young people would acknowledge that they *never* expect to go further in the educational system; it is neither personally nor socially acceptable for them to admit that they have closed off life's options. When the question is changed to "What is the primary reason you are attending this college at this time?", significantly fewer, usually one-third, say that they are in college to prepare for transfer, while one-half say that they are in college to gain occupational skills. Most of the latter group also expect eventually to gain higher degrees but see job entry as their first aim. In fact, many students mark both "bachelor's" as the highest degree they expect to obtain and "gaining occupational skills" as their primary reason for attending. They may need the bachelor's degree to enter the occupational field to which they aspire, so that their responses are perfectly consistent.

Various studies reveal the proportions of those intending to transfer. According to 1986 Illinois Community College Board (1986) figures, in 1968, 56 percent of the community college students in that state declared transfer intent. By 1970, the figure had dropped to 44 percent; in 1974, it was 37 percent; and in 1978, 32 percent of the matriculants declared transfer intention. The Maryland State Board for Community Colleges (1983) found similar proportions: 32 percent in 1974 and 1976; 31 percent in 1978. In a study of 6,500 students entering California community colleges in 1978, 36 percent reported that they intended to transfer, and even among those who designated transfer as a goal, one-third planned less than a two-year tenure at the community college (Sheldon, 1982). These studies drew samples of *all* entering students, not just first-time, full-time freshmen, and asked why they were entering college *at that time*.

Attempting to determine transfer intentions by counting enrollments in classes yields similarly inconsistent data. Around half the students in the academic transfer credit classes in the

Los Angeles district indicated transfer as their primary goal, but most of the other half also take credit classes to fulfill occupational program graduation requirements or for their own personal interests. The California *Statewide Longitudinal Study* showed more than one-fourth of the students enrolled in occupational programs indicating that they intended to transfer and more than one-fourth of the students enrolled in transfer credit classes indicating that they were attending college to gain job-related skills (Sheldon, 1982).

In summary, consistently over the years, three-fourths of the students entering community colleges say that they intend eventually to obtain baccalaureate degrees. However, when the students are asked their primary reason for attending college, the number who indicate "prepare for transfer" drops to around one-third. The actual transfer rates are considerably lower.

Why Do More Students Not Transfer?

The answer to the question of why more students do not transfer probably lies in a combination of personal and institutional characteristics. More students do not transfer because their academic backgrounds, course-taking patterns, and involvement in the institution tend to be different from those of their freshman counterparts who begin collegiate studies at universities. Furthermore, the universities typically cost more, are further from home, do not offer as many courses at night, and may not welcome students who work full time and want to take classes on a part-time basis. Institutional characteristics include various problems in articulating courses with senior institutions and the practice of allowing students to take courses for which they are not well prepared or that do not lead in sequence to the completion of a program of study. This latter practice is laudable for its maintaining access, but it does militate against a student's transferring to a senior institution.

Student characteristics are among the more deceptive data. In the aggregate, the community college students are certainly different from traditional university students. The very fact of their being in community colleges makes them different; either they could not qualify for senior college admission or they chose to enter a community college for their own reasons. And here again, which students are counted among those who might transfer? Those for whom the community college is a forced choice, or those who go there of their own volition? Those taking only one class for their own personal interest or two or three classes to upgrade certain occupational skills? Students enrolled in adult basic education or high school makeup classes? The list of reasons for associating with the institution could be extended to great length.

Most data that are reported use figures based on class enrollment, rather than head count. That weights the data toward the students taking more than one class, because when the enrollment counts are made, those students have more than one chance to be counted. Using the enrollment figures, half the students taking classes nationwide are aged twenty-four or younger. The other half cover the full span of ages from twenty-five onward; they tend to be older than their counterparts in the freshman and sophomore classes at universities. They are more likely to be members of ethnic minority groups as well; the proportion of blacks in public two-year colleges is twice as high as the proportion in public universities, and the distribution is even more skewed among Hispanics, with the proportion in public community colleges three times higher than in public universities.

The data on student age and ethnicity relate somewhat to the reasons why students do not transfer, because, historically, it is the younger students from the Anglo majority who have obtained the highest proportion of bachelor's degrees. However, certain other characteristics of community college students may have an ever greater effect. According to CIRP data and data obtained from students in twenty-four urban colleges, community college matriculants present undistinguished high school achievement records. One-third of those entering universities were *A* students in high school, but only 10 percent of the community college freshmen were in that category. Furthermore, the CIRP data for 1984 showed the median two-year-college freshman family income at around $25,000, whereas the median family income for students at all institutions was closer to $30,000. Other studies have corroborated the lower income levels; for example, one-third of the students in Washington's twenty-seven community colleges in 1980 came from families whose income was less than $11,000, and that same figure was reported by students in 1983 in the twenty-four urban colleges that enrolled high proportions of minorities.

College attendance patterns of community college students also differ. Two-thirds of the students in the twenty-four–college sample were employed, and nearly half of those who were working had jobs that occupied them for from twenty-one to forty hours per week. The part-time attendance pattern is ubiquitous; across the nation, around five of every eight community college students attend part time. The figures on part-time attendance go as high as 78 percent in Arizona, 74 percent in Virginia, 73 percent in California, 72 percent in Maryland, 71 percent in Michigan, 70 percent in Illinois, and 69 percent in Texas— all states with large, well-developed community college systems.

These demographics suggest a student group drawn from segments of the community that historically have not attended college or, if they did matriculate, have not gone through in the traditional four years: low-income, older, and ethnic minority students. However, good students could be derived from those with such demographic patterns. The more serious limitation on their progression toward the baccalaureate is that they tend to have poor prior academic records, attend part time, and are only marginally associated with the institution. The poor prior academic records mean that students may be required to take remedial courses that do not qualify for graduation or transfer credit, thus adding to the overall course load. The part-time attendance pattern adds additional years to the time between entrance and transfer, years when alternative pursuits loom as more attractive than further studies. The marginal association with the institution means that the courses must carry the full burden of involvement with the college; counseling, clubs and other activities, informal contacts with faculty members and peers, and similar potential learning encounters are minimal.

Students who would transfer should be encouraged by being involved in a full complement of collegiate activities. They
should take classes similar to those that they would find in the
universities, should take more than one class at a time, since
progression toward the baccalaureate is certainly easier for
students in full-time attendance, and should take advantage of
the various transfer-related services that the colleges offer. However, most community college students exhibit behaviors that
belie their stated intentions. They tend to participate in the
liberal arts only to the extent that their programs require, steer-
ing away from science unless they are in health fields and studying the humanities only if they need those courses for graduation. They gravitate toward the social sciences, because they
want classes that place few demands on their capacity for using
mathematics. An examination of the transcripts of nearly 9,000
students enrolled in the Los Angeles district, reviewing all
courses in which those students were enrolled over a five-year
span, revealed that just over 40 percent of them had completed
one or more science courses. A follow-up survey of students in
that same district found that 23 percent of them had been above
the sample average in their participation in high school science
courses but were below the average in the number of college
science courses taken.

One of the CSCC studies tested the proposition that student degree aspirations may not be a relevant measure of transfer
potential. Estela M. Bensimon, at the time an associate at the
Center, developed the construct "predisposition to transfer"
and took the lead in creating a measure of individual attitudes
and behaviors that could facilitate a systematic classification of
potential transfer students on the basis of commitment. The construct was verified in the center's survey of 1,613 students in
twenty-four urban colleges (Cohen, Brawer, and Bensimon,
1985).

In summary, the transfer rates are affected by certain
characteristics of the students. On average, when compared with
university matriculants, community college students have done
less well in high school; they are not accustomed to academic
success. Their aspirations for baccalaureate degrees are lower,

and they have not had practice in studying academic fields in depth. They are more likely to be in college to prepare for direct employment; their tolerance for extended years of study may be lower. They take fewer courses in the sciences and humanities.

Several characteristics of the institution similarly militate against transfer. Because most of the community college leaders have given primary attention to the access dimension of their institutions, they have allowed the students to use the college in ways that do not foster progression toward the baccalaureate. Most of the liberal arts classes offered do not have prerequisites or, if they do, the prerequisites are not enforced. Students who want to fulfill graduation requirements with minimal effort may select only those classes with the fewest reading and writing assignments. Students whose commitment to college is marginal are not required to participate in extracurricular activities that might better connect them with the world of academics. Those with undistinguished prior academic records are often counseled into or required to take remedial courses that do not carry transfer credit. The combination of the students' insouciant view of the higher learning and the institution's commitment to open access makes for a potent force operating against transfer.

The imperfect connection between community college and university academic programs, described in detail in Chapter Eight, is a further institutional sanction. When a student's degree cannot be taken at face value, when course-by-course approvals must be granted, when the grades earned in some classes make those acceptable for transfer credit while the grades in other classes are used to deny credit, transfer is difficult. In brief, when students whose commitment to collegiate studies is marginal are enrolled in an institution that makes minimal demands on their time and depth of participation, the flow from community college to university is held to a trickle.

What Happens After Transfer?

The story of transfer has a happy ending. Most community college students who go on to the four-year colleges and universities do quite well. There is an initial transfer shock, with the students' grade point averages generally dropping slightly in their first term after transfer, but most of them persist on to the baccalaureate, and, by the time they complete it, their records are little different from those who began at the senior institutions.

An examination of the transcripts of 3,955 (2,187 native and 1,768 community college transfer) students who received baccalaureate degrees at the University of California at Los Angeles between 1976 and 1978 showed that the native students earned grade point averages approximately 0.2 of a point higher than the transfers. The transfers took 1.4 years longer to earn a degree. When academic ability was controlled for by matching a subset of natives and transfers on an entering ability test, the natives showed a grade average 0.15 of a point higher than the transfers (Menke, 1980).

A study of all Illinois community college transfers to senior institutions in that state found that 31 percent of the transfers had received associate in arts or associate in science degrees at the community college. Of that group, 67 percent received the bachelor's degree within five years, whereas 48 percent of the transfers with no degree or with associate in applied science degrees received the baccalaureate. That study, based on a cohort of students entering community colleges in 1978, yielded results similar to those found when the records of students entering in 1974 and in 1967 were analyzed (Illinois Community College Board, 1986).

The Maryland State Board for Community Colleges (1983) reviewed the records of students who had transferred to senior institutions in that state in 1978 and found that after four years, 76 percent of those who had declared transfer intent and 15 percent of those who had other goals had transferred. The average number of credits transferred in was only 38.5, indicating that a sizable number transfer without receiving the associate degree. Many students in the Maryland cohort reported losing some credits when they transferred; 38 percent lost four or more hours.

Several studies have considered the phenomenon of transfer shock and concluded that it may be due to the newness of the campus. Community college students may not know which courses to take or may be unfamiliar with the university and its course demands. But some studies have suggested that, because the extent of the decline is less for students eventually earning baccalaureate degrees than for those who do not earn degrees, the students doing less well after transfer may be inclined to drop out, thereby leaving the better students in the data set.

As with the data on numbers of students transferring, those regarding transfer success may be variously interpreted. But it is certainly idle to charge the community colleges with the success or failure of their students who transfer to universities if those students took only a few courses at the community college. All the efforts to equate students on the basis of entering academic ability or other dimensions founder on that rock. The community colleges can reasonably be held responsible only for those students who have completed all of the institution's requirements for obtaining the associate degree. If the universities demanded the associate degree before a student was allowed to transfer in, the community colleges could mandate course sequences that would enhance the students' chances for success. They could impose requirements for remedial and general education course sequences and could restore a full array of specialized courses for sophomores. As long as the universities take transfers who have not completed degree requirements at community colleges, the sending institutions' power to impose such requirements is attenuated.

Answers to questions of whether community college courses are less demanding or other institutional factors are operating to mitigate the collegiate experience must await a more closely articulated form of student flow. In states such as Florida, where the community colleges provide a major proportion of the university undergraduates, and in instances of paired institutions where close links between sender and receiver have been established, the transfers show few ill effects from having begun at a community college. In states such as California, where the flow of students to and from community colleges and universities is essentially unregulated, valid information on the community colleges' contribution to their students' success cannot be established.

There is a paradox in the community colleges' approach to collegiate studies. Most community college leaders understand the desirability of transfer education; it maintains the link with higher education that they developed throughout the early decades of the institution, and it fits the expectations of many of their constituents who still look to the college as a low-cost, readily accessible point of entry to postsecondary study that itself leads to better social and career positions. On the other hand, occupational education is presumed to ameliorate social problems by providing a trained work force that enhances the nation's economy and to assist individuals by preparing them for higher-paid employment than they could receive without specialized training. Accordingly, and especially since the passage of the vocational education acts in the 1960s and 1970s, community college leaders have seized upon the idea of career education and the monies available for it, and many of their constituents also accept career education as an equally valid function for the institution.

The paradox appears when the transfer and occupational programs are compared. Typically, students enrolled in programs leading to associate in arts degrees and/or transfer with a major in a traditional academic subject receive less guidance and are faced with fewer specific requirements. In many instances, they may choose any humanities, science, or social science course from a list of a dozen options in order to fulfill a one- or two-course graduation requirement in each of those areas. The liberal arts classes typically have open entry; students may matriculate even when their goals are indistinct. Within the classes, they may face minimal demands for reading and writing. The size of classes in the humanities and social sciences tends to be limited by the size of the room or by negotiated faculty contracts that specify maximum class size. Few instructors desire or have access to paraprofessional assistants who would aid their students' learning. The occupational programs are much more structured. Their facilities include specialized laboratories and workshops, along with equipment and tools. Their curriculum is restrictive, with courses required to be taken in sequence. Admission to the programs is selective; students may often be required to take a year or two of college-level courses before being admitted to the allied health or high-technology programs. Each program typically has a lead faculty member, instructors who work together as a group, and a cohort of aides.

Granted that the occupational programs operate within different sets of accreditation guidelines and that state and federal monies are often earmarked for them, if both they and the transfer programs were considered of equal utility, they would not be organized as differently as they are. Prior to the 1960s, the liberal arts curriculum was the more highly regarded. Facilities for occupational education were poor, and the faculty in those programs were in some cases prohibited from fully participating in academic governance activities. More recently, career education has been ascendant, with a concomitant reduction in the status of the traditional freshman and sophomore courses. If both were equally valued, they would be more proximate in terms of teaching load, requirements for student entry, enforcement of prerequisites in curriculum, and academic support services.

Still, the occupational studies are not antagonistic to transfer education. Sizable numbers of students who complete community college programs in nursing, allied health, engineering technologies, data processing, agriculture, forestry, and many of the other advanced technologies eventually transfer and complete baccalaureate studies; it may well be that more students transfer from occupational programs than from the liberal arts curricula. That speaks well for the portion of the collegiate dimension that rests on the transfer function, but it says little for the liberal arts as a way of organizing the curriculum.

Overall, the colleges' role in transfer is as mixed as their success in performing that role. On the positive side, the transfer function makes it possible for all students to go as far as they can in the formal educational system. This does nothing to overthrow the class- or ethnic-based stratification of American society, but it does enable any individual to move between classes, not a small contribution. The transfer function assists the colleges in maintaining their credibility as legitimate partners in providing education for everyone. Without it, political and fiscal support for the colleges would rest entirely on their function of preparing people for immediate employment. A different form of institution would be the result, and the path to the baccalaureate would be as narrow as it was in the nineteenth century.

On the negative side, the transfer function allows the universities to dictate the colleges' curriculum policy. As long as the senior institutions have the ultimate say in which courses are acceptable for baccalaureate credit, the community colleges' freedom to reform the liberal arts is restricted. The transfer function also perpetuates the temptation to limit access to only those students who show the greatest promise. And it affects the colleges' other roles, especially adult education, which tends to be minimized unless it is provided through entirely separate organizational structures.

On balance, the transfer function will be maintained because of its importance in providing an avenue to the baccalaureate for students who might otherwise be shut out of the system. It is especially important because the associate degree has not yet gained recognition and credibility as a terminal degree signifying certain competencies. Proportionately, it is not as dominant as it was before the colleges embraced occupational and adult education, but it is a key component of the services they provide. Its ebb and flow in the various states and institutions depend on the vigor with which college leaders pursue it, the funding available for it, and the extent of competition for students that neighboring institutions mount. But it will persist because without it the colleges would lose their place in the mainstream of the American graded educational system. It is essential to their collegiate connection.

Curiously, this original community college function is not well understood, nor has it been sufficiently explored. Better data are needed, and they may be forthcoming because of state agency interest spawned by concern over the costs of higher education and the community colleges' role as a link between the lower schools and the higher learning. The current trend toward mandatory testing, detailed in Chapter Six, will also yield useful data as information about the entering and exit abilities of students is correlated with their progress through the institutions.

6

Testing
as a Tool for
Placement and Transfer

Tests exercise an obvious influence on both aspects of the collegiate connection. They affect the liberal arts curriculum when they are used in placing students in introductory or remedial classes. Within the classes, they serve as student motivators and as explicators of subject matter. They also affect transfer, because they play a large part in determining grades, passage from one class to another and, eventually, success or failure in attaining the associate degree and moving on to the university.

Issues in testing fall into a few broad categories. Few question testing within the classes; most instructors and administrators alike defend tests for their value in motivating and sorting students. But should an open-access institution with a mandate to admit everyone test students at entry? Should there be districtwide or statewide uniformity in test administration? Should the staff rely on homemade instruments or on tests built by testing bureaus? Should they implement capstone or achievement testing to assess the effects of their curricula? In this chapter, we consider those questions and suggest ways of using testing to enhance the collegiate function.

Background

In an open-access institution, the need for testing is acute. The community colleges have no assurance that their students possess even the most rudimentary academic skills. Therefore, the most prevalent use of tests outside the classrooms is to direct the students to programs where their basic skills might be enhanced. This use of testing has a long history in community colleges. During the 1950s and 1960s, many institutions offered several levels of English classes into which students might be placed, depending on their entrance test scores. The use of tests and the number of different courses fell in the 1970s as students were allowed to enter courses at will. In the 1980s, testing as a screening device for various levels of courses came again to the fore, most probably because single classes held students whose reading abilities ranged from the third to the thirteenth grade. Nothing is more dispiriting for an instructor than to have such a heterogeneous class. Testing at entry makes feasible the placing of students into classes where their peers have similar abilities and enables the instructors to plot learning exercises and select reading materials that at least somewhat match the students' abilities.

The retention of students also arose as an issue during the 1980s. When college enrollments were advancing year by year, college managers were less concerned with keeping students; those who left would be replaced by new enrollees in the coming year. But as the population of eighteen-year-olds in the United States decreased for several successive years beginning in the late 1970s, the importance of retaining students increased. It was considered more feasible to keep the students already enrolled than to seek new recruits. The belief that students would be less likely to leave if they were placed in classes where they had a chance to succeed became pronounced. Thus, the colleges had an additional incentive for placement testing.

Testing practices in community colleges during the 1970s and 1980s revealed these shifts. Rounds (1984) reviewed several surveys of testing practices and found that, in the early 1970s, around one-third of the institutions had no formalized assessment practices. In many of the others, testing was not mandated by the institution; students might be advised to take tests at entry if they wished to be assisted in selecting courses to enter. When Rounds conducted her own study of ninety-nine California community colleges in 1983, she found fifty-five of them requiring assessment for English placement and another thirty recommending it; twenty-five colleges required a mathematics test, and another forty-two recommended it. A 1983 study of Illinois colleges found four out of five testing students for admission to composition classes (Illinois Community College Board, 1984b).

The testing program increase in the 1980s centers on measures for placing students in English and mathematics classes. The most frequently used tests are for reading ability, since that skill correlates most readily with all the academic subjects. Tests of English usage run a close second to the reading tests in frequency of use, because the language skills they measure similarly relate to academic abilities. Examinations in English as a second language and in mathematics are also being used as required entrance tests.

Using Tests for Student Placement

Since most entrance testing is done for purposes of placing students in the proper course level, the staff continually seek instruments that are highly correlated with course retention and course grades. Sometimes, researchers will attempt to compare the validity of two tests by giving both and seeking correlations with grades; such a study was done at Oakton Community College (Michigan) using individual student scores on the Test of Written Expression and the Nelson-Denny Reading Test (Bers, 1982). The staff at Wytheville Community College (Virginia) compared the predictive ability of the English Qualifying Examination and the Science Research Associates Assessment Survey (Beavers, 1983). However, although greater predictive validity can be shown for one or another instrument, staff tend not to readily accept the results, because the correlations are usually low.

Obtaining higher correlations is difficult, because the variables are inconstant. The psychometrists ask that the dependent variable, the course grades, be more reliable; the faculty seek tests that will predict student success regardless of the shifting criteria for grades. The result is that the faculty prefer to rely on their own measures, particularly of student writing skills. For obvious reasons, writing assessment is considered a better predictor of student grades in the English classes; the same staff who are marking the writing samples on the entrance examination are marking the writing assignments in the classes. The writing sample as an entrance test, then, is a behavior equivalent to that expected of students in class, while performance on a quick-score test of word usage is at most analogous behavior. At best, the correlation studies verify what the faculty have always known: student performance is related to reading ability and hence to course grades in nearly all collegiate studies.

Some of the more astute institutional researchers and faculty members have recommended using assessment tests that more closely approximate the behavior demanded of the students in class. They also seek reasonably common criteria for grading. Thus, a testing program would have instructors closely involved in testing for the specific skills needed to succeed in a given class as identified by analyzing lectures, instructional materials, and assignments. Such a process has not been popularly adopted.

These problems with uniformity of criteria pervade all issues of testing. Are the different classes offered in a single department equivalent? Faculty members generally have resisted efforts at uniformity in texts and assignments, and they tend to be reluctant to subscribe to the idea of departmentwide or collegewide criterion tests. As long as they guard the criteria on which they award student grades and allow those criteria to shift according to the abilities of the students in their classes, correlations between grades and any type of entrance test must remain low.

Similar problems appear when testing programs are instituted on a districtwide level in multicollege districts. When the San Diego Community College undertook a project to develop a consistent placement testing program using the same instruments and cutoff scores, significant correlations were found between placement scores and grades in only one English class (San Diego Community College District, 1983). St. Louis Community College attempted to validate the Nelson-Denny Reading Test as a districtwide instrument by relating it with course grades at the three campuses but found little correspondence among them (Hartman, 1981).

Still, testing goes on, and it affects instruction in all areas, especially in courses where reading and language use are prominent. Since most learning in the liberal arts is based on the apprehension of texts, that area is affected most acutely. The single most persistent difficulty named by instructors is their inability to plan instruction for students who cannot comprehend the language being used in classroom, textbook, or assigned readings. Their frustration increases as the range of student abilities in a single class increases. Just as they deplore policies that allow any student to enroll in any class, they welcome mandated testing that sorts students into classes according to their ability to understand the written word. High correlations or low, at least the range of student ability has been narrowed.

Often without being aware of alternative positions and without being able to articulate their own, the staff members take actions that reveal their ambivalence about the use of testing in educational program design. Many of them eschew tests with a commonality of items and criterion scores because of an unease with the effects of such measures. They are dismayed at their students' lack of ability to conceptualize sufficiently to write a coherent abstract of something they read. They are convinced that there is a set of qualities that enable students to succeed in the collegiate classes—the ability to read and comprehend, to organize and communicate in writing, to suspend judgment and analyze arguments—but they know of no quick-score instrument that assesses these qualities reliably. They do not want to jeopardize progress for minority-group and non-native-English-speaking students. They fear rigorous standards that would result in so few students surviving the introductory courses that the second-tier courses would be depopulated. And they use all these arguments to justify a pattern of relativistic testing that puts students in competition with each other for grades and places in desirable programs.

Bias in Testing

The early 1980s saw the arguments about test use and student placement move to a broader arena. The state of Florida imposed a College-Level Academic Skills Test (CLAST) that must be passed by all students seeking an associate degree or transfer to the junior year in the state's public universities. New Jersey instituted a College Basic Skills Placement Test for all freshmen entering the state's public institutions. South Dakota mandated that all colleges gather evidence of the "value added," the learning attained by every graduate. These measures arose because of legislators' dissatisfaction with the grade inflation that had afflicted all programs except those where externally administered examinations were common, as in accounting, engineering, law, medicine, nursing, and pharmacy.

The use of tests for admissions, placement, and graduation drew particular attention from commentators who contended that the tests discriminate against various cultural and ethnic groups and are thus antagonistic to the public policy of equal access. The Mexican American Legal Defense and Education Fund in 1983 filed petitions with the major testing agencies requesting that they refuse to send scores to colleges that use such scores as the measure of admissions. The testing bureaus responded that it would be difficult to deny scores to the colleges, since they are sent only at the request of the student seeking admission (Farrell, 1983). The controversy over admissions was less pronounced in community colleges. The fears of discrimination were as great, however, because the colleges sort students into various programs on the basis of test scores, and, since some programs are more desirable than others, claims of discrimination still can be made. In 1984, the American Association of Community and Junior Colleges (AACJC), spurred by its Council on Black American Affairs, conducted a study to determine the uses of testing in admissions and placement in community colleges nationwide. It found an increase in placement testing but no evidence to support the contention that minority students were being denied access.

Institutional Testing Efforts

The large-scale testing programs introduced in the community colleges in urban areas evidence both the move toward enforced sorting of students and the beginnings of an interest in correlating student sorting with college outcomes. Miami-Dade Community College has used tests both as admissions screens and as measures of institutional success. During the college's early years, the 1960s, the Florida Twelfth Grade Test was used along with the School and College Ability Test and the Nelson-Denny Reading Test to place students in remedial or transfer-level classes. That program remained in effect until 1974, when the Florida Twelfth Grade Test was discontinued. Testing was relatively uncoordinated during the middle 1970s, but the college gradually reinstated mandatory placement testing between 1978 and 1981. Full implementation of the program meant that first-time students taking three or more classes, any student having earned fifteen credits, or anyone wanting to enroll in a math or English class was required to take the test battery.

The college developed a basic skills assessment program, with the Comparative Guidance and Placement Test, published by the College Board, as the primary instrument. The test has three sections—math, reading, and writing. Students failing a section were directed to take the remedial classes in that area. Follow-up demonstrated that retention rates were greatest for students who passed all three exams, with nearly two-thirds staying in school, compared to fewer than half the students who passed none of the exams. Graduation rates differed as well. Two years after entrance, only 4 percent who passed none of the three subjects had graduated, whereas 26 percent of those who passed all three had graduated (Miami-Dade Community College, 1982).

Concerns were expressed when the program was introduced that it would discriminate against minority students. The black student retention/graduation rate did decline for the first two years of the program but soon came to parity with the graduation rate for all students before the program was installed. For black students entering in 1979, the graduation rate after three and a half years was as high as the rate after six years for those black students who had entered in 1976 (Losak, 1983).

Much of the Miami-Dade effort coincided with the Florida College-Level Academic Skills Test. When scores made on the CLAST were related to student activity in college, some distinct patterns of Miami-Dade students emerged. When students who failed two or more sections of the CLAST were compared with those who passed all four sections, the ones who failed proved more likely to have been in the bottom quartile on the entrance test, graduates from foreign high schools, older, and enrolled in the college longer, with lower grade point averages. In addition, those who failed were more likely to have withdrawn from many of their classes, suggesting that they were having trouble while they were going through school. Forty-five percent had been in developmental reading classes, 64 percent in developmental writing classes, and 36 percent in developmental math. The comparable figures for those who had passed were 4 percent, 9 percent, and 13 percent.

Similar if not as far-reaching measures to control student entry and progress have been undertaken in other large urban community college districts:

- All the Dallas colleges use tests. Those students who do not want to take the tests may sign a waiver accepting responsibility for their actions.
- Each of the seven colleges in the Maricopa district has some type of student placement testing program centering on English and reading proficiency. In addition, some of the campuses administer such esoteric instruments as the Myers-Briggs Type Indicator because of the staff's interest in cognitive-style mapping.

- Every campus of the City Colleges of Chicago mandates entrance testing for placement in English and mathematics, as well as some tests for specific programs, such as accounting. Olive-Harvey College tests all new students who are taking more than six hours of classwork, scores the tests immediately, and places the students in courses before they leave the testing room.

- The Los Angeles district's Project ACCESS (Action for Community College Enhancement of Student Success), coordinated by the American College Testing Program, tests for reading skills, language usage, and numerical skills. The same tests are given throughout the district, but each of the nine colleges makes different use of the scores. Placement in courses tends to be advisory, not mandatory.

- The three campuses of St. Louis Community College mandate placement tests for all full-time students but set their own cutting scores. Although the campuses may use different tests, all are coordinated so that students taking placement tests on one campus do not have to repeat them if they transfer to another campus. The Florissant Valley campus mandate for students who have completed fifteen hours of course work includes the Nelson-Denny Reading Test, an English writing sample, a comprehensive basic skills tests, and certain locally developed tests.

In summation, the thirty-eight colleges in the six large urban districts were using at least forty-four different placement tests, many of them developed on the local campuses. All but Miami-Dade allowed local autonomy regarding the use of scores in placing students. Most of the English, reading, and mathematics tests were being administered prior to or during registration so that the results would be available for academic advising. Follow-up subtests were sometimes administered in some academic areas once classes were under way in order to determine more exactly a student's level of ability. In more than three-fourths of the colleges, the tests were mandatory for certain classes of students, usually those with no prior college credits who were registered for English or mathematics classes or who had taken more than four or five courses at the institution.

Across the large urban districts and, indeed, in most colleges, the 1980s trend was toward mandatory entrance testing. In the case of multicampus districts, the trend was toward increased uniformity of measures but with local campus autonomy in using the scores, with such autonomy guarded because of the variation in mean student abilities among campuses. This pattern was mirrored in smaller, single-campus colleges, with academic departments demanding the right to set minimum entrance levels. There, the cutting scores might well be frequently adjusted to reflect enrollment patterns; no department's faculty wanted to be left without students.

Measuring Outcomes

Although placement testing helps achieve homogeneous classroom groupings, it does little for learning. Any instrument that yields normative scores used to direct students toward certain curricula gives rise to the illusion that the students in those curricula are achieving more than they would elsewhere. But most of the achievement is related to selectivity, not to more efficient instruction. The practice of selecting students on the basis of one measure and administering a comparable measure later yields high correlations, but those correlations are useless as an indicator of the worth of a curriculum.

Outcome-, achievement-, and curriculum-related measures should be scored differently, with predetermined scores evidencing certain learning levels and all the students who achieve a certain score then being considered to have learned what the curriculum was designed to teach. Under such systems, the students do not compete for scores; the scoring is not for the purpose of selection but for curricular verification. The more students attaining the criterion (hence the term "criterion-referenced testing"), the more effective the curriculum. Most educators are unfamiliar with criterion-referenced testing, because all their experience has been with tests given for the purpose of sorting among applicants to curricula and among students within classes. This accounts for a portion of their discomfort with districtwide or state-level testing. Such tests typically are criterion referenced. They can be taken repeatedly until passed. And they seem to turn responsibility for learning back to the faculty and the curriculum. Instead of being pitted against each other, the students as a group are giving witness to the effects of the curriculum in which they were involved.

Some good arguments may be made for beginning criterion-referenced testing in the colleges. Should statewide tests of student attainment such as Florida's CLAST spread, the effect on the curriculum will be baneful. Tests that must be taken by every student moving from one grade level to another invariably measure only the most rudimentary skills. They cannot measure specialized learning without penalizing the students who have not had such experiences. Hence, they drive students toward classes in the basics, away from electives in the arts and other favored areas.

Educators should anticipate these developments and prepare for them by increasing their own staffs' and the public's awareness of the possibilities and limitations of broad-scale testing programs. A general college community familiarity with criterion testing, test types, competencies to be measured, and test administration procedures can allow the staff to take the initiative when such tests are mandated. Moreover, if a good measure in the liberal arts has been refined within the colleges prior to the mandate, it stands a chance of being adapted for more widespread administration. Since mandated tests invariably influence students' course-taking patterns, any measure that ignores the liberal arts has a negative effect on the curriculum in the liberal arts.

There are additional reasons for beginning collegewide testing programs in the liberal arts. Periodic administration of a liberal arts measure can yield an estimate of the secondary school preparation of the students coming to the college. It can lead to cooperative curriculum-development projects between college and secondary school departments. It can reflect how well the students that the college is receiving are prepared in certain academic areas.

The testing program can also provide an estimate of what people are learning at the college. Taken over time, the difference in scores made by entering and exiting students, or by students who have been at the college for one or two years, shows knowledge gained. The recent flurry of interest in "value added" is an indicator of the importance of these types of estimates. The college can pursue a pattern of public relations based on what students learned. This can assist the public in understanding that their local college is still a collegiate institution and that it is possible for students interested in the higher learning to find useful experiences there.

How much do students learn in community colleges? The question is usually answered obliquely. Many colleges and some state systems maintain estimates of the success enjoyed by their matriculants who transfer to senior institutions; Radcliffe (1984), Illinois Community College Board (1984a), Fernandez and others (1984), Doherty and Vaughan (1984), and Young (1982) present recent examples of such studies. Program planners in most colleges also have an idea of the number of students obtaining jobs in the field for which they were trained; see, for example, Lee (1984), Scott (1985), New Hampshire State Department of Education (1984), and Lucas (1984). And some colleges periodically survey their alumni, asking whether they were pleased with the experiences provided them by the college. Such studies are reported by McConochie (1983), Nespoli and Radcliffe (1983), Staatse (1983), and McMaster (1984).

But the question of student *learning* seems the one measure of value added that is *least* likely to be answered. Comparing the grades earned by community college transfers with those made by students who began at the universities is of marginal utility, because relatively few students transfer. Measures of job gaining are better, even though most of the reports reveal serious methodological flaws relating to both response rates and the validity of the questions asked. Even less useful are the studies in which former students are asked whether they felt that they had learned. The answer to that question is too often confounded with the student's generalized attitude of satisfaction with the entire college experience.

Most tests are inadequate to answer questions of what knowledge is being gained by cohorts of students because they were designed for different purposes. Tests administered in individual classrooms are almost invariably course specific; students who did not take those courses are at a disadvantage in answering the questions. Nationally normed tests in various subject areas are somewhat better, but they suffer the defect of having been built for purposes of screening students. To the traditional test maker, the perfect hundred-item test is one that, when it is administered to any number of students, yields a mean, median, and modal score of 50, with no student missing all the answers and no student getting all the items correct. By definition, then, half the students are below average and half are above. But the test has not measured the learning attained by the entire group, because items that everyone can answer are routinely discarded. Some nationally normed tests do show promise: the American College Testing Program's College Outcomes Measures Project, for example, was devised to gain an estimate of student knowledge in general education, and several college and university systems are beginning to use it (Jaschik, 1985).

The General Academic Assessment

It is feasible to assess community college students' knowledge in the liberal arts by building an instrument for that purpose and by designing the procedures for administering it to fit the realities of community college student attendance. The Center for the Study of Community Colleges did just that in 1983–84 in cooperation with the faculty and staff in the Chicago, Miami-Dade, Los Angeles, and St. Louis community college districts. The results of this administration are instructive in what they reveal about student knowledge at various stages in the community college programs and how this knowledge relates to student demographics. But its greatest contribution is in demonstrating a procedure that can be employed readily in administering tests of this type.

The center had been tracing trends in the liberal arts and transfer in community colleges by surveying students and faculty and by tabulating information on curriculum and instructional practices. In conjunction with these projects, the center staff developed, field tested, and administered a survey and content test that would reveal student knowledge in general education and the liberal arts. This General Academic Assessment (GAA) was designed to assess knowledge among cohorts of students, not the learning of individual students. The items were selected so that a student's general knowledge could be assessed regardless of where or when that knowledge was gained.

The GAA included representative items in the humanities, sciences, social sciences, mathematics, and English usage. The survey portion of the instrument asked students such background questions as age, number of credits earned, educational and occupational aspirations, number of liberal arts courses taken, and self-assessment of their skills in those areas. These questions were selected from those that had proved useful in the center's earlier surveys of more than 12,000 students in Washington and California. Items for the content portion were drawn from several sources: the National Assessment of Educational Progress provided numerous usable items in science, social science, and mathematics; the Educational Testing Service made items in the humanities and social science available on loan for purposes of the project; the City Colleges of Chicago provided items in English usage; and Miami-Dade Community College provided items in the humanities. Center staff members culled the items with the help of instructors, counselors, and administrators from several community colleges. Final selection was made by panels of faculty and administrators from the colleges in which the instrument was to be given.

The items were arrayed in five forms and tried out with around 1,300 students in five community colleges in California and Kansas. After revision, the final instrument included nineteen demographic and student-experience questions and fifty-seven items in humanities, sixty in English usage, fifty-two in mathematics, fifty-nine in science, and seventy-one in social science. The items were distributed at random across the five forms so that each form had a sampling of items in the five areas and each could be completed within one fifty-minute class period.

Class sections were used as the unit of sampling because that is the most feasible way of getting a random sample of students enrolled in credit classes. The method has the disadvantage of skewing the sample in the direction of full-time students, because a student taking four classes has four times as many chances of being in a sampled class section as a student who is taking only one class. Nevertheless, the sample, based on duplicated head count, is an accurate representation of general student knowledge, since the full-time students represent higher proportions of the full-time-equivalent enrollment in the college.

The General Academic Assessment combined item sampling with population sampling. Not all students in the population took the test; no student taking the test took all the items. The value of this sampling and testing procedure is that testing time is reduced; it became possible to administer 336 items on five forms, with no form having more than 69 items, so that all could be done within one class hour. And as the class section was used as the unit of sampling, the problem of getting representative numbers of each student type was mitigated.

A total of 8,026 students in twenty-three colleges (nine in Los Angeles, four in Miami, three in St. Louis, and seven in Chicago) completed the form. Their responses were tallied according to total score and to scores on individual subtests in humanities, sciences, social sciences, mathematics, and English usage. Scores were converted to ten-point-scale scores for each of the areas, and a cumulative scale score was tallied. While the findings illustrate the diversity among community college students, they suggest that student knowledge is related both to age and to the number of courses that students have completed in particular areas. The age relationships showed up primarily in English usage, social sciences, and humanities; the older the student, the higher the score on those scales. These age-related differences did not occur in mathematics or science (see Table 16). All of the five scales showed a direct relationship between the number of units a student had completed and the scores made (see Table 17). The highest scores were made by students attending college for their personal interest, with

Table 16. General Academic Assessment
Survey: Mean Scores by Age.

	GAA Scales					
Age	Mathe-matics	Literacy	Social Science	Human-ities	Science	Total Liberal Arts
20 years or younger	5.01	5.00	4.79	3.17	5.16	23.13
21–30 years	4.89	4.79	4.86	3.29	5.19	23.01
31–40 years	4.61	5.06	5.31	3.75	5.23	23.96
41–50 years	4.08	5.30	5.33	4.07	5.35	24.12
Over 50 years	4.61	5.71	6.19	4.88	5.38	26.77

Table 17. General Academic Assessment Survey:
Mean Scores by Number of Completed College Units.

	GAA Scales					
Completed Units	Mathe-matics	Literacy	Social Science	Human-ities	Science	Total Liberal Arts
0–14	4.45	4.73	4.64	3.02	4.89	21.73
15–29	4.84	4.84	4.80	3.13	5.05	22.65
30–44	4.88	4.90	4.88	3.31	5.25	23.23
45–59	5.18	4.96	5.13	3.54	5.27	24.07
60 or more	5.51	5.55	5.58	4.24	5.84	26.71

those preparing for transfer making the second-highest scores on the combined scales (see Table 18). And scores tended to increase for each of the scales to the extent that students took courses in those areas, with the greatest difference being in the humanities and the least difference in English usage as related to number of courses completed in English composition (see Table 19).

There was no surprise in the finding that students who take more courses in an area are likely to know more about that area than students who take fewer courses. The age-related scale scores proved interesting in that mathematics and science knowl-

Table 18. General Academic Assessment Survey:
Mean Scores by Reason for Attending College.

| Reason for Attending College | GAA Scales | | | | | |
	Mathe-matics	Literacy	Social Science	Human-ities	Science	Total Liberal Arts
Transfer to a four-year institution	5.14	4.98	4.95	3.32	5.26	23.63
Entry into specific occupation	4.47	4.72	4.77	3.16	4.93	22.05
Advance in current occupation	4.54	4.83	4.86	3.37	5.16	22.75
Personal interest	4.57	5.43	5.32	4.25	5.46	25.03

Table 19. General Academic Assessment Survey: Mean Scores
by Number of Completed Courses in Scale-Related Curriculum.

| Number of Completed Courses | GAA Scales | | | | |
	Mathe-matics	Literacy	Social Science	Human-ities	Science
None	4.41	4.87	4.60	2.88	4.88
One	4.63	5.00	4.74	3.16	5.26
Two	5.08	4.97	4.95	3.44	5.30
Three or more	5.91	5.01	5.65	4.31	5.88

edge showed little age-related difference; those areas seem to be school related, whereas the humanities, social science, and English usage abilities may be enhanced merely by living in and interacting with the culture. But one of the more surprising findings from the GAA administrations was the accuracy of the students' self-assessments (see Table 20). Students were asked to compare themselves with other students at their college in terms of their ability to "use algebra to solve problems," "edit written material," and demonstrate similar competencies that suggested knowledge in the various liberal arts areas. The ex-

Table 20. General Academic Assessment Survey:
Mean Scores by Self-Rating on Scale-Related Skill.

	Ability Rated				
Self-Rating	Use Algebra to Solve Problems (Mathematics)	Edit Written Material (English Usage)	Understand Political Ideologies (Social Science)	Understand Art, Music, Drama (Humanities)	Understand Scientific Technological Development (Science)
Poor	3.82	4.16	4.22	2.66	4.44
Fair	4.49	4.58	4.60	2.99	4.81
Good	5.16	5.08	5.17	3.48	5.25
Excellent	6.17	6.28	5.82	4.22	6.34

tremely high correlation between students' self-ratings and their scores made on the corresponding scales suggests that community college students are quite realistic, at least in regard to their academic prowess. Students know what they know.

Toward Better Testing Practices

The administration of a General Academic Assessment demonstrated the feasibility of a form of cohort testing that is rarely employed in community colleges because it cannot be used to assign students to classes or to make any other decision about individuals. However, it can be useful for estimating the differences in knowledge exhibited by entering students as compared with the cohorts that have completed a year or two of course work at the institution. It can be used to assess entering or graduating students' abilities from year to year, thus gaining a measure of value added to the student body as a whole in a time series. It can be used to show how the courses in particular liberal arts areas contribute to knowledge in those areas. It can focus attention on curriculum in the college and in its feeder secondary schools. And it can be used as the centerpiece of a public relations effort showing that the college is concerned with student learning in a collegiate context.

The General Academic Assessment administration was certainly not the first time such an effort had been made in higher education. Pace (1979) reported the methodology and findings of studies done in the prior fifty years, recounting in particular the detailed results of a set of tests given in Pennsylvania colleges beginning in 1928. There, tests of liberal arts knowledge were administered to sophomores and seniors, whose scores related directly to the number of college courses taken. The more hours the students had completed in the humanities, natural sciences, and social sciences, the higher the scores on those subtests. The students' language ability accounted for nearly half the average humanities score. The score on natural sciences was most related to courses taken in that area. Seniors knew more than they had known as sophomores; seniors as a group knew more than sophomores as a group. Pace concluded that comparisons of groups of students at different levels (cross-sectional studies) produce results similar to those obtained in comparisons of the same group at different times (longitudinal studies).

Why, then, are these types of measures not used more frequently? Pace attributed the lack to the costs of preparing, administering, and scoring the tests, saying that students can be asked to bear the costs only when they themselves stand to benefit, as in admission to a preferred program. But that reason seems insufficient to explain the dearth of such measures in community colleges. There, the reasons might be that educators fear interinstitutional comparison, feeling that their colleges have unique missions and student populations and, especially, that their fiscal and popular support may be tied to the results. They may be skeptical of their effects when they control so few hours of any student's life. They may fear that any measure of student knowledge in general may be used in arguments against courses in particular fields. Test scores that are central to grading and used for sending data to succeeding classes and to prospective employers dare not rely on item and population sampling lest the students who fail charge that their items were more difficult than those answered by the students who passed. Above all, cohort testing does not square with the educators' self-appointed mission of sorting people for the benefit of employers, the senior institutions, and the professions for which they are preparing them.

Many community college leaders are annoyed because they feel that the public misunderstands their colleges' role, saying that inappropriate criteria are used to judge them. However, they share the blame. They reject the use of transfer data, because they serve numerous students who have no intention of transferring: students in occupational certificate programs, those who already have degrees, adults taking occasional classes for their own interest, and so on. When asked about program effects, they usually refer to the number or percentage of students graduating or gaining jobs, without considering how closely those effects are tied to selection at entrance and attrition within the colleges. And they skirt questions of student learning because they neither have nor seek valid measures of what students as a group knew when they enrolled as compared to what they knew after they had taken a number of courses.

Tests are typically used for placing students in certain classes or programs. Most educators and members of the lay public understand testing as a placement measure. In fact, they tend to be reassured by single-score measures that rank people relative to each other. Testing for the effects of a curriculum is hardly ever done in higher education. It demands careful construction of tests, a skill difficult to find among a staff unfamiliar with the concepts involved. It rests on practices that few within the colleges consider: controlling for the abilities of students entering the program, administering different forms of the same instrument to students at the beginning and at the end of the program, accounting for student dropout, item and population sampling, and numerous other controls that are completely outside of most staff members' experience.

The state agencies, reflective of the public and the legislators, deserve data. How many students learned how much in what period of time? Normative tests do not provide answers, and statewide achievement testing programs of necessity yield bland, highly generalized information. The community college leaders who see value in measuring their college's effects would sponsor criterion-referenced, multiple-matrix testing programs on their own campus and thereby gain information on student learning and program outcomes that they could send to the state agencies. Better that than the other way around.

The current issues in entrance testing will subside as collegewide test administration is more widely employed to screen students into classes that are consonant with their abilities. The practice of allowing any matriculant to enter any class is in headlong retreat, and selection measures other than testing have made practically no headway. Testing is economical and generally accepted by staff, students, and the public. To the extent that it assists students in succeeding in their classes, it is actually one of the first academic support services that they encounter. Other supports that the colleges provide to enhance student flow are described in Chapter Seven.

7

Services Supporting
Academic Goals

The classroom is the home of the curriculum, but outside-of-class supports to learning enhance student achievement and transfer rates. This chapter reviews orientation programs, advising services, remedial instruction, supplemental instruction offered through learning laboratories, and honors programs. It concludes with a report of student use of these services and recommendations on the types of services most feasibly installed and most likely to enhance the collegiate function.

Orientation Programs

Orientation programs are designed to moderate the transition from high school to college. Some institutions mandate program attendance, but most qualify this requirement by applying it only to first-time, full-time students. Attendance varies, depending on how adept the program managers are at integrating the orientation activities with registration and assessment procedures, or at including them as part of required course sequences.

Thirty of the thirty-four large urban colleges surveyed by the Center for the Study of Community Colleges reported having an orientation program for new students. Twelve of them mandated attendance, but this requirement was usually qualified by conditions such as "if a student is enrolling for six or more units and is attending college for the first time." Eight institutions estimated new-student attendance for their programs at 75 to 100 percent, while twelve colleges reported attendance by fewer than half the students. Several colleges reported high participation rates because they presented their orientation programs as part of, or just prior to, the registration and assessment process.

By offering Human Development 100 as a mandatory course for all new full-time students, Mountain View College (Texas) incorporates orientation into its academic structure. This course, taught by counseling center staff members, familiarizes students with the colleges' policies and procedures. West Los Angeles College (California) and South Mountain Community College (Arizona) have developed video presentations to convey their orientation message, while Jefferson Community College (Kentucky) offers a sixteen-week transfer orientation course. Compton (California) College's honors program for ninth- to twelfth-grade students as well as its own students features a Family Orientation Program that focuses on program requirements and student responsibilities.

Is orientation effective? In 1983, Phillips County Community College (Arkansas) studied the impact of freshman orientation classes on students' persistence and academic performance (Jones, 1984). Participants were all first-time, full-time freshmen who entered during fall 1982, spring 1983, or fall 1983. During the registration process, students were encouraged to enroll in an eight-week orientation class that included information on academic policies, college regulations, career counseling and testing, placement, financial aid, student services, and study skills. Performance and persistence data were analyzed for an experimental group of 337 students who successfully completed the orientation class and for a control group of 433 students who either did not enroll in or did not complete the class. Results indicated that 80 percent of the experimental group had been retained at the end of one semester, compared to 43 percent of the control group; 45 percent of the fall 1982 experimental group had been retained at the end of one academic year, compared to 23 percent of the control group; and the combined first-semester mean grade point average for the experimental group was 2.28, compared to 1.72 for the control group. On the basis of these findings, increased efforts were made to enroll freshmen in orientation classes, improve the consistency of those classes, and promote the classes among faculty and students.

A different view of orientation and support programs was reported by Friedlander (1984). Napa Valley College's (California) Student Orientation, Assessment, Advisement, and Retention (SOAAR) program consisted of evaluating first-time students' math and reading skills, advising about enrollment in regular or developmental courses on the basis of test scores, and providing information on college services, policies, and procedures. In fall 1983, 866 students participated in the SOAAR program. An analysis of student course transcripts, test scores, and survey responses indicated that in comparison with students enrolled in comparable courses before the implementation of the SOAAR program, SOAAR students were less likely to complete their developmental courses in English and mathematics, finish their introductory-level courses, and earn a grade of *C* or higher in their developmental or regular classes. Although a number of factors might have contributed to the decline in student performance from fall 1982 to fall 1983, participation in the SOAAR program did not seem to have a positive effect on student performance or persistence in their English and math classes. Furthermore, test scores did not appear to be accurate predictors of student success, and SOAAR did not seem to increase student use of support services.

These types of mixed effects have been reported in several other studies, although the students who participate usually do better in their other college work. Most colleges continue to offer orientation. The more integrated programs are included in a class; for example, beginning psychology. Less frequently, they are offered in advance of the academic year. While these orientation programs are far from being the popular support source that they are in many four-year colleges and universities, they seem to help by familiarizing students with the college world.

Advising

Student advising is a key, ubiquitous component in helping students find their way through the college. In 1979, a national survey of administrators in 1,600 colleges and universities found that the most common institutional response to reducing student attrition was an attempt to improve academic advising and counseling programs (Beal and Noel, 1979). More recently, (in Koltai, 1981), the chancellor of the Los Angeles Community College District called for the revitalization of academic advisement in order to increase the number of students who satisfactorily progress toward completing their educational programs. And the report of the Study Group on the Conditions of Excellence in American Higher Education recommended that "all colleges should offer a systematic program of guidance and advisement that involves students from matriculation through graduation. Student affairs personnel, peer counselors, faculty, and administrators should *all* participate in this system on a continuing basis" (National Institute of Education, 1984, p. 31).

The three major functions of community college academic advisement programs are to help students plan educational programs commensurate with their abilities and interests; to alert students who are experiencing difficulties in their courses and bring them into contact with appropriate institutional resources; and to provide students with continuous, up-to-date information on the progress they are making toward completing the requirements of a specific program of study.

Over 60 percent of the colleges in the six districts surveyed by the CSCC reported that academic advisement is usually mandatory for students taking more than a certain number of units or for all new students. But Chicago is the only district among the six that mandates academic advisement for all students. Students attending any of the eight City Colleges of Chicago must have their program planning cards signed by a faculty adviser before they can register for the next term. At South Mountain Community College (Arizona), students must have an educational plan on file in the counseling office before registering for classes. Miami-Dade requires all students who have not yet declared a major to seek out academic advisory services. Both Maricopa's Phoenix Community College and Dallas's Richland Community College allow students to bypass the academic advising requirements if they sign a waiver accepting full responsibility for their decision. In nearly every college, the counseling office is open during the evening in order to reach part-time and evening students. Some colleges have peer advisers who visit certain evening classes to inform students of the kinds of evening services available. Others send letters to students describing the academic advising services available at the college after 4 P.M.

Faculty participation in advising varies from perfunctory to a high level of coordination with the academic advising services of the campus counseling center. Faculty members in the City Colleges of Chicago play an integral role in the academic advisement process, and faculty are directly involved in advising students during the registration process at Dallas's Mountain View, Forest Park in St. Louis, and Maricopa Technical. Most institutions reported that faculty members advise students majoring in their academic area. Some colleges incorporate faculty training programs in preparation for academic advisement responsibilities, while others prepare handbooks to provide guidelines.

Still, advising is not all it might be. Counselors tend to be overworked, many faculty members tend to be only marginally involved, cooperation between the two groups is often minimal, and it is impossible for either group to keep up with all that they should know about program requirements in their own college and in the feeder and receiving institutions. Traditional advisement systems are unable to keep pace with the multiplicity of requirements associated with the numerous college programs, the frequency of changes made in those requirements, and the clerical task of maintaining current tracking records on each student.

Can the major obstacles to an effective advising system for students be removed by incorporating computer technology into the academic advisement process? Trombley and Holmes (1980), Aitken and Conrad (1977), and Harper and others (1981) allege that they can. Computer-assisted advisement involves a computer program to store the degree requirements and match them with the student's academic record. The record produced is a report showing the degree requirements and the student's progress in completing those requirements. Perhaps the most significant aspect of computer advisement programs is the capability to provide students and academic advisers with an immediate assessment of student progress.

The Academic Graduation and Information System at Miami-Dade Community College provides information on suggested and required courses in seventy-two associate degree programs (Harper and others, 1981). Each advisement report is based on the year and term that the student enters Miami-Dade and the graduation requirements in effect at that time. In addition to the college's requirements, the computer provides a listing of transfer courses recommended by each of the colleges and universities attended by most of the students who transfer. Computer programs also provide a detailed evaluation of all graduation requirements for each individual, citing requirements that are completed and those still to be taken. If the student has satisfied all graduation requirements, the Miami-Dade system will automatically inform the student and place the graduation notation on the permanent academic record (Harper and others, 1981).

Miami-Dade has incorporated an Academic Alert and Advisement System into its advisement program. At midterm, all faculty members indicate whether the progress of each student in their classes is satisfactory or unsatisfactory. The system then generates personalized letters to each of the students, informing them of their classroom performance and, if appropriate, where they can receive assistance, what they need to accomplish prior to the next registration, and whether they are eligible for the honors program. Anandam (1981) notes that if the advisers at Miami-Dade were to meet individually with each of the 40,000 students and provide them with all the information produced by the computer in the midterm progress report, it would take thirty-one working days—if the advisers dedicated all their working hours to this task, if they gave fifteen minutes per student, if they had a miraculous way of scheduling the students every fifteen minutes, and if every student kept his or her appointment.

The advantages of computer-assisted advisement over traditional methods include reduced time in evaluating student transcripts, improved accuracy in advisement, ease in obtaining and providing information, reduction in costs, and more efficient use of adviser time. Researchers at Miami-Dade estimated that using the computer system saves the college a minimum of $100,000 a year in wages paid to professional staff members to work overtime in approving graduation certifications and in time spent on conducting preliminary grade checks during the academic year (Harper and others, 1981).

Remedial Education

Remedial education is offered in three categories: classes for non-native-English speakers; remedial studies for young matriculants whose high school preparation was inadequate; and basic literacy training for functionally illiterate adults. In some colleges, all three are offered through the same set of classes, but in most they are demarcated. The non-native-English speakers take classes in English as a second language; the inadequately prepared students seeking college-level studies participate in remedial classes, often provided through learning laboratories; and the functionally illiterate adults take separately funded classes in basic reading and writing.

The problem of inadequate academic skills has been exacerbated by the great number of students who come to college with a native language other than English. Glendale Community College, a leader in the Maricopa district's developmental education efforts, conducts English-as-a-second-language programs through two different instructional approaches: one for the student who has had little formal education and another for students who have had secondary and postsecondary schooling in their native language. The adult basic skills program consists of reading and writing skills training as well as a counseling component, which helps students develop an awareness of their resources for effective decision making. The college also offers a full complement of remedial courses in reading, English, and mathematics, featuring a coordinated assessment and advisement process designed to ensure effective student program placement.

Los Angeles City College has the largest number of limited and non-English-speaking students in the nation. Sixty-one percent of the 1981 freshman class came from homes where English was not the principal language; and more than fifty languages are spoken at one neighborhood high school that sends students to this college. In expanding its ESL program, the Los Angeles district established three five-unit core classes—supplementary classes in conversation, vocabulary, and advanced reading. At several colleges, heavy emphasis for all ESL students is placed on using writing laboratories, while all the Los Angeles colleges offer ESL speech classes.

Native-born illiterates pose a similar problem. On April 21, 1986, the front page of the *New York Times* carried a headline reporting that 13 percent of American adults are illiterate in English (Werner, 1986). In many states, the burden of teaching them has fallen to the community colleges. Central Piedmont Community College has achieved some success with its Project ABLE (Adult Basic Literacy Education). Adults advance one grade level in reading after 25 to 30 hours. One grade-level advancement in mathematics is attained in about the same length of time. These achievements compare with the average of about 150 hours in a traditional classroom and 50 hours in the one-on-one tutorial method to achieve the same grade-level advancement. ABLE's teaching methods center around microcomputers and other communication devices. The project's three centers use the best available instructional materials, plus others created by college personnel. The first ABLE center was located in a shopping mall to provide easy access and student anonymity. It is the nucleus for a developing system of neighborhood centers. Expansion into new neighborhoods is a phased process. The college's mobile laboratory is moved into a target neighborhood, and then, after three days, it is moved to another area. Experience has shown that after six months of this sequencing in two neighborhoods, at least one has recruited enough clients to justify a permanent center. The mobile lab then moves on to another neighborhood.

The well-documented decline in high school graduates' literacy has forced the colleges to expand their efforts to prepare their students to embark on collegiate studies. As one example, the City Colleges of Chicago run a two-tiered developmental education program in which entry is based on reading and writing assessment. The first tier consists of a twelve-hour block of courses for students reading and writing below the seventh-grade level. The second tier of the program is for students reading and writing between the seventh- and eleventh-grade levels. A six-hour reading/writing communications core is augmented by completer courses in human development, social science, math, business, and humanities. In addition to being given intensive counseling and tutoring, the students are carefully tracked in their academic progress by specially selected faculty and support staff. Retention and achievement levels in both tiers of the block are from 20 to 40 percent higher than in nonblocked courses for similar groups of students.

Funding is a continuing problem in remediation. Many states fund remedial classes at a lower level than the academic credit classes, because remedial studies are presumed to cost less. Historically, they were taught in the lower schools, where the per-student costs were lower than they were in the colleges. The colleges have had to adjust. The San Diego colleges mandate remedial classes for students whose entrance test scores fall below a certain level but offer the classes through their continuing education division, which is funded at a lower rate and where instructional costs are correspondingly lower.

Should remediation be mandatory? If so, for whom? The voluntary approach involves making comprehensive support services easily accessible but leaving the decision to participate completely up to the student. This approach is based on the assumption that students who need help are mature or sophisticated enough to seek assistance from an appropriate campus resource; that students deficient in reading, for example, will seek help through developmental reading courses, tutoring, or some other related resource. The supporters of voluntarism maintain that students who seek help will be more highly motivated to improve their skills than those who are forced to participate and that instructor morale will be higher among those working with students who choose to be in their classes rather than with students who are forced to do so. On the other hand, critics of this approach contend that many students will not get needed help because they will not voluntarily enroll in basic skills courses.

The colleges do not want to restrict admission, but they must make special provision for students who cannot manage the collegiate curriculum. If the colleges refuse admission to the academic classes, the students whose programs are filled only with remedial work tend to drop out. The best combination for retention seems to be some remedial, some general studies, and some specialized course work. Students seem to need the mix of basic skills classes and courses offering college graduation credit. But the more progressive view of remediation calls for allowing students into the collegiate classes and then building a great variety of supports so that they can succeed in those classes, a procedure known as supplemental instruction.

Supplemental Instruction

Tutorials and related instructional activities coordinated through learning laboratories are the most popular forms of supplemental instruction. Nearly all the colleges in the six urban districts provide formal learning centers and/or tutoring arrangements for their students. The philosophy of Maricopa's Glendale College is that the services are available for students who appear of their own volition, not mandated, as in some other districts. Its Learning Assistance Center is open fifty-six hours weekly and serves several purposes. Evening instructors as well as some regular daytime instructors use the facility to administer makeup tests. Tutors visit instructors to ask about students needing help, and the center surveys instructors to ask about the types of help that students require. Over 700 individual students are tutored per semester. The college also has a special program for minority students, in which retired adults from Sun

City are paid at slightly over minimum wage rates for up to nineteen hours per week for tutoring, although many retirees are so enthusiastic that they work without pay. Thus, the faculty, who may not seek out paraprofessionals to help them teach, are actually being provided with targeted tutorial services in another guise.

A structured tutorial system operates in Chicago, where all tutors must meet with instructors regarding course requirements, while the tutoring coordinator meets with department chairpersons. Tutors also work directly with students in their classrooms, thus integrating support services with the same academic programs that they were designed to augment. Supplemental instruction is carried on by peer tutors, and these activities actually extend the learning time of high-attrition classes.

Miami-Dade's RSVP (Response System with Variable Prescription) program produces feedback to students in the form of personalized letters. The RSVP computer software package assists in individualizing instruction and record keeping and permits the maintenance of a record on each student, which includes name, address, personal attributes, students' responses to a "survey" or exam, the number of exams and assignments completed, and the number and kinds of responses received by students. The RSVP program also prints feedback reports to students, informing them of their test scores and prodding those who are negligent. It also provides instructors with reports on student performance and collective class data. For example, the use of RSVP in the basic mathematics lab provides a course description and sample feedback report for a student who achieved a passing score on one fractions exam, a perfect score on a decimals exam, and a failing score on another exam. For each test item, the feedback report identifies the particular skill being tested, tells how well the student performed, and, if the item was solved incorrectly, assigns a set of personalized exercises focusing on that skill.

St. Louis Community College at Florissant Valley has developed ways of identifying students who might experience difficulty in a content course. Students in all sections of American Politics as well as certain other classes are given a reading test during the first week of class and an exam on the content covered to date at the end of the third week. After the test results have been returned, a reading instructor attends the class and lets students know how their performance can be improved by enrollment in the adjunct skills class for the course, which begins the fourth week of the term. Students get one hour of credit for this class, and they must pay for the additional credit to enroll. The skills instructor sits in all class sections of the content course, takes notes, and goes over the reading materials. He or she then uses this information to teach study skills in the adjunct course.

At Chicago's Kennedy-King College, students with grades of D or F or students who have poor attendance records receive a midterm letter instructing them to set up appointments at the counseling center. At their interviews there, the counselors arrange for them to receive the extra tutoring and assistance they need to complete the courses in which they are experiencing difficulty. The program has been so successful that in all sections of an introductory social science class, 90 percent of the students doing D or F work at midterm who came in for extra assistance went on to complete the course, compared to only 13 percent of those who did not receive extra academic assistance.

The Midterm Enhancement Program at several Chicago colleges provides supplemental instruction by the faculty member teaching the college-level content course. At midterm, the faculty member has the option to offer an extra hour of instruction for those students who need assistance. This supplemental class is taught by the faculty member but is funded and offered as an adult education course. There is no charge for this participation in the extra-hour class, because adult education courses at the City Colleges of Chicago are free to all students who are enrolled for six or more hours of credit. Studies on the effectiveness of this program have shown that students with unsatisfactory midterm grades who participated were much more likely to complete their course than those who did not elect to take the extra hours of instruction.

Some colleges have initiated block programs that consist of basic skills courses, academic support services, and a college-level content course. Students enrolled in the Alternative Services to Raise Achievement (ASTRA) Program at Greater Hartford Community College have their schedules planned for two semesters. In the first term, they are enrolled in an interdisciplinary program of composition, reading, and speech, which is designed by the college's English faculty. Students work on similar objectives each week from the perspective of their reading, writing, and speech courses. The second term comprises an interdisciplinary course arrangement of Western civilization, reading, speech, and composition. In the reading class, students improve their reading and study skills by using the text from the Western civilization course. In the composition course, they write themes, answer essay questions, and work on a research paper for the content course. In speech, student presentations are based on their research papers and the content of their Western civilization course. Tutors are used regularly during class time and also are available in the learning center. Counselors meet weekly with the instructors to monitor student progress in their courses (Eddy, 1979).

The first semester of the Individual Needs (IN) Program at Chicago's Loop College (Barshis, 1979) consists of a twelve-credit-hour block of work in reading, composition, psychology (self-development), educational and vocational counseling, and a content course chosen by the students to correspond to their educational objectives. In many instances, the content course (for example, biology, sociology, child development) is team taught and coordinated with the basic skills course in reading or writing. For example, in the combination biology–English composition course, the English instructor uses materials from the biology course for assignments, and the biology instructor requires writing assignments in an outside class. As with the ASTRA Program, academic assessment, tutoring, counseling, learning laboratories, and the close monitoring of student progress are integrated into the IN Program.

Academic support services are typically funded through a fixed percentage of the college's total operating budget. At many colleges, this allocation does not allow for the number of staff members needed to provide a full complement of support services to all students. Among the approaches being taken at some colleges to overcome the constraints of limited staff and resources are the placing of responsibility for student academic advisement in the hands of the faculty; assigning interested faculty members to teach and advise in the learning skills center as part of their regular work load; and generating funds for the college by having learning skills staff members provide their services to students in one- or two-unit college-credit courses.

A limitation on supplemental instructional services is that the colleges must find a way to be reimbursed for the extra, nonclass time that is spent in assisting students with their course work. In 1984, the board of governors of the California community colleges revised regulations for tutoring services. Attendance for learning assistance in a course may be reported for state apportionment when such activity is required for *all* students and is offered during scheduled hours, thus making tutorial assistance a component of the course. But the issue of having a high-cost instructor who is credentialed in the subjects in which students are being tutored physically present in the learning lab has still to be resolved.

Honors Program

Special services for high achievers are at the other end of the spectrum. By recognizing the better students, honors programs are tangible evidence that the colleges do not deal exclusively with lower-ability or unmotivated students. The programs are initiated because the students can benefit from them, new and better students can be attracted to the college, and the programs can enhance the public image of the institution as a place where superior scholarship is honored and encouraged. A 1975 survey done for the American Association of Community and Junior Colleges (Olivas, 1975) revealed that only 47 of 644 responding institutions had honors programs. But the list has grown recently, as shown by the number of colleges belonging to the National Collegiate Honor Council and/or Phi Theta Kappa, the national honors society for community colleges. In 1982, there were 700 chapters of Phi Theta Kappa.

In fall 1982, Miami-Dade initiated its first formal honors program. This program includes special sections of courses, interdisciplinary courses, honors seminars, special honors projects, faculty mentors, and special enrichment activities. Students enrolled in the honors sections are asked to read more primary source materials and write more papers than those engaged in regular classes, cover the subject areas in greater depth and breadth, and develop a contract with the instructor on an individual project to be completed for the course. Miami-Dade offers all its honors students academic scholarships that cover matriculation fees. It also makes special notations (the letter *H*) on the transcripts for all honors classes completed by students. And all honors students receive special assistance in exploring upper-division studies and/or career options. Each honors student is assigned a mentor, a faculty member from within the student's major area of interest. The mentor assists students with registration, program conflicts, and career preparation, as well as in such individual honors explorations as Miami-Dade's special Capstone Project—a three-credit creative or scholarly project. This enables the student to demonstrate research skills as well as the ability to apply and present material and to develop a portfolio or major paper to present to four-year institutions, scholarship committees, or prospective employers.

Other districts take similar approaches to working with their better students. Chicago's Wright and Loop colleges both have well-developed honors programs. Wright's Dean's Scholar Program recruits students with an American College Testing Program (ACT) composite score of 24, a ranking of at least the fifteenth-grade level in a mandatory writing test, and first-year college math placement. This program begins with a block of fifteen to eighteen hours of special honors courses taken in the student's first semester. After that, students who maintain a 3.5 grade point average (GPA) may enroll in individual honors sections offered as alternatives to many of the regular courses. Loop College's Advanced Arts and Sciences Program, which requires that students take a minimum of two advanced arts and science courses per term, relies less on ACT and other test scores than on results of placement tests. And in order to stay in the program, students must maintain at least a *B* average in general education courses. Loop College has a tentative agreement with three private four-year institutions—De Paul University, Mundelein College, and Roosevelt University—to give preferential admissions treatment to students who have completed the Advanced Arts and Sciences Program.

Maricopa's honors program, initiated in 1981, includes honors sections of traditional courses, special honors courses, forums, and seminars, and special performances and social activities. Each year, the district holds an Honors Forum Series, with six notable speakers presenting lectures and meeting with interested students and staff members. The series has a specific theme each year that the speakers—outstanding humanists, scientists, industrialists, and social leaders—address from the point of view of their respective fields. A special honors course is based on lectures given in the Honors Forum Series. This interdisciplinary approach to various individual and social issues is supplemented with readings, and after the lectures, honors students visit with the speakers in small-group settings. Assignments for the course might take the form of written or oral reports in which students summarize the sources and scope of the issue addressed during the term; compare and contrast rationales, perspectives, and conclusions of the authors and lecturers; and define and defend their personal conclusions about the issues. Maricopa's Rio Salado College offers an innovative approach to crediting courses that do not carry honors sections. Students who desire honors credit for a nonhonors course agree with the course instructor to a Course Enrichment Plan, a type of contract in which students complete special assignments (extra reading, library research, field projects, or class presentations) in order to earn honors credit.

Dallas's honors program, initiated in 1982, involves approximately 600 students, some of whom take more than one honors course. Seminars offered to these high achievers are characterized by the reading of primary sources, the treatment of topics in depth, and considerable reading, writing, synthesis, and analysis. The students may enroll in any honors course for which they are qualified, receiving a special designation (*H*) on their transcripts upon course completion. No minimum number of hours or minimum overall GPA is required for such enrollment. However, if students wish to qualify as honors scholars, they must complete seven honors courses, with one course from each of the following areas: English/foreign language, social science, math/science, and humanities. While the three remaining courses may be taken from any other area of the curriculum, seven courses must be completed within two years from the date of the students' enrollment in their first honors course. Admission requirements for the Honors Scholar Program allow students to demonstrate superior ability in a number of ways. A student whose GPA was 3.5 or who placed at or above the ninetieth percentile on two out of three Richland College assessment tests, and who had a combined score of 1,100 on the Scholastic Aptitude Test (SAT) or a composite ACT score of at least 25, would, of course, qualify for the program by satisfying the traditional honors program requirements. However, a student without the high GPA, high percentile ranking, and/or strong showings on the ACT and SAT could also qualify for the Honors Scholar Program by demonstrating special abilities through a portfolio, audition, or paper, or participation in special national conferences and summer institutes. Honors students are frequently selected as tutors through the Center for Independent Study, and Phi Theta Kappa members graduate with special recognition.

An honors program in the Los Angeles district was launched by the faculty of West Los Angeles College. Admission to the program requires that students place at a college freshman level in English and that they be recommended by an instructor. The program is both varied and extensive, offering a number of options for its participants. A core of general education courses is set aside for honors students, as well as a number of interdisciplinary courses to choose from within the general education area. In addition to their honors course work, students are responsible for conducting special projects and are encouraged to participate in off-campus internships. Los Angeles Harbor College has an honors society, gives departmental recognition to special students, offers special courses for special students, and maintains a dean's list, as do other colleges in this district. Top students at Harbor who are involved in the program for biomedical research receive scholarships at California State University, Long Beach.

Lakeland (Ohio) Community College's honors program includes an Honors Student Advisory Council, which meets quarterly and provides a forum for sharing ideas and concerns with honors students and faculty members, provides early registration, and offers honors scholarships. In addition, this program gives students special commemoration as "honors graduates," designates "honors" on transcripts and diplomas, develops a special student portfolio that can be sent to prospective employers, and offers a liaison with honors programs at four-year institutions. Lakeland also offers a program abroad—eight weeks in Oxford, England, where participants earn twelve hours of humanities and social science credits.

St. Louis Community College's Forest Park campus has incorporated a program whereby students may sign a special contract with the instructor of any course in which they are enrolled to do extra work for honors. If all of the honors activities have been completed to the instructor's satisfaction, the participating students are given certificates and receive a notation on their transcripts designating completion of honors work in that particular course.

In summary, the academic support services for high-achieving students include special courses; special sections of courses, usually restricted in size to encourage maximum faculty-student interaction; in-class honors options, which often include the negotiation of a contract to complete special assignments; honors colloquia and special events, which often feature notable speakers from off campus; extracurricular activities, such as recognition banquets, graduation recognition, and opportunities for independent study and research; scholarships; memberships in national honorary societies, including Phi Theta Kappa and the National Collegiate Honors Council; and regular meetings with faculty mentors.

Enhancing Student Use of Support Services

Many students who could benefit fail to use the support services available to them. At Oakton Community College (Illinois), over one-third of the entering students were deficient in their basic skills, but only a small percentage enrolled in basic skills courses. Similar results were reported in studies in Florida (Lukenbill and McCabe, 1978) and Nevada (Friedlander, 1981a). Faculty members in Los Angeles reported that over 50 percent of the students enrolled in their classes were unable to understand course reading assignments, express themselves in writing, learn on their own, solve problems that require arithmetic, or understand science developments. There, as in most colleges, academic support programs were available but were not reaching most of their intended audience. Fewer than 30 percent of those students who reported that they did not feel confident in a skill area took advantage of a support program designed to assist them in writing or reading ability, developmental mathematics, or ability to understand science content. In fact, there was little difference in the use of support services by students who were and those who were not confident in their abilities (Center for the Study of Community Colleges, 1982). The reason most students offered for not using a support service was that they did not feel a need for it. The second most frequently cited reason was that they had no time, and the third reason (cited by over 35 percent of the respondents) was that the service was offered at an inconvenient hour. According to half the faculty, most students who were deficient in reading, writing, and mathematics ability failed to take basic skills courses in those areas because they were unwilling to devote the extra time or effort.

If students who are weak in the basic skills that they need to succeed in their courses do not take the time to participate in the support programs, then the colleges' policy of allowing students to attend class for the minimum number of hours must be questioned. That policy has contributed to the high dropout and failure rates. The colleges might better effect measures that make a specified number of hours spent in the learning laboratory a condition of continued enrollment in the collegiate classes. Every high-enrollment introductory liberal arts class should also have a mandated laboratory component where students learn to read the books and write the papers assigned in that course. Integrating support services with the courses themselves is essential. Other recommendations to enhance student use of support services include:

- Mandating orientation programs for all full-time students and for all students who have completed three or four classes. The students should learn that they are enrolled in a college that has certain expectations, codes of conduct regarding their studies, and interest in their progress toward attaining their goals—that it is not a passive, uncaring environment.
- Involving students with the college by arranging for them to assist their fellows. Repeatedly, studies of college retention of and effects on students have shown that the more that students involve themselves with the college, the more they achieve. Paying students (in coin or in academic credit) to tutor other students individually or in small groups in learning laboratories links those students to the college. Having them serve as readers or aides to the faculty has a similar effect.
- Beginning an academic proficiency exit examination program. This capstone test can be administered to all students who attain the associate degree level. It verifies the degree, allowing the college to demonstrate that students who have completed its program requirements have attained a certain academic proficiency level. Once begun, such a program affects the individual courses by indirectly testing their output. And it can focus student attention on college expectations for their learning, leading them to greater involvement with the academic support services. Testing is itself a form of academic support.
- Automating advising to the extent that every student's transcript and the graduation requirements for every college program are readily accessible to the student and to the

staff. Students should be periodically and routinely advised of their progress toward graduation.

- Publicizing the honors program and offering scholarships to high-achieving high school students in the vicinity. A cohort of such students must be attracted to maintain the college's image as a place of serious study. The program should be broadened to include greater numbers of students and should be connected with the local universities through guaranteed junior-level transfer arrangements.
- Scheduling remedial classes, counseling, and study skills sessions sequentially so that students participate in mutually supportive groups.

If enacted, these recommendations would have several effects. They would mitigate the drop in–drop out pattern of student attendance by linking the students with the college in more ways than just the classroom. They would signal the public and the state agencies that the collegiate function is still important, still worthy of support. And they would alert the university and secondary school staff members to the college's concern about its role as a connecting institution, a theme developed more fully in Chapter Eight.

8

Community Colleges as Connectors Between High Schools and Universities

From their inception, the community colleges have served as connectors between the high schools and the baccalaureate-granting colleges and universities. This chapter reviews the program coordination and joint agreements that have been established between high school and community college and between community college and four-year college and university. This articulation takes many forms, but all arrangements are based on the concept of a linear flow of students from grades 10 to 12 in the secondary schools, through grades 13 and 14 in the community colleges, and on to grades 15 and beyond in the senior institutions.

Strengthening the Preparation of High School Students

Most articulation between college and high school centers on attempts to improve the educational preparation of students who will enter college. Only some community college students continue on to universities, but all of them have attended secondary school at some time in the past. The kinds of preparation that the students have had account more than any other factor for their success and failure with the collegiate curriculum. Astute educators know that improving the quality of their feeder schools is necessary to maintaining their own enrollments and to the effectiveness of their own programs. The high school dropouts rarely become successful college students. The high school graduates with sets of inappropriate courses on their transcripts make the college's job more difficult.

Declines in the quality of precollegiate education were exacerbated by the fact that the high school students of the 1970s took fewer academically demanding courses than their counterparts of an earlier era. According to the National Center for Education Statistics (1975), the total proportion of high school students enrolled in general science courses declined by 30 percent between 1970 and 1972. During the same time, enrollments in general mathematics declined by 15 percent, in regular English courses by 8 percent, and in foreign languages by 4 percent. The proliferation of elective courses and the granting of credit for work experience by high schools had reduced the likelihood that a college-bound student would have taken advanced courses in mathematics, science, or other so-called hard academic subjects.

Efforts have been made by the boards of education in several states to require more academic courses before a high school diploma will be granted or before a student is admissible to the state's universities. The state of Illinois has adopted a uniform set of high school subject requirements (effective in the fall of 1990) for admission to university baccalaureate degree programs and to community college associate in arts and associate in science degree programs. Specifically required are four years of English, three years of social studies, three years of mathematics, three years of sciences, and two years of electives in foreign language, music, or art. In setting these requirements, the state hopes to send high school students "a clear signal" as to what is expected of college entrants. And through their enactment, the state believes that "the quality of high school preparation and the quality of both associate degrees and baccalaureate degrees should also improve" (Illinois Community College Board, 1985, p. 1).

Similar measures have been adopted in other states. California's strengthened standards were phased in over a period of years beginning in 1984. In Florida, had the requirements adopted in 1985 been enforced in 1983, only 7.5 percent of the state's high school graduates would have been eligible to attend the university, but the effect of the ruling was so marked that, by 1985, 25 percent met the standard.

Many individual colleges, too, have endeavored to promote an increase in the number of required academic subjects in the high schools. While the open admissions policies of community colleges militate against changes in their admissions requirements, the colleges have encouraged prospective applicants to take more solid academic subjects in high school, and they have provided prospective applicants and their parents with data on the relationship between the types of high school courses taken and student success in college. In California, the statewide academic senates of the community college system, the California State University and Colleges, and the University of California have published a handbook for parents, teachers, and high school students outlining mathematics and other academic skills that students should have before starting freshman-level college work. The Community College of Rhode Island and several other colleges have distributed similar works. Miami-Dade and the Dade County schools have worked jointly to increase parental and student awareness about the attitudes that students need to acquire, basic skills that they must develop, and academic courses that they should complete to be adequately prepared for college.

Some colleges have made direct efforts to strengthen the skills of their potential students before they arrive. One activity is designed to decrease the number of students in the colleges' remedial courses by bolstering remediation in the high schools. The colleges send student tutors to the high schools and open their learning resource centers and other campus facilities to high school students. Lawson State Community College (Alabama) has designed a series of workshops with its six feeder high schools and its local university. These transfer-related meetings are held with faculties from mathematics and science, English, and humanities. St. Louis Community College faculty meet regularly with high school teachers on the three college campuses to discuss course content, texts, and requirements. They report that their relationship with high schools is much better than their relationship with neighboring universities. Mathematics instructors from Chicago's Malcolm X College have worked on their own with local secondary schools, and English instructors from Los Angeles have gone into the high schools to facilitate articulation between the two levels of schooling.

A joint English and journalism committee operates in Dallas, with college and high school faculty meeting together. Speech and journalism departments sometimes send brochures to high schools, and art faculty advertise special campus events in the high schools. Cuyahoga Community College has joined forces with Links, Inc. (a national organization of black women dedicated to civic, cultural, and educational activities) to administer a program designed to improve the test-taking skills of inner-city high school students and to help them build the skills needed to succeed in postsecondary education (Harris and Rohfeld, 1983).

Clark Technical College's High School Liaison Project has sponsored several programs for local high school students, including a writing-skills competition and a summer "bridge" workshop on college survival skills. Clark has also encouraged local high schools to participate in statewide testing programs that are designed to assess the math and writing skills of high school juniors and to thus encourage students to seek remediation if necessary before high school graduation (Bordner, 1985). And the Community College of Philadelphia has cooperated with a local high school in a program designed to improve the reading, writing, and thinking skills of low-achieving, poverty-level students in the eleventh grade. Professors from the college have visited the high school to conduct classes, and the students also have had the opportunity to visit the college for special lectures and courses (Hatala, 1982).

Sharing Facilities. Strengthening student preparation has also been undertaken by sharing facilities. As one example, the counseling staff at South Mountain Community College (Arizona) provides American College Testing Program study sessions for high school students. In the same district, Mesa Community College makes campus facilities available for both the Summer Youth Employment Program and the High School Drop-Out Program to encourage college attendance by students from populations that traditionally have had low college representation.

College courses offered to high school students on their own campuses have also gained in popularity. The nine Los Angeles colleges present college-credit classes in beginning and advanced foreign languages, advanced mathematics, and sciences on proximate high school campuses, thereby offering students a head start toward their college degrees. San Antonio College (Texas) conducts a high-technology program on its campus for junior and senior high school students. College faculty teach science, math, and computer courses, and students receive high school credit.

The City Colleges of Chicago operate a College Acceleration Program for more than 1,700 high school students, who take regular college courses in their high schools from the college instructors before and after regular school as well as during break periods. Students are recommended by their schools and must meet the entry requirements of the courses for which they enroll. In recent years, students in this program have earned more than 10,000 credit hours per year. The Chicago school superintendent pioneered the ''Adopt a School'' program with business and industry when she ran the school system in Oakland, California. After meeting with her, the Chicago City Colleges decided to begin a pilot ''Adopt a High School'' program with Kennedy-King College and two area feeder high schools. This linkage involves exchange of course information, articulation discussions, sharing of resources, and special recruitment programs.

Miami-Dade's many efforts to strengthen the high school–college connection include the Performing and Visual Arts Center (PAVAC) and Emphasis on Excellence. In the PAVAC program, artistically talented high school students spend fifteen hours weekly on Miami-Dade college campuses with faculty from Miami-Dade and the Dade County public schools. As part of its Emphasis on Excellence program, Miami-Dade began offering a Summer Program for the Gifted and Talented in 1980. Two hundred high school students were selected to participate in a six-week summer program, which is designed to provide high-quality college-level instruction with a blend of theory and hands-on experience, utilizing modern equipment and facilities. The PAVAC program proved so successful that, in 1986, Miami-Dade took the lead in organizing the New World School of the Performing Arts, designed to shepherd students from grade 10 through the college and on into Florida International University.

Establishing Program Articulation. Program articulation includes efforts to coordinate and share curriculum, facilities, and staff members. In some cases, it is as informal as the community college instructors' checking with their counterparts in the local secondary schools before adopting a new textbook to ensure that the content and level present a natural progression for the students. In others, it includes formal agreements between school and college districts in which programs are so linked that students take the introductory course in a subject at the secondary school and the advanced courses at the community college. These types of programs, often called "two-plus-two" to suggest the number of years of study at each institution, are designed to maintain student progress with no duplication or gap in instructional objectives. As an example, Bakersfield College and the Kern High School District (California) adopted a two-plus-two plan leading to an associate degree with a concentration on agriculture (Parnell, 1985b).

The Center for High School/College Articulation at F. H. LaGuardia Community College was established in 1981 to serve as an informational network to encourage the exchange of data about high school–college programs. The center has issued a *Yellow Pages Directory* (Lieberman and Greenberg, 1983), which includes information acquired from a survey of 240 institutions. This directory compiles data about articulation programs, funding, student populations, and those four-year colleges and universities to which community college students might transfer. LaGuardia also operates Middle College, a secondary school program completely integrated with its collegiate offerings.

But these types of arrangements are rare. Advanced placement or dual enrollment whereby high school students take classes at the local college are much more common. Already operative in most districts, these arrangements were given a further boost by the nation's governors, whose 1986 report *Time for Results* (National Governors' Association, 1986) recommended that high school juniors and seniors be granted the option of enrolling in public college courses.

Clark (1985) and Parnell (1985b) both note the difficulty of maintaining links between high schools and colleges. Clark suggests that the high school is biased against preparing students for higher education because of several structural features. These include the American commitment to universal education through the twelfth grade, the development of the comprehensive secondary school, the organizational forms that couple high schools with elementary schools rather than with higher education, local control of the schools, and the local monopoly enjoyed by the secondary schools. Finding these features responsible for the poor academic preparation of students entering higher education, he contends that universal education requirements are detrimental, because the comprehensive high schools tend to allow large groups of students to "take undemanding coursework and eventually graduate without ever exerting any academic effort" (p. 395). These characteristics of the system have several baleful effects, one of which is the disincentive for doing well in secondary school. As long as these organizational characteristics of the schools are in place, any recommendations for strengthening secondary schools will have little effect. Clark suggests a greater variety of types of secondary schools, including specialized schools, private schools, schools within schools, and competition among comprehensive institutions.

Parnell cites results of an AACJC survey of community college administrators wherein the respondents were asked about four types of collaborative efforts between their institutions and the high schools in their area:

1. *Joint enrollment.* The primary purpose of this type of program is to provide a stimulating challenge for selected students. In some states, funding formulas reward both

schools and colleges, but such programs may be viewed as taking money from the high school, since they may be perceived as a form of student recruitment.

2. *Sharing of faculty.* Very little program articulation or collaboration is required in cases where faculty are shared or where one institution uses the facilities of another.

3. *Advance placement.* This type of program, which is aimed at motivating talented students, requires little collaborative commitment or articulation. It allows qualified students to matriculate in college classes while they are still enrolled in high school.

4. *Program coordination efforts.* Here the high schools and colleges develop written program articulation agreements. These agreements generally pertain to the vocational/technical courses and programs; they are the most difficult in terms of collaborative efforts. The most commonly cited issues inhibiting and discouraging this type of cooperation are turf, or intrusion into another program, state leadership limitations, inadequate resources, scheduling differences, community college image, lack of communication, and focus upon machinery rather than action.

According to Parnell, three out of four community college leaders report that their colleges are doing little or nothing in coordinating programs and in articulation. The successful programs show some consistent patterns and suggest that policy makers must demand program coordination and articulation; college and school system chief executive officers must take the responsibility for beginning a dialogue and maintaining communication; a program focus must be established as top priority; participants must receive recognition and awards (for example, reduced work loads); and an executive secretary or director must be selected to schedule meetings, edit reports, and so on. Other necessary components for successful programs include outlining specific duties, issuing periodic reports, and developing a written agreement and plan of action.

In summation, efforts to articulate high school and community college courses have been made, but much more could be done. The more successful efforts include joint course planning through intradisciplinary meetings between faculty of both institutions; advanced placement of high school students, sometimes with dual enrollment; after-school activities for students on the community college campus; and college courses offered on high school campuses. No one activity suffices to smooth the path between high school and college. But one feature stands out: the faculty of both institutions must be involved; district-level agreements and "college days" in which counselors visit high schools to talk with prospective students are not nearly enough. The most effective articulation is along disciplinary lines, with faculty planning connecting courses and with advanced placement or deferred college credit arrangements bringing students to the college campus before they have made their decisions about the colleges to which they will apply.

When college courses were taught by high school teachers with dual appointments, articulation was easy. Now, special efforts must be made to ease the transition between institutions. Many community college instructors take their curricular cues from the university; they would be well advised to look back to see how their courses mesh with those offered in the secondary schools. The California Community College Board of Governors' 1984 regulation requiring districts to articulate courses with the high schools may give impetus to that connection.

Connecting with the Baccalaureate

From the early days of the junior college through the 1960s, when the community colleges became comprehensive institutions, articulation with universities constituted a major effort. The primary function of the colleges then was transfer education, and most colleges, as well as their receiving institutions, supported articulation officers who monitored the student flow and assisted curriculum committees to ensure that courses would transfer with credit. From 1965 through 1981, transfer education was de-emphasized in favor of other college functions, and many articulation processes were diminished. By the second half of the 1980s, transfer education was renewed, and articulation once more became an important issue.

The flow of students from community colleges to universities is variously affected by national, state, and local agencies that mandate policies for accepting transferring students, develop informal guidelines regarding course equivalencies, fund special projects, and otherwise impose conditions to link institutions. The national agencies typically fund short-term projects to assist certain curricular efforts or the transfer of special groups of students between certain sets of institutions. The state agencies develop rules affecting the number and type of courses for which transferring students receive credit. Institutions locally develop guidelines for course equivalencies and various forms of admissions guarantees. The pattern is ever changing, and each level impinges on the other. The state mandates loom large as an apparent influence, while the locally derived agreements between institutions seem to have the most direct effect on student flow.

National Efforts. The community colleges and the fate of their students have not been prominent among the concerns of most federal education agencies or those philanthropic associations concerned with education. There are, however, some notable exceptions. Because of its interest in the education of minorities, the Ford Foundation, beginning in 1981, supported several projects that attempted to increase the numbers of minority students from urban areas successfully completing programs and moving on to four-year colleges. One of the foundation's efforts centered on an Urban Community College Transfer Opportunities Program (UCCTOP), which stimulated transfer-related activities in twenty-four colleges with high proportions of minority students. Grants awarded under UCCTOP ranged from $25,000 to $250,000 per college. UCCTOP and its related efforts became landmarks. Although it is always difficult to assess cause and effect, three direct results of the projects are greater publicity for the colleges' transfer function, a general appreciation of the difficulties confronted by students who wish to transfer, and a heightened awareness of the paucity of data about numbers of transfer students and their experiences in the receiving institutions.

The Andrew W. Mellon Foundation has a major interest in assisting liberal arts programs in colleges. In 1985, the foundation began a program to assist ten predominantly liberal arts colleges in attracting community college transfers. With the assistance of the Association of American Colleges, each senior institution was paired with a feeder community college so that articulation problems could be addressed. The colleges have developed articulation guidelines, handbooks, and counseling services for potential transfers and encouraged joint meetings of faculty at two-year and four-year colleges. Some of them also evolved special application and registration procedures for community college transfers.

Several federal agencies assist articulation indirectly. The National Institute of Education's Study Group on the Conditions of Excellence in American Higher Education considered several ways of enhancing student flow. The National Endowment for the Humanities assists articulation through its summer institutes for community college instructors and other activities that support the humanities in community colleges, some of which began in 1975. And in prior years, the National Science Foundation had sponsored programs that brought two-year and four-year college teachers of the sciences together to articulate their courses. Still, most of the articulation effort is in the hands of the states.

The States. Articulation between community colleges and universities in the same state is frequently strained. College staff members often reveal much mistrust and lack of communication: "Universities are dictatorial in what they will accept"; "They restrict us"; "Why should our curriculum be dictated by them?" The universities are accused of challenging the content of community college courses and of requiring students to take additional courses at the university to satisfy grade requirements. They may accept the courses taken or the grades earned by students at one college in a district and not those earned at others. Competition between the universities and colleges is pronounced in some districts, and the relationships are fraught with anger, distrust, and suspicion.

Although most states' publicly supported systems of higher education are organized to provide community college access to students who do not qualify for admission as freshmen to four-year colleges and universities, few have enacted explicit policies that guarantee access to the senior colleges after completion of the associate degree. In states with declining enrollments, the absence of policies guaranteeing admission to associate degree holders is not likely to hinder transfer opportunities, particularly with regard to state four-year colleges, because the senior institutions need the enrollment. However, the absence of such policies may decrease opportunities for transfer to the more prestigious public universities that can afford to be more selective.

Most states set forth some types of articulation policies, many of which (for example, in Missouri, Iowa, Michigan) are merely guidelines, while others (in Nevada, Florida) act as state mandates. In all, the main intent is to encourage cooperation among the various units of a state's publicly supported institutions. In a report identifying fifty types of coordinated programs in fourteen states, states with the greatest number of specific arrangements were those in which higher education agencies played an important role in their development (Southern Regional Education Board, 1979). As an example, a policy adopted by Oklahoma's state regents drew a specific agreement between the state's ten public four-year colleges and all public and private junior colleges (Beerson, 1979).

Articulation problems at the state level have been well documented. Kintzer (1982) describes and assesses the current status of transfer education, points to particular problems and concerns, and highlights specific techniques, activities, and policies regarding issues of transfer. In a later report, Kintzer (1985) presents a taxonomy of statewide agreements for the years 1972, 1976, and 1985. He categorizes the agreements into four types: formal and legally based guidelines and policies, state system policies, voluntary agreements between institutions or within states, and special state agreements on vocational/technical transfer credit. Kintzer and Wattenbarger's *The Articulation/Transfer Phenomenon* (1985) discusses these issues, describing major projects undertaken to promote the study of articulation and transfer.

A handbook designed by the Arizona board of regents (Wright, 1985) to assist college and university representatives from specific disciplines provides information on implementing statewide postsecondary articulation. This handbook defines the role of the Articulation Task Force, which facilitates credit transfer, develops methods to communicate accurate information to students, and establishes a communication process regarding program change—a particularly important endeavor. Arizona's statewide course-equivalency guide lists all courses offered by community colleges, indicating for each their eligibility for transfer credit (general elective, departmental elective, general studies) to Arizona State University, Northern Arizona University, and the University of Arizona. This statewide course-equivalency guide, in effect for many years, reflects only the three state universities as whole units, and not the colleges or departments *within* each university; hence, problems do exist. A more accurate and detailed guide that will automatically update curriculum changes is a state goal. In fall 1985, a statewide common numbering system for like courses was put into effect. This procedure, which includes common course prefixes, numbers, and titles, is making the process of transferring infinitely easier.

California has a long history of efforts to ameliorate intersegmental transfer problems, but the attempt has yielded little. State-level committees on articulation operate, but there are few official state rules governing the movement of students between institutions. The most promising recent effort has been to fund transfer centers at twenty community colleges to identify and assist potential transfers, track them, conduct information workshops, organize study groups, and work on articulation agreements. A California Articulation Number System was begun in 1986 with the intention of making it a statewide course-equivalency guide.

Florida has had formal articulation compacts since the late 1950s. These state agency–coordinated agreements set down rules regarding the definition of all associate degrees and certificates; the awarding of credit for the College Level Examination Program, advanced placement, and the United States Armed Forces Institute; responsibility for general education requirements and preprofessional courses; admission to upper-division programs that are competitive because of space or fiscal limitations; upper-division requirements and lower-division prerequisites; standard transcript forms; and experimental programs. Florida's nine public universities have been required to develop counseling manuals listing the courses by programs that students need to take at the community college in order to qualify for transfer. And one of the most useful of the Florida mandates led to a statewide four-digit common course-numbering system.

Florida requires every public two- and four-year institution to develop a general education program that embraces at least thirty-six semester hours. The state also specifies that students who have been certified by any public institution as having fulfilled general education requirements and who transfer to another institution will not be required to complete any additional lower-division general education courses. Thus, Florida community colleges can certify that their students have completed general education requirements, and the senior colleges are required to honor their certification. However, several universities have added upper-division liberal arts requirements as general education supplements, which means that the universities are modifying the articulation agreements by usurping liberal arts courses from the community colleges. And articulation suffers further where the universities duplicate occupational courses and lower-division liberal arts courses—for example, in pre-architecture and pre-engineering. Nonetheless, the Florida higher education system is as well articulated as any in the nation, a situation that contributes markedly to the relatively high rate of transfer in that state.

A 1970 resolution adopted by the Illinois Board of Higher Education requires that a student who has completed "an associate degree based on baccalaureate-oriented sequences be considered to have attained junior standing and to have met lower-division general education requirements of senior institutions" (University of Illinois, 1978, p. 5). Since the adoption of this resolution, Illinois has refined its efforts to communicate the admissions requirements of senior institutions to potential transfer students and has continued discussion of lower/upper-division course classifications.

According to Maryland's policy statement on transfer students, an individual who has been awarded the associate in arts degree or who has successfully completed fifty-six hours of credit with an overall 2.0 average in college and/or university parallel courses shall not be denied transfer to an institution. When receiving colleges and universities must curtail admissions for oversubscribed programs, they are required to develop criteria for admission that provide equal treatment for native and transfer students. Students who had qualified for admission to the four-year institutions as high school seniors are eligible for transfer regardless of credits earned, as long as they have earned a 2.0 average in college and university parallel courses. When differences of interpretation in the award of transfer credit cannot be resolved between the individual student and the receiving institution or between the sending and receiving institutions, appeals can be made to the Segmental Advisory Committee.

Ohio students who earn the associate of arts degree with a specified number of credits in English composition and literature, humanities, social and behavioral sciences, and/or natural sciences or mathematics are considered to have reached the halfway point in the progression toward a baccalaureate degree as long as they have also completed programmatic prerequisites. Massachusetts's Commonwealth Transfer Compact states that the associate degree will be honored as a unit. It is also construed as completion of at least sixty hours of work toward a baccalaureate degree, including at least thirty-three hours toward fulfillment of the general education requirements for the baccalaureate degree. Texas has been actively involved in developing transfer curricula in selected majors. But since the information provided is limited to the number of credits that should be completed in general discipline areas, students are required to consult with the university or college to which they plan to transfer in order to select appropriate courses. The articulation policy in Texas provides for either the staff of the coordinating board or a specially appointed committee to mediate transfer problems that cannot be resolved by institutional representatives.

Local Arrangements. Regardless of the presence or absence of state mandates, numerous colleges develop independent articulation agreements with the universities in their vicinity. The status of articulation agreements between institutions was reviewed by Walton (1984), who reported the findings of a survey of 1,000 two-year and four-year institutions. Respondents in all the colleges were asked whether their institutions had a written agreement governing transfer; more than half the institutions reported no such agreements in force. More than two-thirds of the senior colleges indicated that they would not accept the associate degree on its face as evidence that a student had had appropriate lower-division preparation. Instead, most reviewed students' prior course work and grades individually, awarding credit toward the baccalaureate only for courses that met certain specifications.

The agreements that are negotiated typically concern guaranteed admission and/or course equivalencies. The City University of New York's policy on students transferring from community colleges to senior institutions states that recipients of the associate degree will be accepted as matriculated students at a senior college of City University. It further provides that, upon transfer, they will be granted a minimum of sixty-four credits toward a baccalaureate degree and that they will be required to complete only the difference in credits between sixty-four and the total credits required in the baccalaureate program in which they enroll. However, this policy goes on to state that the mandated acceptance of sixty-four credits is *not* intended to prevent the senior colleges from establishing major requirements and prerequisites for those requirements, the same loophole that has allowed the departments in universities across the land to add their own additional course requirements.

California's statewide transfer compacts are so weak that the only useful transfer arrangements are those negotiated among sets of institutions. In 1985, the University of California at Berkeley directed about 200 students to four local community colleges, with a promise of admission to Berkeley as juniors if they completed an appropriate program of studies with an adequate grade point average. Students were guaranteed admission not to specific programs but to the university in general. The Santa Monica College Scholars Program involves students who will transfer to the University of California at Los Angeles, and the UCLA Transfer Alliance Program encourages academic alliances between the university and the local community colleges in an effort to increase transfer of members of underrepresented groups and establish faculty-to-faculty dialogue. Santa Barbara Community College and the University of California at Santa Barbara are connected through a Transition Program. The Transfer Opportunities Program provides information, encouragement, and financial aid for students who would transfer between the Los Rios Community College District and the University of California at Davis, while a project conducted by Palomar College and the University of California at San Diego studies and attempts to overcome barriers to transfer encountered by disadvantaged students.

Other projects to facilitate transfer in California include the Sacramento Student Transition Project, which recruits community college students throughout the state to participate in work-experience internships by concurrently enrolling at the California State University, Sacramento; the Merced-Modesto-San Joaquin Delta Student Transition Project, which provides transition services for students at three community colleges as well as concurrent enrollment at the California State University, Stanislaus; and the San Diego Student Transition Project, which offers student transition counseling and orientation seminars at four-year colleges (California State Postsecondary Education Commission, 1983).

Some of California's community colleges have taken matters into their own hands. In order to identify candidates for transfer to a four-year institution, San Diego City College and Los Angeles Harbor College each developed a computer program that would create a file of potential transfer students from the district student data base. This file identified eight variables as criteria: an indicated interest in transferring, a 2.0 GPA, full-time enrollment, number of units completed, age, gender, ethnicity, and address. All students who were selected by these criteria were invited to participate in the project by having their names sent to potential receiving institutions.

LaGuardia Community College transfer efforts have focused in part on what that institution perceives as the major problems surrounding the issue of transfer: the students' lack of knowledge about continuing their education and the benefits of so doing and their options for planning, financing, and obtaining the baccalaureate. Accordingly, LaGuardia has developed and tested a model to provide students with basic transfer information, involved the corporate community in its transfer project, and developed a model of transfer to Vassar, a selective, private, residential college. It has also collected both qualitative and base-line data on its potential and actual transfer students, strengthened its transfer counseling, increased articulation with four-year colleges, and created a framework for a comprehensive, collegewide transfer program.

Miami-Dade Community College developed a highly sophisticated computerized system wherein all course equivalencies for public and private colleges and universities are matched by degree program with courses offered at the college. This system is particularly useful for both students and counselors, because it allows for continuous monitoring of individual progress. For instance, students who have selected computer science as their major can log into the system and receive a printout that lists, in addition to the required general education sequence, all courses required for transferring to the computer science program at the University of Florida. The printout also informs students of the number of courses they have completed in the sequence and the grades earned for each course. Among the many advantages of Miami-Dade's program is that any changes in course equivalencies necessitated by the addition of new courses, changes in course titles or numbers, or changes in transfer requirements can be made quickly through the computer program. The program allows up-to-date information to be entered quickly and economically, making it much more efficient than maintaining printed equivalency guides.

By way of formalizing its articulation agreements with all of the community colleges in its state, the State University College of New York at Plattsburgh developed a course-by-course analysis that serves as the foundation for the entire transfer articulation process (Fairweather and Smith, 1985). Though such analyses require much initial time and effort, once a guide of this sort is completed, very little effort is required to maintain and update it.

In 1984, J. Sargeant Reynolds Community College (Virginia) established an alumni support network for community college students who contemplated transfer. Alumni transfer coordinators worked with university staff members to identify college alumni presently enrolled at the local state university as well as current students applying to enter a baccalaureate institution. A few colleges have also attempted to recruit alumni to work with current students or to act as role models, but this activity is not widespread.

Beginning in fall 1985, John Wood Community College (Illinois) offered its students a guarantee that either courses taken at the college would transfer to other institutions or the students' tuition would be refunded (Drea, 1985). Each student applying for the credit transfer guarantee must meet with a college counselor and must be responsible for indicating the institution that he or she will attend and the courses to be transferred. The counselor consults articulation agreements and other sources and reports back to the student regarding the courses guaranteed to transfer. The student, the counselor, and the dean of student services sign the agreement, which is official and binding. The guarantee is designed to encourage students to attend the college by reassuring them that the credits earned there can be used at other institutions. In addition, the guarantee is intended to deal with transfer issues particular to Illinois, where each institution determines independently what courses it will accept and where virtually no courses are universally transferable.

Program-by-program guaranteed admissions programs have made much headway. A career ladder mobility program in nursing was developed by New Mexico Junior College for articulation with the University of New Mexico. The report of this program (Hafer and Davis, 1985) outlines both the internal institutional factors and the external influences from the nursing field that served as the basis for its development and implementation.

Virginia's Norfolk State University, a predominantly black four-year public institution, and Tidewater Community

College, a predominantly white multicampus two-year public college, developed articulated transfer programs in office administration/secretarial science, accounting, and business education (Mohr and Sears, 1979). Discussions leading to resolution of program duplication were held at the college as well as at the state level. The deliberations resulted in the development of a plan for teaching faculty from the three discipline areas and an articulation model that led to eight agreements in an atmosphere characterized as friendly and respectful. Curriculum modifications and policy changes for the purpose of better meeting the needs of students evolved easily, and the negotiations resulted in agreement on nontraditional credits and fulfillment of requirements, compliance with state and institutional policies, and admission and financial aid procedures.

The Maricopa County Community College District has numerous program-by-program articulation agreements with Arizona State University. High-level administrators, department chairs, and faculty from both institutions participate in periodic meetings to ensure that the transfer process runs smoothly. Guaranteed admission to junior-level programs is a feature of the agreements. The arrangements have been extremely successful in maintaining the flow of students between the institutions. Their most notable feature is that they are maintained at the department level.

In summary, the articulation process is directly related to the transfer process. Most institutions have some sort of articulation plan, whether state mandated or locally developed. These efforts not only focus on the transfer of course credits from two-year to four-year colleges but include programs to better prepare students for college work before they enter the community college, attempts to equalize the academic rigor of lower-division courses taught at community colleges and senior institutions, plans for college matriculation that stress the identification and achievement of student goals, information systems designed to monitor and support student flow from matriculation through transfer, and program-by-program arrangements worked out by groups of neighboring community colleges and universities.

These types of connections between high school and community college and between community college and university are difficult to effect and maintain, because numerous groups must be involved and numerous sets of regulations must be considered and, where necessary, modified. Furthermore, the ground is continually shifting as student preferences and abilities, curricular requirements, and staff member interests and energies change. Maintaining the collegiate connection requires intense commitment by local and state leaders. There is no easy path.

9

Strengthening
the Collegiate Connection

Throughout this work, we have considered the policies that affect the liberal arts curriculum and patterns of student transfer. Here, we discuss ways of monitoring and strengthening the collegiate connection, beginning with a proposal for reconceptualizing the traditional ways of measuring curriculum and student transfer rates and continuing with other recommendations for enhancing the liberal arts and the flow of students through the colleges.

Reconceptualizing the Curriculum

The collegiate curriculum centers on those courses that carry credit toward the associate degree and/or are accepted by the four-year colleges and universities for credit toward the baccalaureate. This liberal arts–based curriculum includes courses in the humanities, sciences, social sciences, fine arts, mathematics, and English. It is often labeled "transfer studies," but that is misleading, because fewer than one-fourth of the students enrolled in the liberal arts courses will go on to further collegiate studies.

169

Occupational studies have played an important role in higher education's development. Just as the universities could never have commanded the share of public support that they enjoy if they had not developed professional schools, the community colleges without the occupational programs would have been severely attenuated, remaining as postgraduate training centers for the secondary schools or as narrowly based screening and sorting centers for the universities. The liberal arts have remained prominent in both university and community college, but, in both, they have been modified to fit institutional realities. They have been compromised by the universities' professional schools and by the community colleges' emphasis on occupational education. Most liberal arts study in the community college is in service to the occupational programs, not only the certificate and associate degree programs but also those requiring that students transfer to universities and obtain higher degrees before entering the work force.

Most of the proponents of the liberal arts recognize their curriculum's service to occupations and accept it, because they know that occupational preparation and general education are their institutions' major functions. They might prefer rationalizing their courses as contributing to their students' love of learning and the scholarly quest, but few are so naive. The curricula that promote social cohesion or economic development are more likely to engage support from legislators than are the courses directed toward individual benefit (enhancing self-concept, filling leisure time), which are likely to be considered self-indulgent. Therefore, the more astute liberal arts proponents assess and publicize their curriculum's usefulness in the workplace and its contribution to the well-being of the community.

The general education aspect of the curriculum is revealed in the way that the courses are presented: general surveys and introductions to concepts and terminology within each subject area. The instructors' marginal affiliation with academic disciplinary associations has helped them avoid most of the excessively specialized instruction designed for people who are going to conduct research in a disciplinary field. The philosophy instructors have shunned an inordinate concern with analytical examinations and have attended to interpretations of concepts of truth, justice, ethics, and logic. The psychology instructors are more likely to direct students toward understanding interpersonal relations and self-motivations, less likely to attend to the measurement of minutiae. The literature instructors have avoided the immoderate emphasis on textual analysis that characterizes their university counterparts.

The result is that the liberal arts in community colleges hardly resemble the contemplative, text-centered courses that are posed as the ideal in the university. They are more likely to be manifestations of general education, designed to teach people to be enlightened citizens. Interdisciplinary or integrated humanities and social science classes have made some headway, but the general education of most students is accommodated through single classes in psychology, history, biology, or literature. Connections among classes are rare, because few students attend in linear fashion, taking one class and another in a predetermined sequence. Each class makes its own contribution.

General education is effective. The students are more likely to gain appreciation for and some facility in language, the arts, and general science than they are to acquire an attachment to contemplative study in depth. The students in Washington community colleges whom we surveyed in 1981 reported those types of gains. The more liberal arts courses they had taken, the more confident they were in their ability to speak and write effectively and their awareness of different viewpoints and the more likely they were to say that they had developed a sense of values, an understanding of social issues, and an understanding of scientific developments. Conversely, the more classes in business that the students had taken, the less confident they were about each of those goals (Center for the Study of Community Colleges, 1982).

A common misconception is to consider these liberal arts–derived courses as a transfer program, a term suggesting sequence and unified purpose. Courses with titles reflecting their roots in the liberal arts are listed in the catalogues, with students advised to take certain classes in order to qualify for transfer to various programs at the universities. But exceedingly few students who intend to transfer take the classes in the recommended sequences; most take them in whatever order suits their personal schedules. They drop in and out of the institutions, taking major program requirements now, distribution requirements another time, and electives along the way. A transfer program cannot reasonably be assumed from a perusal of the sequences as listed in the catalogues.

Furthermore, many enrollees have no intention of transferring. The students in an art class may already have baccalaureate degrees and be enrolled only so that they may paint under the direction of an instructor. The students in a class in child development offered under a psychology course title may be there only to gain credentials entitling them to apply for immediate employment in the field of child care. The students in a biology class may be seeking a vocational nursing license. Most students in physical education classes take them for their personal interest. The fact that all those classes carry transfer credit is an artifact of college accreditation, staffing, and financing. It relates to the perceptions or intentions of only a portion of the students who are enrolled.

The transfer function, integral to the collegiate connection, must be sustained if the colleges are to maintain their place in the mainstream of graded education that characterizes the American educational system. All the calls for more responsiveness to the students' quest for activities that satisfy their immediate desires founder on that rock. Without the transfer function, the community college would take on the form of a neighborhood adult school or occupational training center, thereby reducing its societal value and its support base. However, the misleading terms *transfer program* and *transfer courses* should be abandoned, because they confound student behavior with course content.

Categorizing the curriculum by relating it to student intentions or behavior leads to a succession of errors, from inappropriate criteria for institutional success to a distorted view of curricular effects. The colleges are adjudged unworthy because the student transfer rate is low, even though two-thirds of the matriculants have no intention of transferring. Instead of appreciating the liberal arts–based curriculum for its contributions to the general education of the community, its critics contend that it does not adequately prepare students to become majors in an academic discipline at a university. But few of the commentators realize that there is no transfer program. There are only courses that students may take that will be accepted for credit if they transfer to a baccalaureate degree–granting institution. Judgments of institutional worth, staff and outsiders' perceptions, and institutional support in general are based on a misconception. Curricular content and student intentions are confounded. They should be separated in the interest of better understanding the colleges' contribution to American education.

Measuring Curriculum Content and Student Intent. A new measure of institutional functioning would be based on differentiating curriculum content from student intent. The liberal arts have been distinctly modified in the direction of general education and occupational service and cannot well be understood by using the traditional content categories that the community colleges inherited from the universities. Portions of the content in humanities, sciences, social sciences, and fine arts have moved far from the liberal arts ideal. Much of the content in those areas falls under skill development. The remedial classes in English and mathematics are obviously designed to teach basic literacy, computational, and study skills. Those liberal arts courses that are in distinct service to occupational programs, such as some of the science courses, similarly should be placed under the category of skill development. And the physical education and fine arts courses that are directed toward enhancing the students' recreational skills need also to be separated. Whether these courses are accepted for credit toward bachelor's degrees is irrelevant. The entire curriculum should be categorized as:

Liberal Arts
   Science
   Social science
   Humanities
   Fine and performing arts

Skills
  Basic
  Occupational
  Recreational

The transfer function similarly would be better understood if the students' intentions were more carefully described. Assuming that all students without bachelor's degrees intend to obtain them is naive. Asking students about the highest degree they hope to receive yields the distorted answers that can be expected when no limits are placed; few students believe that they will never progress further than the current term in their education. And many of the students who say that they want to gain baccalaureate and higher degrees and/or to enter professions that require such degrees exhibit behavior that runs counter to their stated aspirations. They avoid the courses that require mathematics or writing skills, and they fail to participate in volitional activities such as seeking counseling, meeting with instructors outside of class, or attending college events that have been organized to smooth the transfer process. They seem to want their classes to do it all, to be the magic carpet that transports them to the university and to the high-status careers to which they aspire.

However, in fairness to the students, the question about the highest degree that they intend to obtain does not assess their actual reasons for attending the college. Such a question should not be open-ended but instead should ask the students about their immediate goals. Furthermore, since students often maintain several goals simultaneously, it should seek their primary goal by posing a forced choice among alternatives.

What is the most important reason that you are attending *this* college at *this* time? (Mark only one answer)
  ☐ To prepare for transfer to a four-year college or university
  ☐ To gain skills necessary to enter a new occupation
  ☐ To gain skills necessary to retrain, remain current, or advance in a current occupation
  ☐ To satisfy a personal interest (cultural, social)

Thus, student intentions should be categorized as:

- preparing for transfer
- gaining skills for a new occupation
- occupational upgrading
- personal interest

By such a separation between curriculum content and student intent, both may be assessed more accurately. The curricular classifications can be made by using the catalogue descriptions of the classes to make the determinations of content. The percentage of college effort devoted to each area of the curriculum can be estimated by tabulating enrollments in the courses that are actually offered each year. Student intentions can be estimated by asking the indicated question of all students who enroll. The question can be placed on every student's registration card or, in colleges where that procedure is unfeasible, asked in a survey of students in a sample of all class sections offered. Measures of success can then be drawn by determining the percentage of students who attained the goal that they sought when they matriculated, with further subdivisions made according to the length of time that it took for them to attain it. If the question of student intent were so posed, the figures regarding the proportion seeking transfer would drop considerably, and calculating the percentage of students transferring would gain a different denominator.

Categorizing curriculum according to its content would assist in understanding each college's role in providing general education, basic skills, recreational skills, and occupationally specific training for the people of its community. Classifying the students' intentions by asking them to state their primary goal would yield a better measure of the types of people who are being served, the purposes for which they come to the college, and the extent to which they achieve them. This form of information could be used by state agencies in allocating funds, within the colleges as an aid to resource allocation, and, not least, as a constant public information resource that would assist college spokespersons in explaining what their institutions actually do.

Measuring Learning. The liberal arts would be better understood also if student learning were assessed more consistently. The measurement of student learning has suffered from its being confounded with grades, transfer rates, and persistence rates. The result is that practically no reliable information is available. However, as reported in the chapter on testing, it is feasible to develop and administer a test of student knowledge in the liberal arts. Content questions from the areas of humanities, science, social science, mathematics, and English usage can be collected, alternative test forms generated, and the instrument administered to the students at varying stages in their academic careers. In the colleges that have mandated orientation sessions, the instrument can be administered to all matriculants. If there is no occasion when all students are brought together, the test can be given in the various classes, with students indicating the number of course credits that they have already attained. In that procedure, the cohorts of beginning students and students with some number of units already completed can be generated for purposes of analysis after the results are in.

The results of this form of measuring student learning in the liberal arts can be used to estimate the "value added" to each student's knowledge, currently a seductive concept. More important, the greater knowledge exhibited on the test by students who have taken certain numbers of courses in the various content areas would provide a verification of curricular effects. The curriculum's contribution to the students' general education could be noted and publicized. And revisions in curriculum and academic support services could be undertaken with reference to a useful data base.

The Liberal Arts in Occupational Education. The concepts on which the liberal arts classes are based are too basic to individual and social welfare to be reserved only for the students who intend to obtain associate in arts or science degrees. Half the students entering community colleges seek either job entry or job upgrading; by definition, they are "occupational students," whether or not they are enrolled in formally designed occupational programs. The liberal arts are as important for them as they are for any other types of students.

The teaching of concepts stemming from the liberal arts to students in occupational programs is most feasibly done by requiring that those students take a certain number of liberal arts classes. Perceiving the value of the liberal arts for the general education of all students, the AACJC in 1986 took a strong position on their behalf. They recommended that the graduation requirements in all associate in applied science degree programs, the programs provided especially for students seeking immediate employment opportunities, include a minimum of 25 percent of courses in the social and behavioral sciences, communications, and the humanities. The association did so even while continually urging that its member colleges be recognized for their contribution to the economy and a trained work force. The association's president and board members were aware that contemporary job training must include literacy, awareness of the environment, and appreciation of America's heritage.

Other procedures for merging the liberal arts with occupational studies that have been attempted have proved more difficult to sustain. In a few colleges, the liberal arts faculty have developed short lessons that they teach to the occupational students, but questions of faculty course-load credit have retarded the spread of that idea. The faculty at Triton College (Illinois) solved the problem of work-load assignment by building a set of one-unit short courses that are required in the various occupational programs. But in most colleges, the graduation requirements, often state mandated, are all that keep occupational students enrolled in liberal arts classes. The AACJC's recommendation that these requirements be sustained in programs leading to the associate in applied science degree deserves support.

Setting Goals in the Liberal Arts. The community colleges exist within a framework of conflicting expectations. They are to enlighten the citizenry through general education, enhance the productivity of the work force through occupational studies, provide the basis of successful transfer for students opting for the baccalaureate, and remedy the defects occasioned by the lower schools' inability to teach literacy. The liberal arts must fit within those broader institutional goals, but few practitioners consider them in that broad a framework. They are more likely to specify the goals and activities maintained discretely within each course. Linking all together demands a level of abstraction that is difficult to translate into specific curricular objectives.

When curricular goals are articulated, the general drives out the specific. Statements such as "The students will gain an appreciation for democratic institutions, the ability to think critically, and skills enabling them to function effectively" decorate the pages of every catalogue. But few curriculum organizers have been able to translate those types of goals into the specifics of numbers and percentages of students who will achieve them and the ways that goal attainment would be measured. On a collegewide basis, the general does not accommodate the specific.

On the other hand, within the classrooms, the specific drives out the general. The classes are dedicated to teaching students to solve computational problems, translate vocabulary words, write coherent sentences and paragraphs, list and comment on the causes and results of major historical events. If all the objectives in all the courses were viewed together, a lengthy list of disconnected individual tasks would appear.

How can the gap between the general college goals and the objectives toward which each class is directed be bridged? Assuming that the primary value of the liberal arts in community colleges is in enhancing the students' acculturation and sense of social responsibility, the broad social goals and course objectives can be linked through the core concepts of general education. In order for that to be effected, the goals must be drawn less from the academic disciplines, more from the notion that learning gains should be reflected in the students' actions.

In many institutions where the definition of general education as leading students to more responsible individual and social activity has been accepted as the desired pattern for curriculum organization, committees composed of people from all positions within the college have put together such goals. The Dallas County Community College District's Common Learning Committee (Armes, 1984) and the Maricopa district's Arts and Sciences Task Force (Meixner, 1984) are examples. The sets of goals brought forth by these groups have been used in deciding on the content of entrance examinations to the various programs, communicating to secondary schools the types of abilities desired of entering students, constructing courses that would lead students to obtain subsets of those goals, pointing the way for faculty to specify objectives that would reveal progress toward those goals in individual courses, and setting a forum for describing and assessing college outcomes.

Designing and using the tenets of general education as curriculum organizers is difficult, because few people in the colleges have been prepared to conduct such exercises and because the academic department–dominated universities persist in reviewing the community college curriculum to ensure that it fits the model of the academic discipline. Nonetheless, some progress has been made, and more can be done as the community college educators recognize that their institutions are sufficiently important to warrant their own form of curriculum organization. The liberal arts in community colleges will thrive to the extent that they are converted to the realities of those institutions.

Strengthening Articulation with the University

Curriculum articulation varies considerably between states and between institutions and college districts in the same state. Some colleges have clear-cut articulation agreements with their neighboring universities. Functioning articulation committees, composed of staff members from both institutions, meet regularly to maintain the details of curriculum and transfer. But in other sets of colleges and universities, there are constant confusion and varied interpretations about which courses are transferable to what programs.

In some states, common course-numbering systems in all publicly supported colleges have been adopted as a way of enhancing the process of student transfer from one institution to another. They offer the most feasibly arranged, influential supports to student flow, and they should be pursued in every state. But although such systems are essential, as long as the senior institution staff members have the right to accept or refuse courses in their academic departments for graduation credit, common course numbering is by no means sufficient. As an example, a common course-numbering system covers all public higher education in Texas, but students who transfer from some colleges in the Dallas Community College District to the University of Texas at Arlington may have their courses accepted at full value, whereas transfers from other colleges in the same district may not.

Since most states provide articulation guidelines only, without the force of a mandate, program-by-program links are necessary. Miami-Dade's mode of maintaining computerized records of the requirements for juniors entering any program in any university in Florida affords one model. Maricopa's frequent joint meetings with the staff in each department at Arizona State University presents another.

Influencing Transfer Rates

Articulation with the local university demands constant attention, but it is only part of what can be done to increase transfer rates. Many students do not intend to transfer, but those who do must be identified early in their collegiate career; by the time they have applied for graduation or for their transcripts to be sent, it is much too late. If a potential transfer cohort is defined when the students matriculate, the many services that support them in their quest can be targeted, strengthened, and effectually mandated. These services include special transfer counselors, periodic sessions where the students meet university representatives, materials describing university programs and requirements, and on-campus lectures by university professors, to name only a few. The students' participation can be required just as regular class attendance is required.

Furthermore, a full array of second-year, sophomore-level courses must be offered so that students encounter fewer scheduling difficulties in progressing toward completing their programs. The colleges that have particular commitment to student flow provide those courses even when they attract but a handful of students. Where they are offered, the students have greater incentive to stay enrolled without transferring until after they have attained the associate degree.

Other efforts to enhance transfer can be made. Miami-Dade Community College has received much publicity for its rate of student retention and transfer. Since 1975, the college has had a distinct commitment to enhancing its transfer numbers and to holding students for the full two years or even longer, if necessary, to prepare them for transfer. Miami-Dade awards associate degrees to its students at a rate considerably higher than that of any other large public institution. It boasts also that it provides one-sixth of all the transfer students in the state of Florida, a number all the more notable in view of the geography of the state: Florida's flagship universities are between 250 and 500 miles from Miami.

How did Miami-Dade do it? Identifying particular student cohorts is part of the story. The college built an honors program to attract the better students from the Miami high schools and offered full-tuition scholarships to students from the top 10 percent of their graduating classes; Miami-Dade enrolls nearly 40 percent of that top student group. For students on the other end of the scale, it designed a full complement of remedial courses and mandated placement on the basis of test scores and prior academic achievement. It also imposed a limitation on drop-in students by not allowing students to enroll in more than four courses until they have taken a placement test in English and mathematics and entered a designated program leading to a degree or certificate. It invoked standards of academic progress and enforced probation and suspension of students who were not making satisfactory progress toward completing a degree. It designed a computer-generated Response System with Variable Prescription that informs students each semester of their progress toward completing the program in which they are enrolled. It built an Academic Graduation Information System that shows students exactly which courses are required for transfer to each branch of the state university and each department within that branch. This latter system is readily accessible, so that students may walk into a counseling office, have their record placed on a screen, and see exactly which courses are needed to complete the transfer requirements in any program. All these activities were pointed toward facilitating transfer rates. All were coordinated rather than implemented on a piecemeal basis.

Involving the Students. Despite the claims made for distance learning, most of higher education's successes have depended on teaching students who matriculate in courses on a campus. The more closely the students are involved with the college, the greater the institution's effect. Because most community college students work off campus, commute to school, and attend part time, their primary interests and allegiance rest elsewhere. The instructional and academic support services that the colleges provide benefit the students only to the extent that they participate.

Keeping the students involved takes special efforts. Students can be linked to the college through work-study experiences, specialized student clubs, block scheduling so that they have greater opportunities to develop relationships with their peers, consistent program advising, and more opportunity for interaction with faculty members outside of class. Since most students need paid employment, many more jobs on campus should be provided and off-campus internships arranged, including work experience–based liberal arts programs (Center for the Study of Community Colleges, 1983). The colleges cannot duplicate a residential experience, but they can simulate some of its better features.

Rewarding the Colleges for Their Student Flow. Supporting transfer is expensive: students must be provided with special testing, counseling, and instructional and academic support services. It is unquestionably more economical to let the students drift in and out of classes at will, even though that policy is decidedly detrimental to program completion. Some state systems have provided funds to promote retention and program completion. Twenty colleges in California, for example, received a total of $1,873,000 in supplemental funds from the state in 1985 for the first year of a three-year project to organize transfer centers wherein students and student support practices are guided in coordinated fashion (Dyste and Miner, 1986). However, these types of sporadic funding efforts are not nearly enough.

Student flow might be more efficiently enhanced by directly

rewarding the colleges that increased their student flow rates. State funds could be set aside for colleges to receive an override of a specified percentage of the instructional costs for each student who completed a prerequisite course and enrolled in the next course in a curricular sequence. An additional bonus could be provided for each student who received an associate degree and each student who transferred to a senior institution within a specified time. The amounts need not be large. The intention would be to demonstrate the state's commitment to the transfer function.

A per capita bonus plan would have notable effect. The colleges would begin vigorously recruiting the more able secondary school students and seeking funds for scholarships. They would enforce prerequisites in curriculum and provide more sophomore-level courses. They would coordinate supplemental instruction activities, mandating them for students in the high-enrollment introductory classes. They would develop information systems so that students and counselors could tell at a glance the courses still needed for graduation. And, not least, because student progress was related directly to dollars, they would be stimulated to collect and maintain data on student progress through the college and on into the universities. For the first time, student follow-up studies would gain practical value.

External Supports for the Collegiate Connection

Campus leaders who seek to enhance the collegiate connection can find assistance from off-campus agencies. Every state has official committees and associations working continually on data-collection procedures, interinstitutional program articulation, course-equivalency problems, and related issues of curriculum and transfer among its public higher education units. Less pervasive but still influential are the efforts of private foundations and federal agencies.

A prime example is the Andrew W. Mellon Foundation, which has long had an interest in the liberal arts and has funded numerous endeavors to support these programs in universities and other settings. Funding projects to help strengthen the liberal arts in community colleges is a natural extension of their work. The foundation has sponsored consortia such as the Community College Humanities Association and a project linking the six large urban community college districts that have been cited in this book: Chicago, Dallas, Los Angeles, Maricopa, Miami-Dade, and St. Louis. The latter project, coordinated by the Center for the Study of Community Colleges, identified the best courses and organizational forms to enhance the liberal arts; analyzed the colleges' curricula; identified the extent to which the liberal arts are required for and offered to students in the career programs; determined the manner in which courses and requirements are initiated, coordinated, organized, and set in place; and publicized in workshops the more successful practices, sharing them among the staff in the thirty-eight campuses.

The Ford Foundation has been more concerned with the transfer function. Their projects to increase the number of minority students entering community colleges and transferring eventually to universities stem from their prior commitment to minorities in other educational sectors. The CSCC's project, Facilitating Student Progress Through Community Colleges, and the Urban Community College Transfer Opportunities Program (UCCTOP) are examples of projects receiving the foundation's support. In addition to developing articulation plans with neighboring universities and secondary schools, the colleges involved in those projects undertook numerous internal changes to keep students in college and help them prepare for transfer.

Federal agencies committed to areas of the liberal arts have sponsored community college-related projects. The National Science Foundation is dedicated to supporting the sciences, social sciences, and mathematics in all areas of American life. The foundation has extended such support to community colleges through fellowships and summer workshops for science instructors and by funding research on the state of the sciences in those institutions. The National Endowment for the Humanities, with a comparable mission on behalf of the humanities, has supported workshops and fellowships for community college instructors, along with various research and advocacy endeavors. The funds awarded by these agencies seem modest when they are spread across more than 1,000 institutions, but they have significant impact on faculty morale. The Endowment has a very high success ratio for community college grants, because relatively few community college staff members apply.

Various state agencies have an interest in maintaining curricular balance. When the Washington State Board for Community College Education perceived that the humanities were in decline in that state's colleges, they directed their attention to gaining funding for a project to work on that area of the curriculum. The National Endowment for the Humanities supported their project from 1979 to 1982, breathing new life into the humanities, stimulating faculty morale and professionalism, and establishing the Washington Community College Humanities Association.

The AACJC has sponsored numerous activities on behalf of the liberal arts, including a major redefinition of the associate degree and publications supporting the humanities in their member colleges. Their 1986 Public Policy Agenda includes an item pledging the association to help member colleges strengthen the humanities, arts, and sciences by encouraging linkages with other community agencies that are committed to culture, supporting the study of these curricular areas, and encouraging communication between the faculty in the humanities, arts, and sciences and those in technical education (American Association of Community and Junior Colleges, 1986).

Continuing support for the liberal arts is available also through such national groups as the Community College Humanities Association and the Community College Social Science Association. These groups draw most of their support from the faculty and other concerned individuals within the institutions. Other support groups have been formed and maintained as part of institutional associations. The League for Innovation in the Community College has sponsored several retreats, leadership programs, colloquia, and similar projects as a service to its member institutions; some of these training and development endeavors involve themes emanating from the liberal arts. The League for the Humanities in Community Colleges affords an example of an institutional membership association with a focus as distinct as its title.

The outcomes of these types of endeavors can be traced. In general, the projects spawned by the various foundations, agencies, and associations publicize the liberal arts as a curriculum area. Through the continual informing of prospective students and community groups of the vitality of the collegiate curriculum, a flow of students and tangible support is maintained. The publicity helps to mitigate the possibility of the liberal arts being shrunk to a point at which they are no longer viable within the institutions.

The endeavors also have an effect on faculty morale. Instructors who might feel that their efforts are undervalued can be encouraged when they perceive that others are interested in the subject areas they teach. The projects award recognition for what the faculty are doing, providing them with the intangible rewards of public acclaim and the tangible rewards of a sufficient cohort of students to fill their classes. Externally directed activities also develop communication links for the faculty. The invisible college that has tied university professors in common disciplines across colleges has never been well developed in community colleges. However, the associations that link community college liberal arts instructors can serve that function, helping to break down the isolation and parochialism that are otherwise endemic to the community college. These intercampus links often spawn conferences and other opportunities for faculty to associate with their counterparts in other institutions, opportunities that typically would not exist were it not for externally sponsored endeavors.

The agency and association activities also yield the intangible benefits of a sense of professionalism among faculty who begin communicating through the journals, forums, and conferences. They share ideas on teaching, commiserate with each other on the decline in student literacy and administrative support in their specific curricular areas, congratulate each other on new techniques that have stimulated enrollments. They gain a sense of camaraderie and the realization that other people also are concerned with that to which they have dedicated their professional lives.

Various tangible benefits also appear when agencies and associations direct their attention to the liberal arts. As a direct outcome of several projects sponsored by the National Endowment for the Humanities, a number of community colleges have formed lay advisory boards or committees that meet regularly and act to support the humanities and the liberal arts. Composed of citizens from the surrounding communities, these committees confer with the staff within the colleges to discuss curricular modifications, requirements for graduation, and various co-curricular activities that may involve other community agencies. They assist in organizing joint projects between the college and the local museums, galleries, theaters, libraries, and similar extramural liberal arts–related organizations. This not only enhances the regular program by providing publicity and support but also extends the liberal arts into community service areas. The San Diego Community College District's annual Humanities Week is an outgrowth of the work of such a committee interacting with the faculty.

Lead, Follow, or Get Out of the Way

Leadership in strengthening the collegiate connection can be assumed by staff members in any position. Ideally, the top administrators would lead in developing plans for the numbers of students to be recruited and the manner of testing and placing them, the enforcing of curricular standards, the numerous activities that enhance transfer rates, and the research efforts essential for gathering data on the college's effects. However, many chief executive officers and vice-presidents in charge of instruction are more supportive of other college functions or fail to consistently support any of them. In such cases, other proponents of the collegiate connection may come forth.

Different forms of leadership have various effects. Some colleges have taken steps to integrate their liberal arts curricula and their activities that promote student transfer; others have well-developed occupational programs with strong links to local industries; and still others fall short in both areas. Most colleges with firm commitments to defined transfer or occupational goals have presidents who maintain consonant initiatives on behalf of their favored programs. But in others, the presidents have so concerned themselves with the budgets and business of college operations that they have effectually abandoned the field to staff members with more directed views of desirable curricular outcomes. The focused colleges seem to have presidents who either are educational leaders or have withdrawn and allowed others, often strong faculty members, to become the leaders. The colleges with no identifiable commitment to anything other than the ceremonially articulated "comprehensive programs that meet everyone's needs" are usually managed by administrators who, perhaps inadvertently, dabble in educational plans only to the extent of thwarting the staff members who might otherwise pull together the many necessary parts of a coherent program.

Strengthening the collegiate connection can be undertaken by presidents who sincerely desire to do so. As the president of a California college that is fully involved with integrated general education put it, "I can't believe how far you can move people if you have an educational plan. Direction is far more effective than drift" (Carhart, 1982). The collegiate connection may also be furthered by presidents who stand aside from educational planning, provided that they are sufficiently sensible to avoid subverting the plans of others.

The Future of the Collegiate Connection

The community colleges' resiliency has been a source of their strength. As the demands grew for curricula designed to lead to job entry, the colleges expanded their occupational programs. As the cohort of marginally literate students grew, they increased their remedial efforts. As further social and demographic changes appear, they will continue to adjust.

The collegiate connection has waxed and waned intermittently over the decades. Prior to the 1970s, the community colleges maintained policies that had the intent of channeling students in the direction of completing programs: entrance tests, course placement, required class attendance, mandatory orientation courses, midterm grades, penalty drop after the eighth week, academic probation and suspension for students who were not making satisfactory progress, failing grades, and mandatory exit interviews for dropouts. In the 1970s, these were replaced by policies of allowing students to enter any course and to with-draw without penalty up to the last week of the class, with no penalty for readmission. The *F* grade and the "incomplete" were rarely seen. Grades went up dramatically on average, not because students were doing better but because anyone who was not earning a *C* or better tended merely to drop the course rather than to get a low grade; hence, the lower portion of the grade curve was effectually dropped off. By the end of the 1970s, the students had responded to the colleges' allowing them to drop into any course without bothering about prerequisites by drop-ping out of any course without consideration of the consequences. The students' sporadic attendance was reflected in reduced transfer rates and in a curriculum composed primarily of in-troductory courses.

Both the transfer function and the liberal arts curriculum will be strengthened in coming years, because the forces that debilitated them will be mitigated. One force has been the decline in literacy. Since the liberal arts historically have been based on the apprehension of texts, when students cannot read or can-not conceptualize through print, it is difficult to teach the liberal arts. A second detriment has been the deliberate intention on the part of many college leaders and state and federal agencies to have the institution seen as a contributor to the economy of its community rather than to the intelligence of its citizenry. This placing the college in a framework of economic analysis constantly shrinks the proportion of effort that it devotes to the higher learning.

Also antagonistic to the collegiate connection, but in a more subtle way, has been the notion of individualized studies. Under the guise of allowing all people to develop to their highest potential, it suggests that every student can be excellent in the area of human performance selected. Its proponents suggest that colleges be judged on the extent to which each student has shown some gain in any aspect of development. However, if the stu-dents are free to design their own programs, the college has sur-rendered its authority over the most basic element in educa-tion: the scope and direction of student learning. Why then should the students accept any of its demands? Taken to the ultimate, the quest for individualization denies not only curriculum formation but also the very ground on which the liberal arts stand. If every student can be excellent in a unique way, determined only by the student's predilections, the door is open to augmenting the student's wickedness, dishonesty, greed, slothfulness, lethargy, mendacity—precisely the areas that education throughout history has sought to mitigate. If goals of enhancing the student's goodness, kindness, honesty, dedication to task, perseverance, truthfulness, and so on are set, the foundation of a liberal arts curriculum has been built. But what then of the individual's special desires?

Individual differences exist. They cannot be willed away. But they are not an argument for differential outcomes of college. They speak only for different instructional methods and various patterns of student support services. Those who favor a plethora of outcomes measures, one for each student, are only in effect granting absolution to the educators who are unable to agree on desired institutional outcomes beyond the most global, unwilling to assess students on the basis of definite objectives, fearful of being held accountable for anything that is quantifiable.

More recently, a striving toward effecting sequence and program completion, along with a belief in the importance of acculturation, has come again to the fore, fostered by a renewed American concern with social justice. The colleges' spokespersons have pointed to their enrolling high proportions of ethnic minorities and students from the lower-income strata and gained support for college efforts to teach literacy and stimulate progress toward the baccalaureate. The collegiate connection's contributions to social cohesion and entry to the professions have become prominent. Acculturating the young and the immigrant is expensive, but it is not a luxury. It is as much one of society's necessities as a well-functioning public transit system or a free press.

Several other shifts in emphasis that relate to the collegiate connection seem imminent:

• As financial aids are reduced, more qualified students who intend to obtain bachelor's degrees from private colleges will matriculate at community colleges in order to save money. This will increase both the number of literate students in the classes and the transfer rates.

- The reforms currently under way to strengthen basic education in the lower schools will allow the colleges to reduce the proportion of effort they currently expend in remedial studies for traditional college-age students.
- The sizable recent flow of immigrants from non-English-speaking nations will make English as a second language and other studies to enhance acculturation more prominent.
- The liberal arts curriculum will be further modified by an emphasis on language, reasoning, and ethics for students in career programs and by their being integrated into programs presented as career options for students who are not preparing for jobs requiring specific skills.
- More advanced placement of high school students will occur, and more colleges will build programs that enroll students at grade 11 and take them through general or career education terminating at grade 14.
- A greater variety in the liberal arts will be provided for the personal interest of older students who may have missed them when they were in college earlier or who want to continue studying them in a disciplined environment, but legislative scrutiny of college expenditures will force a more distinct separation of credit and noncredit studies.
- Articulation with universities will operate more smoothly as greater proportions of their students transfer in from the community colleges. The process will be accelerated by state-level mandates for coordinated higher education systems.

The recent efforts to restore a linear form to the curriculum and to sustain student flow have borne fruit. The liberal arts are stronger than they have been at any time since the 1960s. The 1970s pattern of intermittent student attendance with its resultant inchoate curriculum is being reversed as the collegiate connection comes once again to the fore. But the result will not be a return to the junior college of the 1950s. More likely, the collegiate connection will be effected as an integrated curricular form centering on the general education aspects of the liberal arts, and student flow, so long neglected, will become a measure of institutional pride. But occupation-related studies will not be diminished; in fact, they too will be strengthened as occupational upgrading and relicensure become more prevalent. The two basic functions will coexist, each enhancing the other, each being recognized for its contribution to the colleges' constituency.

Appendix

Details of the Arts and Sciences Curriculum

This appendix augments the information on curriculum presented in Chapter Two. Those disciplines that fall under the rubric of the liberal arts are arranged alphabetically according to five categories: the sciences, the humanities, the fine arts, mathematics, and reading and writing. Although mathematics and reading and writing may be categorized as part of other disciplines of the liberal arts program, they are treated separately because many of these courses are remedial and basic to other courses. Thus, in many ways, they represent a different type of content.

The Sciences

Table A-1 presents the distribution of courses in the sciences and social sciences in the community colleges.

Agriculture and Natural Resources. Relatively few colleges include courses in general agriculture, natural resources, forestry, wildlife, and food service. Differences in offerings tend to be related to region, control, and size. Region presents the most striking breakdown, with more of the northeastern colleges and

Table A-1. Science and Social Science
Courses Offered in the Community College.

	Percentage of Colleges Listing Course in Schedule		Percentage of Total Sections in the Discipline	
	1978	1986	1978	1986
Agriculture and Natural Resources	61%	52%		
Agriculture—general	27	19	8%	8%
Animal science	31	27	21	29
Plant science	39	36	35	34
Soil science	40	21	14	10
Natural resources—general	16	0	6	1
Forestry	13	6	8	9
Wildlife and wildlands	14	6	6	3
Food science	10	5	3	6
Biology	100	98		
Introductory	90	87	36	28
Advanced	25	16	1	2
Botany	62	45	6	4
Zoology	64	44	7	4
Human biology	91	85	31	35
Microbiology	79	71	9	12
Entomology	8	3	< 1	0
Ecology and environment	39	28	5	4
Related topics	47	65	6	11
Chemistry	97	96		
Chemistry for non-science and non-technical students	53	22	17	5
Chemistry for allied health/biology occupations	49	27	14	7
Chemistry for engineering, technical, and related occupations	10	NA	2	NA

Table A-1. Science and Social Science
Courses Offered in the Community College, Cont'd.

	Percentage of Colleges Listing Course in Schedule		Percentage of Total Sections in the Discipline	
	1978	1986	1978	1986
Preparatory chemistry	26	36	10	17
General chemistry for science and engineering	83	83	38	45
Analytical chemistry and instrumental methods	25	21	3	4
Organic chemistry and biochemistry	64	64	11	21
Clinical chemistry	16	5	2	1
Earth and space sciences	79	72		
Geography	65	44	39	22
Geology	43	46	27	30
Interdisciplinary earth and space science	22	21	9	17
Astronomy	37	36	14	24
Meterology and climatology	15	7	4	4
Oceanography and limnology	11	7	6	4
Economics	99	97		
Introductory/general	33	33	11	16
Principles	93	82	60	77
Business-related	34	18	12	4
Technology-related	22	7	8	1
American	16	3	5	1
Special topics	9	18	5	3
Engineering	81	72		
General engineering	27	24	2	4
ngineering graphics and design	77	46	18	15
Civil engineering	50	23	6	8

Table A-1. Science and Social Science
Courses Offered in the Community College, Cont'd.

	Percentage of Colleges Listing Course in Schedule		Percentage of Total Sections in the Discipline	
	1978	1986	1978	1986
Electrical/electronic technology	73	46	41	37
Materials	46	35	6	6
Mechanical engineering	71	48	17	13
Industrial engineering	41	13	7	3
Aeronautical, automotive, and combustion	5	15	<1	12
Other fields	10	13	1	3
Environmental sciences	51	21		
Courses for nonscience majors	33	11	52	29
Environmental technology	13	3	18	13
Air pollution	8	2	5	8
Water pollution	17	3	20	17
Noise pollution	2	0	1	0
Solid waste	4	0	2	0
Radiation	1	1	1	6
Agriculture and soil	2	4	1	10
Other	1	4	<1	17
Mathematics	99	100		
Introductory and intermediate	97	97	44	34
Advanced	86	87	9	9
Applied—technology-related	67	64	13	5
Mathematics for majors	95	77	23	7
Statistics and probability	75	78	5	4
Computer science and technology	71	88	7	28
Remedial	NA	54	NA	14

Table A-1. Science and Social Science
Courses Offered in the Community College, Cont'd.

	Percentage of Colleges Listing Course in Schedule		Percentage of Total Sections in the Discipline	
	1978	1986	1978	1986
Physical anthropology and interdisciplinary social sciences	67	53		
Physical anthropology	22	16	NA	8
Social science (survey)	17	24	51	42
Archaeology	15	13	NA	5
Environmental	7	7	10	5
Aging	16	4	13	2
Special groups	6	11	5	17
Social research	3	7	2	5
Thanatology	9	3	6	1
Urban planning	5	4	3	2
Other	8	18	9	15
Physics	89	92		
Physics for nonscience and nontechnical students	31	29	12	11
Physics for allied health/biology occupations	19	18	4	6
Physics for engineering technology–related occupations	42	53	31	34
Preparatory physics	7	23	3	9
General physics (non-calculus)	75	73	29	37
Engineering and general physics (calculus based)	53	18	21	5
Psychology	99	100		
Elementary/general	97	98	60	49
Developmental	87	86	21	21
Abnormal	36	31	5	4
Social-industrial	39	54	5	9

Table A-1. Science and Social Science
Courses Offered in the Community College, Cont'd.

	Percentage of Colleges Listing Course in Schedule		Percentage of Total Sections in the Discipline	
	1978	*1986*	*1978*	*1986*
Personality/adjustment	35	49	5	8
Experimental	8	9	< 1	1
Educational	28	23	2	2
Contemporary issues	10	35	1	6
Physiological	3	12	1	1
Sociology	100	95		
Elementary	7	48	2	25
General/principles	94	44	57	31
Social problems—general	70	51	13	10
Marriage and family	69	59	14	14
Social institutions—general	10	7	3	2
Social problems—specific	41	34	8	11
Social institutions—specific	4	7	1	2
Sociology of group	11	18	2	3
Other	9	5	1	2

only a few middle-states colleges offering courses in agriculture and/or natural resources. The fact that western colleges do offer courses in all these categories might be a function of their larger size. Private colleges hardly ever offer such courses.

Most courses included in this category are general education courses to orient the student to the scope of the agriculture industry, introductory core program courses for majors, and courses to introduce students to the history of environmental conservation or forest technology. The classes are targeted for both transfer and nontransfer students, as well as for adults who desire to further their education. The lecture-lab format is dominant, and few courses demand prerequisites. Understanding the interrelationships of science and technology with society, understanding the principles, concepts, and terminology of the disciplines, and developing the ability to think critically are qualities that faculty in this area desire for their students.

Anthropology/Interdisciplinary Social Sciences. Anthropology is split between physical and cultural content. Courses in physical anthropology are usually listed as sciences. Neither accounts for a sizable component of community college enrollments. Except for agriculture and physics, physical anthropology is the smallest area in the sciences; it is offered in slightly more than half the colleges. Physical anthropology includes introduction to the study of anthropology, along with some archeology or prehistory classes. Because demand for these classes is so small, instructors in some colleges have integrated elements of this area into classes in introductory or interdisciplinary social science. Such classes are sometimes used to fulfill the social science general education requirement.

In the humanities, cultural anthropology is the smallest discipline except for religious and ethnic studies, offered in fewer than half the colleges. The cultural anthropology courses are almost exclusively composed of introductory or survey courses for students who intend to transfer and who are taking the classes as social science electives.

Biology. Biology accounts for 11 percent of all enrollment in the sciences, ranking behind only mathematics and psychology. Within the field, introductory biology registers 28 percent of the enrollment and human biology 35 percent. Courses directed toward students who plan to major in the sciences account for 44 percent of the offerings. Even though few students transfer as science majors, that is the university transfer function that instructors and curriculum planners perceive as essential. Courses for nonmajors and occupational students enroll another 38 percent of the students.

Class size in biology is higher than the norm for the sciences, and women outnumber men by a two-to-one ratio. The number of biology sections directed toward allied health students undoubtedly accounts for this pattern. A combination of lecture and laboratory dominates the instruction: around three-fourths of the classes include both forms. In biology, the emphasis is less on mastery of a skill, as in chemistry and mathematics, than on acquaintance with concepts of the discipline and on recall of specific information. There is less dissection in the classes, more observation and memorization of terms.

Chemistry. Practically all the colleges offer chemistry, at least at the introductory level. One-third of all these chemistry classes are general chemistry, one-third other introductory types, and one-third advanced courses. Chemistry is one of the few disciplines in all the liberal arts to show a sequential pattern of introductory and advanced courses; enrollments in introductory classes outnumber those in advanced courses by only two to one, a ratio indicating the sequential pattern of chemistry instruction. Courses for nonscience majors account for 12 percent of all offerings.

A significant proportion of chemistry is presented for students in allied health, agricultural, and similar occupational programs. These courses tend to be less intense, more specialized, and to have fewer prerequisites. The allied health chemistry courses have grown most rapidly in recent years, and they are often taught in conjunction with allied health faculty members. Specialized chemistry classes are also offered for engineering technology students and for students in chemical technology programs.

Chemistry is also distinguished among the sciences for its having remedial classes taken in advance of or concurrently with the general chemistry courses; more than one-third of all the colleges offer these types of courses. Because chemistry classes serve both the female-dominated allied health programs and the male-dominated engineering programs, overall they tend to enroll approximately even numbers of men and women. Around 80 percent of the classes are taught in a combination of lecture and laboratory.

Earth and Space Sciences. Both the college size and its type of control (public or private) have direct relationships with the specific earth and space sciences courses. Larger public colleges tend to offer courses in all areas subsumed under this discipline. According to their instructors, usually all of these courses are parallel to lower-division college-level courses at transfer institutions. Yet most of the courses are designed for nonscience majors, for general education for nontransfers, and for personal upgrading of adults as occupational students. About 30 percent of these courses mandate prerequisites. Lecture courses predominate.

Instructors in this area emphasize not mastery of a skill, as, for example, do chemistry and mathematics instructors, but rather acquaintance with disciplinary concepts, recall of specific information, and an understanding of the significance of certain works. Gaining qualities useful to further education and understanding the interrelationships between science and society are important course goals.

Economics. Courses in economics tend to be directed toward students preparing to transfer. Nearly all the economics courses offered are at the introductory level. Most of the courses emphasize principles of economics. Half the colleges that offer both macro- and microeconomics courses require the former as prerequisite to entering the latter. But the emphasis on economics for students preparing to transfer indicates that basic economic principles are more often taught in courses in business. Economics courses tend not to be required for the associate degree or for vocational certificates. The courses are taken primarily by students majoring in business administration.

Engineering. Courses in various fields of engineering account for 9 percent of the science enrollment. Around three-fourths of the colleges list one or more engineering courses in their class schedules. However, few of the classes are general or introductory to the field; most are distinctly service courses to the trades: electrical or electronic technology, engineering graphics and design, mechanical engineering, industrial engineering, and similar specialized offerings.

Around two-thirds of the engineering classes have prerequisites, most often some course in mathematics or a prior course in engineering. However, only one in five courses in aeronautical, automotive, and combustion engineering has a prerequisite, suggesting that those courses are directed toward the practical application of engineering principles to specific trades. More than 80 percent of the instructors describe their courses as intended primarily for occupational students in science technology programs.

Environmental Sciences. This is the smallest category of courses in the sciences offered by two-year colleges. The courses in this area typically fall under the rubric of interdisciplinary or integrated sciences. They generally occur in general education programs or in environmental technology programs, organized primarily in the 1960s in response to national energy problems.

Prerequisites (for example, mathematics) are listed for about 10 percent of these courses. Laboratories are the predominant mode, and the courses are offered chiefly in the West, the Midwest, and the middle states. Most courses are offered in the large, public institutions. Course objectives generally emphasize the relationship of science to society and the interrelationships of science and technology.

Interdisciplinary Sciences. Some of the colleges offer interdisciplinary natural sciences or environmental studies to satisfy student interest in those areas. These courses typically are not designed for students who would major in the sciences; they tend more to be science for nonmajors and courses that meet general education science requirements. Most of the classes in this area combine studies from all of the sciences and focus on the problems of the natural environment. There is some history, philosophy, and sociology of science content as well. Over half of the colleges offer classes in interdisciplinary studies of the environment. But these classes account for a minuscule proportion of the enrollment. Environmental science courses for technicians declined precipitously in the 1980s, drying up along with the special funding that created them.

Courses in interdisciplinary sciences tend to be taught by the more experienced instructors, those who feel secure enough to build innovative courses and sufficiently confident in their colleagues' ability to teach as they do. Class sizes are small. Field trips are sometimes used as instructional devices. Prerequisites are rarely seen. Instructors want their students to be able to relate science to the world around them and to gain ability to think critically. The integrated social science and interdisciplinary science classes are the closest to reaching the promise of general education in the community college.

Physics. Physics, another major discipline in the sciences, is notably underrepresented in community colleges. Although around 90 percent of the colleges offer some classes in physics, enrollments are relatively small, averaging only around thirty students per college nationwide. This is a lower figure than that for any other of the twenty-one disciplines in the liberal arts except for religious studies or ethnic studies. The main reason for this paucity of enrollment is that, of all the disciplines, physics is the one most demanding of mathematical skills.

More than one-third of all physics courses offered are noncalculus general physics, another 40 percent are courses for the engineering occupations, and the remainder are service courses to nonscience and allied health areas. Some of the technical physics courses are taught by technology teachers, not by instructors with their own degrees in physics. There are few preparatory physics classes, but even those frequently specify prerequisites in mathematics.

Psychology. Psychology, accounting for 12 percent of science enrollments, has increased notably in recent years. It is taught more as a social science than as a life science; experimental and physiological psychology, the only categories with a distinct scientific orientation, are offered only infrequently. Elementary and general psychology classes have few prerequisites. Around half the classes in other areas, such as developmental and social or industrial psychology, include prerequisites.

Patterns in psychology course offerings and emphases illustrate curricular purposes. Educational psychology has declined as the number of students using the community colleges as an entry to teaching careers has declined. Offerings in abnormal psychology have increased along with the growth of programs for mental health workers. The decline in physiological and experimental psychology reflects the paucity of psychology-major transfer-oriented students. There has been an increase in courses in personality adjustment and contemporary issues, but introductory courses in elementary and general psychology account for half the enrollments.

Except for the few classes in experimental psychology, practically none of the psychology courses include laboratory sections. Lectures are the primary mode of communicating information. Textbooks and quick-score examinations dominate, although classroom discussions account for nearly 20 percent of class time. Students are frequently asked to form study groups, take field trips, and design their own experiential internships. Psychology's tendency toward teaching students to become self-reliant shows up also in the importance that instructors place on students' relating knowledge acquired in class to real-world systems and problems and in their ability to understand themselves. In fact, the goal of student self-understanding outranks that of assisting students to gain qualities useful in further education by a two-to-one margin.

Sociology. Nearly all community colleges offer courses in sociology. Most of the courses are in elementary or general principles of sociology, with others specialized into general social problems, marriage and family, and specific social problems. The social problems classes tend to have prerequisites, usually the general course in sociology. The sociology curriculum typically includes traditional classes transferable to senior colleges.

Instruction in sociology differs from instruction in the other sciences and social sciences in that class discussion accounts for nearly 25 percent of class time. Furthermore, sociology instructors assign more pages of textbook reading than do instructors in any other discipline in the sciences or social sciences. Even though the classes are directed toward transfer students, there is a definite orientation toward societal problems. More than half the instructors feel that their students should gain an understanding of the interrelationships of science and society and relate the concepts to their own values, and nearly 80 percent feel that their students should gain the ability to relate knowledge acquired in class to real-world systems and problems.

The Humanities

Table A-2 shows the distribution of class sections within each subject area in the humanities.

Table A-2. Percentage of Class Sections Offered Within Each Humanities Subject Area During Spring Term.

	1983	1986
Art history/appreciation		
Introductory/history/appreciation	89%	88%
Specialized	11	12
Cultural anthropology		
Introductory/survey	82	78
American Indian	10	6
Other specialized	8	16
Foreign languages		
French	18	15
German	10	7
Italian	2	3
Russian	<1	1
Spanish	35	29
Career-related Spanish	<1	<1
English as a second language	30	43
Classics	<1	<1
Other	3	2
History		
State and local	5	3
Western/world	27	27
United States	53	54
Other world regions	5	4
Special groups	7	5
Social history	3	8

Table A-2. Percentage of Class Sections Offered Within
Each Humanities Subject Area During Spring Term, Cont'd.

Interdisciplinary		
Introductory/survey	66	68
Theater	13	15
Film	20	9
Specialized	NA	8
Literature		
Introductory/survey	63	60
Genre	14	23
Authors	6	6
Group	7	6
Bible	3	2
Popular	3	3
Classics	2	1
Music history/appreciation		
Introductory/survey	92	83
Jazz	5	5
Specialized	3	12
Philosophy		
Introductory/history	46	39
Ethics	12	15
Logic	25	22
Religions	9	17
Specialized	8	6
Political Science		
American government	63	53
Local/city/state	9	14
Comparative	4	4
Tools and methods	6	1
Specialized (topical)	8	8
Jurisprudence	9	19

Art History/Appreciation. Often used as an elective to satisfy graduation requirements in the humanities, art history is offered in around three-quarters of the colleges. Class sizes are slightly larger than the average. Most of the art history classes are introductions to the entire scope of art, but there are a few specialized classes in modern art and the art of Mexico, Africa, and other regions. Visual material is widely used in instruction; most of the classes include the presentation of art works through slides and videotapes. The intent is to have the students gain an appreciation for art as a means of human expression.

Art history is sometimes combined with aspects of history, literature, and philosophy to make interdisciplinary courses in the humanities. Nearly 70 percent of the colleges present integrated humanities classes, usually allowing students to use them to satisfy the humanities general education requirement. Class sizes typically are the largest of all those in the humanities areas.

Cultural Anthropology. This area is discussed in the section dealing with the sciences.

Foreign Languages. Instruction in the foreign languages has shown some notable shifts. Around 80 percent of the colleges offer some foreign language instruction, with Spanish and French most frequently seen. Although English as a second language is offered in fewer than 40 percent of the colleges, it is well out in front in enrollments and has shown the most marked increase in recent years. Between 1983 and 1986, it overtook Spanish for first place in language study, accounting for 43 percent of the language classes presented. Overall, foreign language enrollments have increased, but all of that increase is due to the flourishing of English as a second language, evidencing the community college role in educating immigrants.

History. History, typically required for graduation, is found in nearly all the colleges. United States history accounts for more than half the enrollments and Western or world civilization for more than one-fourth. Courses in state and local history and the history of the other world regions or special groups comprise the rest of the offerings, but fewer than one-third of the colleges offer any courses in those areas.

Integrated Humanities/Liberal Arts. Patterns of course offerings in integrated humanities are quite varied. Following is a list of some of the titles offered and the disciplines involved.

Course Title	Disciplines Involved
American Military History	Economics, history, literature, philosophy, political science
Medical Ethics	Philosophy, nursing
Contemporary Humanities	Literature, music, art, philosophy, drama
Contemporary Understandings	Literature, sociology, economics, administration of justice
Business History	History of business
Biological Revolution	Philosophy, psychology, biology
Religion and the Arts	Religion, philosophy, art, music, drama
Greek Achievement	Poetry, drama, art, philosophy
Art Literature and History: Study of the Old Testament	Literature, history
Energy and Society	History, sociology, science
The Indian and American History	History, anthropology
Civilizations of Asia and Africa	History, anthropology
Human Sexuality	Sociology, anthropology
British History	Literature, history
Medieval History	Literature, history
Arts and Civilization	Art, history, composition
Puerto Rican Society and Culture	History, sociology, English composition

Black Biographical Sketches	History, art, English composition
Business in Literature	Business, literature
History of Mathematics	History, mathematics
The Human Condition Through Literature	Nursing, English literature, history, anthropology
Ways of Knowing	Literature, art, psychology, science
The Art of Being Human	Literature, philosophy, fine arts
The Life Cycle Through Literature	Literature, psychology
Personality in Literature	Literature, psychology
Environment Amid Changing Values	Literature, history, philosophy, natural sciences
Art, Music, and Ideas	Art, music, literature, history
Awakening of Individuality	Literature, philosophy, music, psychology
Understanding Cultures	Religion, economics, business, sociology
Religious Themes in Literature	Literature, religion, philosophy

Two disciplines were involved in around one-third of the classes, three disciplines in one-fourth, four disciplines in more than one-fourth, and five or six disciplines in around one in seven of the courses. Nearly 60 percent of the interdisciplinary classes were team taught, but one of the problems in preparing such classes was in assigning teaching-load credit to one or another department. In nearly half the cases, the department organizing the course received credit, and in the other half both or all the departments involved received course credit. Full hourly credit was awarded to each faculty member involved in teaching an interdisciplinary course at half the colleges that offered them.

Literature. Courses in literature account for a sizable proportion of the enrollments in the humanities, exceeded only by history, political science, and foreign languages, but enrollments have declined in recent years. The general survey or introduction to literature course, offered in three-fourths of the colleges, accounts for most of the enrollments. However, certain specialized classes have attracted students who are interested in particular aspects of literature. Genre classes dealing with the novel or poetry have picked up students, especially adults attending for their personal interest. Similarly, classes dedicated to the works of a particular author or to a group such as women or minorities have a special appeal. Literature's overall decline may be attributed at least in part to the interdisciplinary humanities classes that have cannibalized their enrollments.

Music Appreciation. Music appreciation is another curricular area offered typically as an option to fulfill a humanities graduation requirement. However, only around 1 in 100 students takes a class in music appreciation, typically an introductory or survey class covering many aspects of music. Music performance accounts for a much higher proportion of enrollment, including curricular sequences leading to mastery of technical skills in popular instruments and voice. The percentage of colleges offering courses in music appreciation has declined as the percentage offering interdisciplinary humanities has increased.

Philosophy. Philosophy has not been a popular area of study. The smaller colleges have difficulty in finding enough students to enroll in any philosophy class; fewer than 40 percent of the colleges with under 1,500 students offer any philosophy at all, but nearly all the larger colleges do. Overall, the total is around 75 percent.

The philosophy instructors have been somewhat more successful than those in other disciplines in the humanities in directing their offerings toward students interested in special topics. Courses in ethics and in logic account for over one-third of the enrollments, and religious studies attract a number of students. Philosophy is primarily considered as a humanities elective, but some of the courses are presented as service to occupational areas. Medical ethics for students in the health fields are popular and in some cases required by the occupational program directors. Business ethics is presented in several colleges, and logic is sometimes offered as a service course to students in computer science.

Political Science. Political science enrollments have held steady. Nearly all the colleges offer it, with around half the enrollment accounted for by American government, a course frequently required for graduation. State and local government and foundations of political science are also popular, the former sometimes being listed as a graduation requirement, the latter as an introduction for those who would major in the area. The political science offerings are also popular among the managers of courses for police or correctional officers; administration of justice programs frequently include a course in the history and philosophy of jurisprudence, an area that has shown marked increase recently.

Religious Studies. Courses in religious studies are most often found in the private institutions that are affiliated with religious denominations. In the public institutions, religious studies tend to be blended with courses in philosophy, but in most of the parochial schools, they are required courses, basic to the students' progress in the institution; there, requirements in religious studies might account for as much as twelve hours of a sixty-hour program. Only around one in four of the public institutions offers even one course in religious studies, usually something in the philosophy of religion, a survey of religions, or the Bible as literature.

The Fine Arts

Studio art is well developed in the community colleges. Most have classes in drawing and painting, and many have elaborate facilities for making pottery. Most of the colleges also sponsor dramatic productions through their departments of theater arts and teach dance through the performing arts divisions, sometimes in liaison with the physical education departments. The colleges teach all aspects of performing music: sight singing, musical ensembles, choral singing, and solo instrument playing.

The performing arts have been part of the community colleges since their early years, when they entered the curriculum because they had been offered in secondary schools and universities. They are justified for their contribution to student knowledge, occasionally for their usefulness in helping students gain professional careers in the performing arts. Some colleges emphasize the career aspect of the arts; Mt. Hood Community College (Oregon) has an extensive performing arts program, and Kirkwood Community College (Iowa) has an independent study program in the fine arts for students wanting to market their artistic talents.

The performing arts are prominent in urban institutions as well. Buckner (1979) surveyed the arts in thirty urban-based community colleges and found art, music, and theater the top offerings. Two-thirds of the institutions offered an associate in arts degree with a major in fine arts. Half the institutions were cooperating with community agencies in arts instruction, and one-fourth had programs for students with limited background in the arts.

Many colleges offer instruction in the performing arts for particular groups of students. Children's theater productions are often seen, and some colleges have organized extensive programs for teaching children art, music, and dance. The colleges also have formed links with community agencies such as state arts councils in presenting the arts as a cultural contribution to the public. These may take forms of campus-based productions or of traveling shows taken to outlying areas.

Mathematics

The literature dealing with mathematics in the community colleges is better developed than the literature regarding most other academic fields taught in those institutions, so that shifts in enrollment patterns, student preparation, and curriculum in that area can be easily traced. Among the associations directing papers toward people teaching and planning mathematics in the community colleges is the Committee on the Undergraduate Program in Mathematics, a standing committee of the Mathematics Association of America. Major sources of information also include such journals as the *Mathematics Association of Two-Year Colleges Journal* and the *Two-Year College Mathematics Journal*.

Many of the reports coming from the Committee on the Undergraduate Program in Mathematics in the 1960s and 1970s related to what the group perceived as deficiencies in the curriculum in two-year colleges. They reported on the need for additional courses in calculus, linear algebra, and other advanced levels of mathematics and on the preparation of instructors in mathematics. However, more recently, such concern for the upper reaches of mathematics in two-year colleges has given way to consideration of mathematics for general education or the severely underprepared student.

Studies of remedial mathematics have included nationwide surveys on teaching techniques, faculty qualifications, time spent on various aspects of mathematics, and related issues of general concern. Chang (1983) found elementary algebra offered in 82 percent of the remedial courses, arithmetic in 68 percent, and intermediate algebra in 53 percent. Most of the colleges surveyed did not offer credit for remedial courses. Nearly all the colleges provided tutorial services for the students, and, in just under half the cases, the remedial students finished their developmental programs within one semester; just over half of them went on to complete at least one college-level mathematics course.

The literature on remedial education in mathematics revolves around questions of definition, placement of students, granting of credit, course content, and effective instructional practices. Nearly all two-year colleges offer courses in developmental mathematics. In the 1970s, fewer than half the colleges required a placement examination; in those that did, few mandated that students take a remedial course. That was the era when the students were to be given the right to fail, a procedure and value system that has changed notably in the past few years. Now, a rapidly increasing number of two-year colleges are returning to the 1950s pattern of mandated placement tests and course placements in English and mathematics.

Many reports from individual colleges are available. Developmental mathematics at Lower Columbia College (Washington) was described in a report indicating the various ways that students might complete the mathematical requirements through courses offered in laboratory and classroom. As in many other colleges, the high attrition rates in developmental mathematics were combated by extensive placement testing, math anxiety workshops, and several levels of review courses (Crepin, 1981). Math avoidance was revealed in a study of students' course-taking patterns in a large urban community college district in which a high percentage of the students who had noted an interest in science-related careers had completed no mathematics courses even after having completed more than thirty units of college work (Friedlander, 1981b).

Information about the operation of laboratories and centers that teach basic mathematics is widely available. Mitchell (1980) reported on the operations of the Mathematics Center at Pima College, indicating that its staff of twenty to twenty-five people served 400 to 500 students. It had a faculty member coordinator responsible for employing and scheduling instructors, assistants, and tutors; training the staff; establishing record-keeping systems; developing curriculum; managing the preparation of materials; determining grades; and "serving as the instructor on duty several hours each week" (p. 43). The center had a differentiated staff, with other fully certified instructors, clerical assistants, and peer tutors. Problems at the center included computing faculty work load and training peer tutors. The Mathematics Learning Center at Cerritos College was examined from the standpoint of its financial base. The center was cost efficient, because its course sections were large and because it employed paraprofessional personnel to maintain student records. The author recommended keeping the staff lean and ensuring that students understand the center's policies (Baley, 1981).

The independent study Math Resource Center program at Lane Community College offers seven courses on an "open-entry/open-exit" basis: Math 1, 2, and 3; Elementary, Intermediate, and College Algebra; and Dosage Computation. Students may enroll at any time, learn at their own rate, and leave class when they have developed their skills to the desired level. Differentiated staffing (aides, assistants, instructors, and director) provides many levels of instruction through self-study texts, single-concept videotapes, tutoring, and small-group instruction. Course procedures include pretesting and the use of students' records, a study guide, and a student reference manual. Additional reports of the mathematics centers and laboratories describe the special services offered for students with various types of deficiencies in mathematics understanding (Habib, 1981; Yawin, 1981; Rotman, 1982). Others focus more intently on the organization and operation of the laboratories themselves (Emerson, 1978; Fast, 1980; Palow, 1979).

Tacoma (Washington) Community College's mathematics learning center offers three programs: an independent-tutorial study system, a student tutorial system, and a basic arithmetic skills laboratory. Thirty independent-tutorial study mathematics courses, ranging from arithmetic to calculus, are available within the structure and control of the mathematics department. Students proceed at their own rate using a commercially available active-involvement text. If they do not complete the course by the end of the quarter, they earn an incomplete grade, which must be made up during the next quarter.

Some work has been done recently on competencies expected of entering freshmen, with particular attention to tests that would place students in mathematics courses in which they have a reasonable chance of succeeding. Many of the questions swirling around student placement have to do with the relative merits of homemade placement tests versus tests that are prepared and distributed by a national agency. Several articles on faculty dissatisfaction with nationally normed tests have been published. Wood (1980) reports the switch made at the University of Houston, Downtown Campus, more than fifteen years ago from the ACT mathematics placement test to an instrument developed at the campus. The college used that fifty-minute test to shunt students scoring below 70 percent to a course reviewing algebra. The effect on retention and achievement was notable.

A minimum level of mathematics literacy for all college-level students was specified in the 1981 annual report of the American Mathematical Association of Two-Year Colleges Developmental Mathematics Curriculum Committee (Dyer, 1981). In several states, the community colleges have been cooperating with the universities and secondary schools in announcing competencies expected. The academic senates of the California community colleges, the California State University, and the University of California addressed a statement to parents, teachers, counselors, and administrators of high school students indicating the competencies in algebra, arithmetic, geometry, and advanced mathematics that students should demonstrate in preparation for college (*Statement on Competencies* . . . , 1982). Miami-Dade Community College prepared a booklet for distribution to junior high school and high school students in its service area indicating expected competencies in mathematics and English usage. Community colleges elsewhere have undertaken similar projects.

A different approach is revealed in the articles carried in *The Two-Year College Mathematics Journal*. For four years beginning in 1980, the journal carried tips on teaching, mathematics concepts for classroom use, mathematics games, and a few articles on mathematics avoidance. There was an occasional article on merging mathematics with other fields, as, for example, ''Integrating Writing into the Mathematics Curriculum'' (Goldberg, 1983), and a few reports of classroom experience; for example, one involving basic mathematics and women in which the investigator found that women in an all-female section of a basic algebra class did better than women in mixed-sex classes (Brunson, 1983). But most of the papers were distinctly addressed to instructors of advanced classes, whereas the ERIC system and the journals especially slanted toward remedial studies in mathematics and English usage carry papers describing the operations of learning laboratories. And other differences appeared in the Center for the Study of Community Colleges' national surveys. Instructors of remedial classes indicated that they spent less time in lecture (36 percent versus 49 percent) and were less likely to administer letter grades (52 percent versus 76 percent). As a group, they tended to be younger, with less teaching experience, and much more likely to use tutors (60 percent versus 48 percent) and paraprofessional aides (27 percent versus 13 percent).

Other curricular differences have arisen because of the growth in the use of computers and hand-held calculators; the five-foot demonstration slide rule has gone the way of the coal stove that once similarly graced college classrooms. But mathematics remains a handmaiden to the sciences and computer-based technologies. It is hardly ever taught as an integrated component of the other disciplines in the liberal arts. Smith (1984) pleaded a case for revitalizing the traditional "great ideas" mathematics course, proposing a curriculum reorganization that would include basic skills courses, courses for career-oriented students, and survey courses covering the application of arithmetic processes, geometry, algebra, statistics, logic, and computer technology to algorithmic processes, generalizations, and problem solving. He contrasted traditional instructional approaches with alternative contracts methods, emphasizing hands-on experience in the laboratory and the community, and discussed the potential of liberal arts mathematics to meet the competency needs of the 1980s by combining the main features of the "great ideas" mathematics course and basic skills training. Such courses appear occasionally as noncredit options, hardly ever in the transfer and occupational programs.

Reading and Writing

Separate courses to teach reading are frequently found, but they are usually offered as part of the adult basic education or less-than-college-level remedial program. One of the nagging questions facing English departments and general curriculum planners concerns the extent of reading instruction that can be offered through the collegiate curriculum. Remedial writing similarly comes in for its share of controversy. The basic question is the matter of funding: Should remedial studies be paid for through the portion of the budget that goes for transfer or that which goes for occupational studies? In some states, Illinois, for example, remedial instruction is funded according to a separate formula. Since most remedial instruction is in English and mathematics, this effectually separates the less-than-college-level activities from the courses that are funded as baccalaureate studies. Still, there is much overlap and continuing concern for the minimal level of literacy that can be tolerated in the collegiate courses.

Most often, remedial English instruction takes place in learning laboratories and is self-paced, with students expected to complete one workbook or area of study satisfactorily before proceeding to the next. Are the laboratories successful? Bell (1983) contends that their most useful practice is to put students together with tutors who can help them realize what writing is—a difficult, engrossing activity that demands successive rewrites and a self-critical eye. The aspect of the laboratory that allows students to work individually on separate writing difficulties has also been cited as a positive feature.

Diagnosing difficulties in composition is a continuing problem. Which students should go into the remedial classes? Which tests should be used? Should placement into the classes be mandatory or optional—that is, should the test be for the purposes of placement, or should it be advisory? A 1983 Illinois study found 82 percent of the responding colleges in that state administering some form of test to place students in composition classes. Around half of the respondents reported that the writing skills of entering students had remained constant over the prior ten years; the other half reported declines in skill. All but one of the colleges offered at least one remedial writing course (Illinois Community College Board, 1984b).

The further issue of how to teach writing to students once they have been placed in classes is the reciprocal of the placement process. Entire journals, such as *Teaching English in the Two-Year College,* are devoted to articles on teaching. Scanning the table of contents in these journals reveals the concerns. How to teach the various specialized composition courses comes in for a fair amount of coverage. The colleges offer business and technical writing, business communications, and similar courses in service to curricula that enroll large numbers of students. How closely should those courses reflect the dictates of the occupation? How closely the tenets of composition as a form? Other articles include tips on helping students to write; managing the writing laboratories; diagnosing students' difficulties with writing, from their own ability to manage the mechanics of the written form to their negative attitudes toward writing and their anxiety as writers; using tutors and readers; and the type of preparation that two-year college English teachers should have. Other journals carrying sizable numbers of articles on teaching English in community colleges include the *ADE Bulletin, Research in the Teaching of English, College English,* and state association publications such as *Inside English* (California).

What works in teaching composition? The question is as broad as the field. Some successes have been reported in tutorial situations, others in group activities where students write and then have their work criticized by their peers. Some courses are broken into segments having to do with the various tasks of writing: planning, writing, rewriting, and editing. Separate sections are sometimes organized for special purposes, such as one for students with particular difficulty in the mechanics of writing, another for students enrolled in certain occupational programs, still others for students who need assistance with content and organization. All these sections are sometimes offered under the same general course title, sometimes as separate courses.

Research on the teaching of English considers certain topics repeatedly and inconclusively. The effect of class size on student achievement and motivation is a perennial favorite as the instructors seek validation for their contention that they have too many students to teach, too many papers to read. The effect of instructors' comments on student compositions is another: Are detailed comments better than sketchy remarks? Are positive comments better than negative? Patterns of student-teacher interaction have also been studied at length: Is peer evaluation of student compositions as useful as instructor evaluation? How much benefit can be derived from individual conferences with students?

Course effect receives its share of examination. How much do students learn in remedial classes and laboratories? The "open-entry, open-exit" Educational Testing and Learning Clinic (ETLC) at Orange Coast College (California) offers an extensive battery of tests and individualized remedial programs to identify and correct learning difficulties. The full mean score of ETLC students on the Wechsler Adult Intelligence Scale was about seven points below the norm, but within normal limits. Reading tests revealed that these students had an average reading level between middle fifth and low sixth grade and commensurate spelling and arithmetic levels. In addition, they had auditory processing and auditory and visual memory problems that were no doubt related to academic deficiencies. After slightly over five hours of remediation per week for approximately five instructional months, statistically significant gains were made in reading (the ETLC groups' word recognition improved 1.2 years, while reading comprehension improved 1.7 years, and word attack skills improved 1.2 years); spelling (the ETLC students made 1.4 years' growth); and arithmetic (students made 0.5 years' growth) (Ortiz and others, 1978).

During the 1960s, numerous English teachers reacted negatively toward the poorly prepared students entering their classes. They felt inadequate to teach them and resented particularly the notion that they should convert instruction into small segments that could be measured independently. Teaching college-level English to students with varying interests and/or poor academic backgrounds is difficult and frustrating.

Curriculum modification has since mitigated the problem; for example, technical communication courses emphasizing short reports, business correspondence, job application materials, and short papers of process have become prevalent (Pickett and Angelo, 1986). And the writing laboratory, a different instructional form, has done more, allowing the regularly scheduled classes to proceed according to the instructors' own determination of effective teaching. This has resulted in a schism between the instructors of scheduled sections of English and the managers of the writing laboratories. The instructors may be pleased to have been released from drill and practice components of their work and relieved that another agency has taken responsibility for teaching the marginally literate students. But they may also feel that the laboratory managers are not true instructors, adhering to the principles of the discipline. For their part, the laboratory managers claim that they are professionals at arranging situations in which demonstrable learning is attained.

References

Aitken, C. E., and Conrad, C. F. "Improving Academic Advising Through Computerization." *College and University*, 1977, *53* (1), 115–123.

American Association of Community and Junior Colleges. *Policy Statement on the Associate Degree.* Washington, D.C.: American Association of Community and Junior Colleges, 1984.

American Association of Community and Junior Colleges. *1986 Public Policy Agenda.* Washington, D.C.: American Association of Community and Junior Colleges, 1986.

Anandam, K. *Promises to Keep . . . Academic Alert and Advisement.* Miami, Fla.: Miami-Dade Community College, 1981. 7 pp. (ED 215 726)

Armes, N. *Common Learning at Dallas.* CSCC Bulletin no. 12. Los Angeles: Center for the Study of Community Colleges, 1984. 7 pp. (ED 246 983)

Astin, A. W., Green, K. C., Korn, W. S., and Maier, M. J. *The American Freshman: National Norms for Fall 1984.* Los Angeles: Higher Education Research Institute, University of California, 1984.

Baley, J. D. "What We've Learned in Nine Years of Running a Learning Center." Paper presented at the Conference on

Remedial and Developmental Mathematics in College: Issues and Innovations, New York, April 9–11, 1981. 13 pp. (ED 201 371)

Barshis, D. *The Loop College Individual Needs (IN) Program: An Analysis of Its Success and a Guide to the Implementation or Adaptation of Its Techniques.* Chicago: Loop College, Chicago City Colleges, 1979. 24 pp. (ED 181 946)

Beal, P. E., and Noel, L. *What Works in Student Retention: Summary of a National Survey Conducted Jointly by American College Testing Program and National Center for Higher Education Management Systems.* Iowa City, Iowa: American College Testing Program; Boulder, Colo.: National Center for Higher Education Management Systems, 1979.

Beavers, J. L. *A Study of the Correlation of Selected Data on High School Transcripts, English Qualifying Exam Scores, and Subsequent Freshman/Developmental English Grades at Wytheville Community College.* Report no. 83-2. Wytheville, Va.: Office of Institutional Research, Wytheville Community College, 1983. 19 pp. (ED 231 488)

Beerson, G. E. "A History of the Activities Which Led to a Formal Articulation Policy for Higher Education in Oklahoma." Paper presented at the annual convention of the American Association of Community and Junior Colleges, Chicago, Apr. 29–May 2, 1979. 43 pp. (ED 169 970)

Bell, E. "The Peer Tutor: The Writing Center's Most Valuable Resource." *Teaching English in the Two-Year College,* 1983, *9* (2), 141–144.

Berger, D. M. "Forming a Citizens' Advisory Committee to the Humanities in a Community College." Unpublished doctoral dissertation, University of California, Los Angeles, 1982.

Bers, T. H. *Assessment of Mandatory Placement in Communications: Fall 1981.* Des Plaines, Ill.: Office of Institutional Research, Oakton Community College, 1982. 18 pp. (ED 214 599)

Bordner, M. J. *Early Assessment of High School Juniors' College Skills.* Springfield, Ohio: Clark Technical College, 1985. 10 pp. (ED 263 962)

Brawer, F. B. *Trends in the Humanities in Two-Year Colleges: Final Report.* Los Angeles: Center for the Study of Community Colleges, 1984. 159 pp. (ED 245 724)

Brunson, E. V. "One Plus One Does Equal Two." *Business Education Forum*, 1983, *27* (5), 11–12.

Brunson, P. W. "A Classroom Experiment Involving Basic Mathematics and Women." *Two-Year College Mathematics Journal*, 1983, *14* (4), 318–321.

Buckner, R. T. *National Community College Urban Arts Survey Based on the Cuyahoga Community College Metropolitan Campus Urban Arts Survey.* Cleveland, Ohio: Cuyahoga Community College, 1979. 47 pp. (ED 197 780)

California State Postsecondary Education Commission. *Update of Community College Transfer Student Statistics, Fall 1972. Commission Report 83-11.* Sacramento: California State Postsecondary Education Commission, 1983. 42 pp. (ED 230 257)

Cantor, H., and Martens, K. *The Humanities in Two-Year Colleges: What Affects the Program?* Los Angeles: ERIC Clearinghouse for Junior Colleges, University of California, and Center for the Study of Community Colleges, 1978. 55 pp. (ED 162 686)

Carhart, J. "General Education at Los Medanos." Speech given at West Los Angeles College, Aug. 31, 1982.

Center for the Study of Community Colleges. *An Analysis of Humanities Education in Two-Year Colleges: Phase IV.* Final report to the National Endowment for the Humanities. Los Angeles: Center for the Study of Community Colleges, 1978.

Center for the Study of Community Colleges. *Revitalizing the Humanities in the Community College: Final Report, October 1, 1979–September 30, 1982.* Los Angeles: Center for the Study of Community Colleges; Olympia: Division for Information Services, Washington State Board for Community College Education, 1982. 29 pp. (ED 230 250)

Center for the Study of Community Colleges. *Merging the Liberal Arts with Work Experience.* CSCC Bulletin no. 9. Los Angeles: Center for the Study of Community Colleges, 1983. 6 pp. (ED 237 124)

Chang, P-T. "College Developmental Mathematics—A National Survey." Paper presented at the annual convention of the Mathematical Association of America, Southeastern Section, Charleston, S.C., April 15–16, 1983. 22 pp. (ED 234 841)

Clark, B. R. "The High School and the University: What Went Wrong in America, Part II." *Phi Delta Kappan,* 1985, *66* (7), 472–475.

Clark, B. R. *Academic Life in America: Small Worlds, Different Worlds.* Princeton, N.J.: Carnegie Foundation for the Advancement of Teaching, 1987.

Cohen, A. M., and Brawer, F. B. *The Two-Year College Instructor Today.* New York: Praeger, 1977.

Cohen, A. M., and Brawer, F. B. *The American Community College.* San Francisco: Jossey-Bass, 1982.

Cohen, A. M., Brawer, F. B., and Bensimon, E. M. *Transfer Education in American Community Colleges: Report to the Ford Foundation.* Los Angeles: Center for the Study of Community Colleges, 1985. 313 pp. (ED 255 250)

Crepin, D. M. "A Developmental Mathematics Program for Community College Students." Unpublished report, 1981. 13 pp. (ED 210 076)

Doherty, F. J., and Vaughan, G. B. *The Academic Performance of Piedmont Virginia Community College Transfer Students at the University of Virginia.* Charlottesville: Office of Instructional Research and Planning, Piedmont Virginia Community College, 1984. 33 pp. (ED 246 943)

Drea, J. T. *College Introduces Money-Back Guarantee on Transferability of Credits.* Quincy, Ill.: John Wood Community College, 1985. 10 pp. (ED 257 526)

Dyer, P. A. "American Mathematical Association of Two-Year Colleges Developmental Mathematics Curriculum Committee: Annual Report." Unpublished paper, American Mathematical Association of Two-Year Colleges, 1981. 27 pp. (ED 208 924)

Dyste, R., and Miner, J. *Status Report on Transfer Center Pilot Program.* Sacramento: Office of the Chancellor of the California Community Colleges, 1986.

Eddy, E. M. "Project ASTRA." Paper presented at the annual meeting of the College Reading Association, Boston, Nov. 1–3, 1979. 8 pp. (ED 184 071)

Emerson, S. *RSVP Basic Math Lab: MAT 1992.* Miami, Fla.: Miami-Dade Community College, 1978. 27 pp. (ED 188 649)

Fairweather, M., and Smith, M. E. *Facilitating the Transfer Pro-*

cess: The Need for Better Articulation Between Two and Four Year Colleges. Plattsburgh, N.Y.: Center for Earth and Environmental Science, State University of New York, 1985. 12 pp. (ED 263 934)

Farrell, C. S. "Testers Asked to Deny Scores to Colleges Misusing Them." *Chronicle of Higher Education,* Nov. 9, 1983, *27* (11).

Fast, C. "Making the Best Better: The LCC Individualized Math Story." Paper presented to the Oregon Developmental Educational Association, Eugene, May 1980. 10 pp. (ED 187 371)

Fay, J. M. *The Humanities as Components of Community Services Programs in Selected Community Colleges in Southern California.* Los Angeles: University of California at Los Angeles, 1982. 152 pp. (ED 217 906)

Fernandez, T. V., and others. *Academic Performance of Community College Transferees.* Garden City, N. Y.: Nassau Community College, 1984. 8 pp. (ED 252 268)

Friedlander, J. *Clark County Community College Students: Highlights from a Survey of Their Backgrounds, Activities, Ratings of Skills, Use of Support Services and Educational Attainments.* Los Angeles: Center for the Study of Community Colleges, 1981a. 56 pp. (ED 201 373)

Friedlander, J. *Science Education for Women and Minorities in an Urban Community College.* Topical paper no. 75. Los Angeles: Center for the Study of Community Colleges and ERIC Clearinghouse for Junior Colleges, 1981b. 107 pp. (ED 214 578)

Friedlander, J. "Student Participation and Success in Community College Science Education Programs." Paper presented at the annual meeting of the American Educational Research Association, Los Angeles, Apr. 13–17, 1981c. 15 pp. (ED 201 374)

Friedlander, J. *Evaluation of Napa Valley College's Student Orientation, Assessment, Advisement and Retention Program.* Napa, Calif.: Napa Valley College, 1984. 12 pp. (ED 250 026)

Gallup Organization. *A Gallup Study of the Image of and Attitudes Toward America's Community and Junior Colleges, 1981.* Princeton, N.J.: Gallup Organization, 1981. 66 pp. (ED 213 452)

Garrison, R. H. *Junior College Faculty: Issues and Problems. A Preliminary National Appraisal.* Washington, D.C.: American Association of Community and Junior Colleges, 1967. 99 pp. (ED 012 177)

Gober, L. A., and Wiseman, T. J. (compilers). *Outcomes, Output, and Outlooks: A Report and Evaluation of Project CALL, a Project in Rural Community Education.* Malta, Ill.: Kishwaukee College, 1979. 53 pp. (ED 175 501)

Goldberg, D. "Integrating Writing into the Mathematics Curriculum." *Two-Year College Mathematics Journal*, 1983, *14* (5), 421–424.

Habib, B. "A Multi-Purpose Math Lab: A Place for All Seasons." Paper presented at the Conference on Remedial and Developmental Mathematics in College: Issues and Innovations, New York, Apr. 9–11, 1981. 10 pp. (ED 201 361)

Hafer, N., and Davis, S. "Development of a Career Ladder Mobility Program in Nursing." Paper presented at the annual National Conference on Teaching and Excellence and Conference of Administrators, Austin, Tex., May 22–25, 1985. 40 pp. (ED 262 830)

Harper, H., and others. *Advisement and Graduation Information System.* Miami, Fla.: Miami-Dade Community College, 1981. 34 pp. (ED 197 776)

Harris, M. L., and Rohfeld, R. W. "SAT/ACT Preparation Program: A Team Approach." n. p.: National Council on Community Services and Continuing Education, 1983. 13 pp. (ED 234 861)

Hartman, N. E. *Maximizing the Effectiveness of Reading Tests in the Community College.* St. Louis, Mo.: St. Louis Community College, 1981. 55 pp. (ED 237 121)

Hatala, C. C. "Community College of Philadelphia + A Humanities Component + Collaboration = The Four C's in Kensington High School." Paper presented at the National Endowment for the Humanities/Beaver College Summer Institute for Writing in the Humanities, Glenside, Pa., July 1982. 21 pp. (ED 220 853)

Illinois Community College Board. *A Statewide Follow-Up of Fall 1973 Transfer Students from Illinois Public Community Colleges (Phase III Progress Report).* Vol. 2, no. 11. Springfield: Illinois Community College Board, 1977. 54 pp. (ED 140 894)

Illinois Community College Board. *Fall 1979 Transfer Study, Report 4: Third and Fourth Year Persistence and Achievement.* Springfield: Illinois Community College Board, 1984a. 25 pp. (ED 254 275)

Illinois Community College Board. *Results of the Survey of Community Colleges on the Teaching of Writing: Illinois Community College Board Report to the Illinois Board of Higher Education.* Springfield: Illinois Community College Board, 1984b. 12 pp. (ED 250 051)

Illinois Community College Board. "Processes for Implementing the New Admissions Requirements in Community Colleges." Springfield: Illinois Community College Board, 1985. 7 pp. (ED 263 969)

Illinois Community College Board. *Illinois Community College Transfer Study: A Five-Year Study of Students Transferring from Illinois Two-Year Colleges to Illinois Senior Colleges/Universities in the Fall of 1979.* Springfield: Illinois Community College Board, 1986. 107 pp. (ED 270 148)

Jaschik, S. "Public Universities Trying Tests and Surveys to Measure What Students Learn." *Chronicle of Higher Education,* Sept. 18, 1985, pp. 1, 16.

Jones, S. W. "Evaluating the Impact of Freshmen [sic] Orientation on Student Persistence and Academic Performance." Unpublished doctoral practicum, Nova University, 1984. 40 pp. (ED 241 089)

Karvelis, D. S. "A Definition, Philosophy, and Self-Assessment Framework for Community Services in California Community Colleges." Unpublished doctoral dissertation, University of California at Los Angeles, 1978.

Kintzer, F. C. (ed.). *Improving Articulation and Transfer Relationships.* New Directions for Community Colleges, no. 39. San Francisco: Jossey-Bass, 1982. (ED 220 146)

Kintzer, F. C. *An Evaluation of a Data Base on Statewide Articulation and Transfer Agreements: Sabbatical Leave Report. Spring 1985.* Los Angeles: Graduate School of Education, University of California, 1985. 37 pp. (ED 263 948)

Kintzer, F. C., and Wattenbarger, J. L. *The Articulation/Transfer Phenomenon: Patterns and Practices.* Horizons Issues Monograph

Series. Washington, D.C.: American Association of Community and Junior Colleges, Council of Universities and Colleges; Los Angeles: ERIC Clearinghouse for Junior Colleges, 1985. 85 pp. (ED 257 539)

Koltai, L. *State of the District, 1981.* Los Angeles: Los Angeles Community College District, 1981. 20 pp. (ED 207 654)

Koltai, L. *Redefining the Associate Degree.* Washington, D.C.: American Association of Community and Junior Colleges, 1984. 24 pp. (ED 242 378)

Lee, B. S. *Follow-Up of Occupational Education Students: Los Rios Community College District, Spring 1983.* Sacramento, Calif.: Los Rios Community College District, 1984. 77 pp. (ED 241 099)

Lieberman, J. E., and Greenberg, A. *Yellow Pages Directory.* New York: Center for High School/College Articulation at La Guardia Community College, 1983.

Losak, J. *Status of Impacts of the Reforms Which Have Been Initiated at Miami-Dade Community College During the Past Five Years.* Research Report 83-13. Miami, Fla.: Office of Institutional Research, Miami-Dade Community College, 1983. 10 pp. (ED 237 136)

Lucas, J. A. *Follow-Up of Occupational Students Enrolled at Harper College, 1982–1983.* Vol. 13, no. 4. Palatine, Ill.: Office of Planning and Research, William Rainey Harper College, 1984. 24 pp. (ED 250 034)

Lukenbill, J. D. *Defining the Associate Degree.* CSCC Bulletin no. 10. Los Angeles: Center for the Study of Community Colleges, 1984. 7 pp. (ED 246 981)

Lukenbill, J. D., and McCabe, R. H. *General Education in a Changing Society: General Education Program, Basic Skills Requirements, Standards of Academic Progress at Miami-Dade Community College.* Miami, Fla.: Office of Institutional Research, Miami-Dade Community College, 1978. 98 pp. (ED 158 812)

McConochie, D. *Four Years Later: Follow-Up of 1978 Entrants, Maryland Community Colleges.* Annapolis: Maryland State Board for Community Colleges, 1983. 37 pp. (ED 234 850)

McMaster, A. *Four Years Later: Class of 1979.* Technical Report 84-04. Trenton, N.J.: Office of Institutional Research, Mercer County Community College, 1984. 47 pp. (ED 245 732)

Maryland State Board for Community Colleges. *The Role of Community Colleges in Preparing Students for Transfer to the Four-Year Colleges and Universities: The Maryland Experience.* Baltimore: Maryland State Department of Education, 1983. 27 pp. (ED 230 255)

Meixner, S. *A New Focus on Arts and Sciences at Maricopa.* CSCC Bulletin no. 15. Los Angeles: Center for the Study of Community Colleges, 1984. 6 pp. (ED 255 270)

Menke, D. H. "A Comparison of Transfer and Native Bachelor's Degree Recipients at UCLA, 1976–1978." Unpublished doctoral dissertation, University of California at Los Angeles, 1980.

Miami-Dade Community College. "Retention Patterns for Full-Time First-Time-in-College Students Based on Basic Skills Assessment Performance." In J. Losak and C. Morris, *Retention, Graduation, and Academic Progress as Related to Basic Skills.* Research Report 82-36. Miami, Fla.: Office of Institutional Research, Miami-Dade Community College, 1982. 29 pp. (ED 226 784)

Mitchell, M. L. "Mathematics in an Individualized Self-Paced Format." Paper presented at the annual convention of the American Mathematical Association of Two-Year Colleges, Washington, D.C., Oct. 1980. 21 pp. (ED 200 287)

Mohr, P. B., Sr., and Sears, J. C. "A Successful Model for Articulation and the Development of Two-Plus-Two Program Agreements Between Norfolk State University, a Predominantly Black Four-Year Public Institution, and Tidewater Community College, a Predominantly White Multi-Campus Two-Year Public Community College." Unpublished report, 1979. 18 pp. (ED 224 381)

National Center for Education Statistics. *The Condition of Education: A Statistical Report.* Washington, D.C.: National Center for Education Statistics, U.S. Department of Health, Education, and Welfare, 1975. 243 pp. (ED 103 991)

National Council for Occupational Education. *Criteria for Excellence in Associate in Applied Science Degree Programs.* National Council for Occupational Education Monograph Series, vol. 2, no. 1. Washington, D.C.: National Council for Occupational Education, 1985.

National Governors' Association. *Time for Results: The Governors'
1991 Report on Education.* Washington, D.C.: National Governors' Association, 1986.

National Institute of Education. *Testing, Teaching and Learning:
Report of a Conference on Research on Testing, August 17–26, 1979.*
Washington, D.C.: National Institute of Education, 1979.
443 pp. (ED 181 080)

National Institute of Education. *Involvement in Learning: Realiz-
ing the Potential of American Higher Education. Final Report of the
Study Group on the Conditions of Excellence in American Higher Education.* Washington, D.C.: National Institute of Education,
1984. 127 pp. (ED 246 833)

New Hampshire State Department of Education. *Graduate Placement Report, 1984: New Hampshire Vocational-Technical Colleges
and New Hampshire Technical Institute.* Concord: Division of
Postsecondary Education, New Hampshire State Department
of Education, 1984. 44 pp. (ED 255 255)

Nespoli, L. A., and Radcliffe, S. K. *Follow-Up of 1981 Graduates.*
Research Report no. 33. Columbia, Md.: Office of Research
and Planning, Howard Community College, 1983. (ED 231
498)

Olivas, M. A. *A Statistical Portrait of Honors Programs in Two-Year
Colleges.* Washington, D.C.: American Association of Community and Junior Colleges, 1975. 16 pp. (ED 136 890)

Ortiz, K., and others. *Educational Testing and Learning Clinic Year-
End Statistical Report. Third Annual Report, 1977–1978.* Costa
Mesa, Calif.: Orange Coast College, 1978. 33 pp. (ED 169 961)

Pace, C. R. *Measuring Outcomes of College: Fifty Years of Findings and
Recommendations for the Future.* San Francisco: Jossey-Bass, 1979.

Palow, W. P. "Technology in Teaching Mathematics: A Computer Managed, Multi-Media Mathematics Learning Center." Paper presented at the annual meeting of the National
Council of Teachers of Mathematics, Boston, Apr. 1979. 8
pp. (ED 184 609)

Parilla, R. E. "Gladly Would They Learn and Gladly Teach."
Southern Association of Community and Junior Colleges
Occasional Paper, Jan. 1986. 6 pp. (ED 263 949)

Parnell, D. (ed.). *Associate Degree Preferred.* Washington, D.C.:

American Association of Community and Junior Colleges, 1985a. 90 pp. (ED 255 266)

Parnell, D. *The Neglected Majority.* Washington, D.C.: American Association of Community and Junior Colleges, 1985b. 189 pp. (ED 262 843)

Peterson, R. E. "Film Forums: On Being Human." In L. Koltai (ed.), *Merging the Humanities.* New Directions for Community Colleges, no. 12. San Francisco: Jossey-Bass, 1975.

Pickett, N. A., and Angelo, F. "Technical Communication in the Two-Year College: A Survey." *Teaching English in the Two-Year College,* 1986, *13* (2), 126–134.

Porter, D., and others. *Report to the Board of Directors of CCHA from the Committee on the Future and Status of the Humanities.* Cranford, N.J.: Community College Humanities Association, 1983. 17 pp. (ED 244 650)

Purdy, L. N. "A Case Study of Acceptance and Rejection of Innovation by Faculty in a Community College." Unpublished doctoral dissertation, University of California at Los Angeles, 1973.

Radcliffe, S. K. *Academic Performance of Howard Community College Students in Transfer Situations.* Research Report 37. Columbia, Md.: Howard Community College, 1984. 29 pp. (ED 244 707)

Richardson, R. C., Jr., Fisk, E. C., and Okun, M. A. *Literacy in the Open-Access College.* San Francisco: Jossey-Bass, 1983.

Rotman, J. W. "Developmental Mathematics and the Lansing Community College Math Lab." Lansing, Mich.: Lansing Community College, 1982. (ED 224 542)

Rounds, J. C. *Entrance Assessment at Community Colleges: A Decade of Change.* Marysville, Calif.: Yuba College, 1984. 13 pp. (ED 243 552)

San Diego Community College District. *The English Placement Test: A Correlation Analysis.* San Diego, Calif.: Research and Planning, San Diego Community College District, 1983. 294 pp. (ED 239 669)

Scott, A. *Placement and Transfer Report, 1985.* Binghamton, N.Y.: Broome Community College, 1985. 139 pp. (ED 263 971)

Seidman, E. *In the Words of the Faculty: Perspectives on Improving Teaching and Educational Quality in Community Colleges.* San Francisco: Jossey-Bass, 1985.

Sheldon, M. S. *Statewide Longitudinal Study: Report on Academic Year 1978-81. Part 5: Final Report.* Woodland Hills, Calif.: Los Angeles Pierce College, 1982. 268 pp. (ED 217 917)

Smith, K. J. "Liberal Arts Mathematics: Cornerstone or Dinosaur?" Paper presented at the Sloan Foundation Conference on New Directions in Two-Year College Mathematics, Atherton, Calif., July, 1984. 13 pp. (ED 245 721)

Solmon, L., Bisconti, A., and Ochsner, N. L. *College as a Training Ground for Jobs.* New York: Praeger, 1977.

Southern Regional Eduation Board. *2 + 2 = Expanded Opportunity. Cooperative Curricular Planning Between Community Colleges and Senior Institutions in Technical and Career-Oriented Institutions: A Staff Report.* Atlanta, Ga.: Southern Regional Education Board, 1979. (ED 178 139)

Staatse, H. *One Year Later, 1982: A Survey of Mercer Graduates of FY 1981.* Technical Report 83-05. Trenton, N.J.: Office of Institutional Research, Mercer County Community College, 1983. 49 pp. (ED 241 1010)

Statement on Competencies in English and Mathematics Expected of Entering Freshmen. Sacramento: Academic Senate for California Community Colleges; Los Angeles: California State University and University of California, 1982. 94 pp. (ED 233 293)

Trombley, T. B., and Holmes, D. "The Changing Roles and Priorities of Academic Advising." *Current Issues in Higher Education,* 1980, *8* (1), 20-24.

Tschechtelin, J. D., and MacLean, A. D. *Student Follow-Up of Entrants and Graduates: Maryland Community Colleges.* Annapolis: Maryland State Board for Community Colleges, 1980. 55 pp. (ED 195 312)

University of Illinois. *Community College-Senior College Articulation in Illinois: Summary of a Report and Recommendations by the Illinois Community College-Senior College Articulation Task Force.* Urbana: Office of School and College Relations, University of Illinois, 1978. 16 pp. (ED 257 498)

Walton, K. D. "Articulation: Transfer Agreements, Minimum

Grades Acceptable on Transfer Courses, and Transferability of Association Degrees.'' *Community/Junior College Quarterly of Research and Practice*, 1984, *8* (1–4), 169–184.

Werner, L. M. ''13% of U.S. Adults Are Illiterate in English, a Federal Study Finds.'' *New York Times*, Apr. 21, 1986, pp. 1–B7.

Wittstruck, J. R. *Requirements for Certificates, Diplomas, and Associate Degrees: A Survey of the States.* Denver, Colo.: State Higher Education Executive Officers Association, 1985. 118 pp. (ED 256 424)

Wood, J. P. ''Mathematics Placement Testing.'' In F. B. Brawer (ed.), *Teaching the Sciences.* New Directions for Community Colleges, no. 31. San Francisco: Jossey-Bass, 1980.

Wright, I. *Handbook for Articulation Task Forces, 1984–85.* Phoenix: Arizona State Board of Regents and Arizona State Board of Directors for Community Colleges, 1985. 32 pp. (ED 257 484)

Yawin, R. A. *Remedial and Developmental Mathematics at Springfield Technical Community College's Mathematics Center.* Springfield, Mass.: Springfield Technical Community College, 1981. 13 pp. (ED 213 456)

Young, F. H. ''Assessment, Historical Perspective, and Prediction of the Academic Performance at Senior Institutions of Transfer Students from a Multi-Campus Community College District.'' Unpublished doctoral dissertation, University of Southern California, 1982. 244 pp. (ED 248 925)

Index